PREDATOR

D0451440

Also by Jack Olsen:

*Available from Dell

PREDATOR

RAPE, MADNESS, AND INJUSTICE IN SEATTLE

■

JACK OLSEN

Island
BOOKS

ISLAND BOOKS
Published by
Dell Publishing
a division of
Bantam Doubleday Dell Publishing Group, Inc.
666 Fifth Avenue
New York, New York 10103

ISBN 0-440-21192-1

Reprinted by arrangement with Delacorte Press

Printed in the United States of America

Published simultaneously in Canada

March 1992

10 9 8 7 6 5 4 3 2 1

OPM

For Su, Sara and Harper, with love

In my dream I saw a old couple bein' visited by their children, and all their grandchildren, too. The old couple wasn't screwed up, and neither were their kids or their grandkids. And I don't know—you tell me this whole dream wasn't wishful thinking.

—*Ex-convict "H. I. McDonough,"* Raising Arizona, *Circle Films*

AUTHOR'S NOTE

In recent years behavioral scientists have focused attention on the social defectives known as sociopaths or psychopaths. Slowly a clearer understanding has emerged, not only of how these dark figures function, but of their creation, their development, and the pain and chaos that follow in their wake.

This book is about one such person, the cruelties he practiced on dozens of women, and the mortal wound he inflicted on an innocent young man. Certain characters, including the predatory Mac Smith, have been assigned pseudonyms in the interests of a larger truth.

PROLOGUE

THE ORDEAL OF ANN CARMICHAEL

i

In the rainy old blue-collar town of Everett, Washington, a rookie real estate agent set out the signs for her first "open house." Less than a month had passed since Ann Carmichael had earned her license, and she'd already sold a $33,000 home on Seattle's Green Lake, chalking up a $577 commission. "Oh, Phil," she'd told her policeman husband in her melodic voice, "it's a whole new world. I'm allowed to work my own hours. I just *love* it."

As she positioned a FOR SALE sign on this chilly March morning, the west wind pressed her long suede skirt against her legs. It was a good omen. When the wind blew down from the wood pulp mill to the north, Everett smelled like old sweat socks. Houses sold better when the wind was off the dark green Cascades to the east or the slate-colored waters of Puget Sound to the west, or even when it blew from busy Seattle, fifteen miles south.

Ann barely glanced at a sports car that slowed and stopped. She was climbing into her blue Datsun 310 to drive to another location when the other car spurted away. The big interstate highway, I–5, was nearby and there was never a shortage of traffic.

She was setting out another sign when the same car reappeared and stopped. A man with a full beard and long, kinky, reddish brown hair called out, "Are you selling a house?"

"Well, yes," she said. "It's a three-bedroom rambler, right over there. The tan one with the dark green trim." She pointed to a simple boxlike structure, no froufrou or gingerbread, the kind of housing thrown up row on row after Boeing started manufacturing 747s in cavernous sheds and the old mill town grew up and out. The house had no vestibule or hall; the pipes banged and the windows leaked and the toilet-and-a-half lacked soundproofing. But the price was only $60,000.

Ann thought how exciting it was to run into a potential buyer before she'd set out her signs. What a business!

The bearded man pulled his RX–7 into the driveway of the sale house and watched as she unlocked the door. "Would you just sign my open house log?" she said. "Then I'll show you through."

Leading the way from room to room, she noticed that the skinny young man wore baggy jeans and a nondescript jacket over a T-shirt. "I work at Boeing's," he told her, marking himself as a local by his use of the possessive. He explained that he was living in a duplex with his ex-wife and they were looking for something larger.

"How did you find out about this place?" Ann asked.

"Are you kidding?" he said with a smile. "If anybody else saw you putting out those signs, they'd be here too."

He excused himself to use the bathroom, then trailed a few steps behind her as the inspection trip moved to the backyard. He asked intelligent questions about financing, interest rates, monthly payment plans. When they stepped back into the house, he commented, "That's a nice skirt you're wearing."

"Thank you," she said, and thought, If you only knew how long it took me to decide what to wear this morning. She'd finally selected the beige skirt, a floppy white sweater, neat brown heels, and light tan panty hose, "the whole nine yards," as Phil had noted admiringly before leaving for his police job in Seattle. One of her mentors at the agency had stressed that tacky attire caused as many lost sales as tacky presentations. Ann thought what a joy it would be to sell this guy on the spot, gather up the open house signs, and be home by noon—a thousand dollars richer.

"Next time you show me through a house," the man said out the corner of his mouth, "I'll be sure to wear baggier pants." Intent on the sale, Ann barely heard.

A few minutes later he excused himself again. How odd, she said to herself. I hate to use a strange bathroom. It occurred to her that the man might be . . . strange. But business was business, and she wasn't suspicious by nature.

The tour took fifteen minutes. She handed him a real estate certificate, good for "free market analysis of property owned by bearer," a few brochures, a fact sheet on the house, and her freshly minted business card with the 800 number. "I hope I'll be hearing from you," she said. "We've got plenty of other houses if this one isn't right."

"I just have to do some figuring," he said. As he

opened the door and stepped outside, a puff of cool air curled about her ankles.

Five minutes later she noticed that the metallic brown Mazda was still in the driveway. She looked around the house to see if he'd left anything behind and spotted the certificate on the kitchen counter. She thought, If he's interested enough to inspect the whole place, he'll want this.

As she approached the car, the man seemed to be staring into his lap. She figured he was doing his arithmetic, a good sign. He was sucking the fingers of his right hand. She took another step and saw what he was doing with his left.

She decided that the safest course was to pretend she hadn't noticed. She handed him the certificate, managed a pleasant "Bye!", and turned away.

"Come back," he yelled as she wobbled across the lawn in her heels. "Hey, wait! *Come back!*"

She turned around at the front door. He was still beckoning. "The ph-phone!" she stammered. "Uh—I've got to get the phone."

She suspected that he was harmless—if he intended to hurt her, why would he have left the house?—but she quickly locked up. The back door was cracked an inch or so. She yanked it shut and engaged both locks.

She edged toward a window and peeked slantwise toward the car. He was still sitting at the wheel. She thought, What a goofball! He'll drive my customers away. Who wants to drive up to an open house and see a pervert in action?

She tried to decide what to do. The situation definitely wasn't covered in her real estate textbooks. She phoned her office for guidance and the broker said, "For God's sake, Ann, don't be so naïve. Call the cops."

Five minutes later the police hadn't arrived and the man still seemed preoccupied with his lap. More time passed—ten minutes, fifteen. This is ridiculous, she said to herself. What can I tell the police when they get here? The guy didn't do anything except act like a degenerate. What can they charge him with? Self-abuse? In this day and age, is that even a crime?

Blue smoke puffed from the Mazda's exhaust as the car eased out of the driveway and headed west on Eighty-fifth. The driver didn't seem in a hurry.

At last an Everett police car pulled up, its siren discreetly silent. Two backup units arrived as she was describing the incident to a calm young officer in uniform. After he'd finished taking her statement, she thought about canceling the open house, but decided not to. A rookie agent couldn't afford to look unprofessional. Why overreact? The guy was just a passing weirdo.

At the office the next morning she accepted a mixture of comment about her experience. "It must be great to be that popular," one of the women cracked, and they both laughed. Ann enjoyed the give-and-take; it meant that she was being accepted, maybe even admired for hanging in at the open house. For four years of her young life she'd worked as a court reporter, a solitary job of recording and transcribing. This new atmosphere was a pleasant change. As she'd told Phil in her first burst of enthusiasm for real estate, "Every day I get a chance to meet different people."

Early in the afternoon the Everett P.D. called to tell her that they'd located the suspect from the information provided on the open house log. The master criminal hadn't even bothered to use an alias. *Gee,* she thought, I hope they're not too hard on him.

While Ann was away from her desk, an excited stranger arrived and demanded to speak to the boss. The woman said that the police had confronted her tearful ex-husband about the incident and he'd immediately phoned her for help. Now she asked the broker to order Ann to back off. "The guy has his problems," the ex-wife insisted, "but he's just not capable of doing what your saleswoman claimed."

Three weeks passed. Ann wasn't vengeful and she wasn't bothered by the lack of action. What had the silly man done except make a fool of himself? Surely he'd learned his lesson.

ii

At twenty-eight Ann Carmichael was still naïve about males. A close relationship with her warm, gentle father had taught her that men were good. In school she'd learned little about dealing with the opposite sex. Who would date a gawky girl who wore corrective shoes for weak ankles and lurched down the halls like Big Bird? She was always the tallest

person in her class; at dances she stared at her partner's scalp and shuffled around in saddle shoes that
never seemed to wear out and felt like snowshoes.
She became introverted and shy. When the other
students went to the cafeteria, she hid behind a
book in the library. When boys made their moves,
she thought they were just being nice. All through
school she dreamed of being a secretary, someone's
right arm. It seemed such a noble ambition. But
who would hire a stork?

At twelve she'd selected her mother's patron
saint, Maria Goretti, as her own. Ann wasn't a fervent Catholic and she was vague on church history,
but it was her understanding that Maria had died a
child-martyr rather than yield to a rapist. Ann's
mother had been violated herself, so the choice of
Maria seemed appropriate.

When Ann turned eighteen, her life changed. Tall-
ness was in, and she now stood five ten in her slip-on
scuffs. She developed a modest bust, small waist,
long slender legs. She took pains with her blond
hair and applied a touch of makeup to large wide-
set eyes of the deepest sapphire. She met Phil, a
good-looking Seattle patrolman, and a year later
they were married.

If there was a discordant note in her life, it was
minor. By the time of her venture into real estate at
twenty-eight, she'd become aware that something
about her seemed to attract degenerates. Leering
men followed her in markets. Anonymous callers
breathed hard and talked dirty. The open house offender wasn't the first stranger who'd tried to show
her his wares. In her second year of marriage, a man

dressed only in tennis shoes danced and preened on a gravel path outside the door of her triplex in suburban Seattle. By the time police arrived, he was gone. A year later she walked to her car in a Safeway parking lot and saw a man exposing himself. It seemed so absurd that she started to laugh, but she thought better of it as he strode up to the door of her car and began yanking in her direction. She sped away.

She prided herself on taking the incidents in stride, including the latest unpleasantness at the open house. Now and then her street-smart husband reminded her that perverts were a fact of life and some were bound to become overstimulated at the sight of such a striking woman. She understood and didn't belabor the problem. She hadn't been harmed and didn't expect to be. Saint Maria Goretti would see to that.

iii

Nineteen days after her first open house, the neophyte real estate agent was back at the same address, this time holding an open house for the trade—a "brokers' open." A FOR SALE sign on the front lawn also solicited drop-in customers, not that Ann expected much action. Real estate was depressed nationally and even more so in this southeast section of industrial Everett. She'd been in the business less than two months and was beginning to realize that interest rates weren't going anywhere but up and home sales anywhere but down. She couldn't have picked a worse time to launch her career.

A few brokers dropped in and left, going through the motions. No one seemed inspired by the little rambler and its low price. She wished she could sell the place on her own; then she wouldn't have to split the 7 percent commission. But that was unrealistic. In this market she needed all the help she could get from other agencies.

Just before noon a bearded man of about thirty arrived and began asking questions about the house. He seemed clean-cut and intelligent, perhaps a professional or an upwardly mobile young manager. His eyes slanted just a little; there was almost a Jesus look about him. His leather jacket, slacks, and shoes matched the brown of his neatly parted hair. He said he and his wife had been house hunting for weeks and this place looked perfect. His voice was low and his manner calm and assured.

The house tour took them to the garage. "Is that a storage area up there?" he asked.

"I . . . think so," she said.

"Do you think you could fit in?" he asked, and quickly explained, "I want to see how big it is."

The opening had been sliced in half by an inner wall and Ann's lanky body wouldn't pass through. The customer was two or three inches shorter than her own five feet ten, but he couldn't make it either. Oh, damn, she thought, I'm gonna lose this sale.

Back in the living room, the straight-haired young man made approving comments as he thumped the walls like a doctor checking for chest congestion. When he asked to use the bathroom, she wondered, What is it about this place that drives men into the bathroom? Could it be something about . . . me?

He returned and informed her that one sticking point remained. Ann held her breath. He said he was in a cash crunch. Nothing permanent. Could she check with the owners and see if they would accept a VA offer?

"I'll do it today," she promised.

She smelled a quick sale. It was obvious that this man knew real estate. "How flexible are the sellers?" he asked.

"About what?"

"Price. Down payment. Terms."

"There might be some flexibility."

"Fine," he said, showing good teeth. "I want my wife to see the place. How long will you be here?"

"When can you be back?" Ann countered.

He looked at his watch. "One thirty at the latest."

"I'll be here."

She asked him to sign the guest log and watched as he wrote, "Mike Drake." He accepted her brochures and drove off in a small red import. As he left, she thought, This looks good.

For two hours she tried not to peek out the window. It was nerve-racking to be on the edge of a deal like this, especially so early in her career.

At 1:15 the man returned, still in the same brown jacket and slacks. "My wife's driving her own car," he explained. "She'll be here in a minute. I just wanted to take some measurements."

He mused aloud about knocking out a wall to

create a master bedroom. "Do you have a tape measure?" he asked. He spoke so weakly that she had to ask him to repeat. She handed him her twelve-foot Stanley tape and watched as he unreeled the metal ribbon across the floor of the back bedroom. He measured the windows and walls and then said he needed to know the total width of the room, including the closet depth.

"Hold that end of the tape, will ya?" he asked, motioning toward the closet.

She dropped to her knees and pressed the tape measure against the closet baseboard. Anything for a sale, she reminded herself.

Something cold touched her neck. "Don't make a sound!" she heard him say.

He slid the knife to her throat and circled her waist with his other arm. "Do what I say," he ordered, "and you won't get hurt." He was breathing in little puffs and snorts.

Her first reaction was confusion, disbelief. Things like this didn't happen to her or the people she knew.

"Undress," he said. "Fast!" The blade tickled her adam's apple.

She fumbled with her jacket. She wanted to stay calm and exercise some control, but her fingers kept twitching.

"I'm—uh—very nervous," she said. "I'll try to hurry."

She thought, I'm bigger than he is, I could give him a hell of a fight. But not with a knife at my throat . . .

The jacket slipped to the floor and she kicked off her shoes. *"Everything!"* he snapped. "Right now." Earlier he'd been so calm; now he seemed enraged. My God, she thought, he sounds mean enough to kill me. She began reciting Hail Marys under her breath.

She was wearing a red cotton terry cloth dress with elastic at the waist and big patch pockets in front, normally an easy outfit to lift over her head, but her hands and fingers were stiff and there wasn't enough room to maneuver on her knees in the closet. "I'll count to ten," he said in that same mean voice. "Then I want everything off."

She imagined the blade slicing her flesh. "I could move faster," she murmured, "if you'd let me out of the closet."

He guided her into the room, then began counting. He'd reached eight before she squirmed out of the dress.

"*Everything!*" he reminded her. She tried to gain time by spreading the dress on the red shag rug, but the chill of the knife made her tear off her slip, bra, panties, and panty hose.

He sucked her right breast, then moved his hand to her bare abdomen. "Stay down!" he ordered. The blade pressed so hard against her neck that she thought she might already be bleeding.

He dropped his brown pants and blue undershorts. "Do you know what to do with it?" he asked. She wondered why he sounded so angry. She thought, I haven't done anything wrong! You don't even know me. She tried to speak to the Virgin. Mother Mary, you're a woman. You'll understand. Hail Mary, full of grace . . .

As the prayers reeled through her mind, the

man began to masturbate toward her mouth. She turned away and said, "Look, I wouldn't be so nervous if you weren't pointing that knife."

"Give me what I want and you won't get hurt," he said. "I just want to get off."

She thought, What would Phil want me to do? Resist to the death? Protect my chastity till my throat gets cut? I have to survive.

"Just . . . don't hurt me," she begged.

He pressed her fingers around his penis and showed her how to jerk it back and forth. Then he shoved it against her half-open lips. She willed herself to be an observer. The point of the knife scratched her throat.

She felt an urge to look up at his face. His dark blue eyes seemed sad and angry at the same time, as though he were far away, raping someone else. She had a crazy thought: We're both here, but we're not here.

She thanked God that it took him only a minute or two. Evidence, the cop's wife thought. She held his fluid in a corner of her mouth.

He ordered her to lie down. She thought, Now I die. Mother Mary, she said to herself, why me? What did I do?

"Don't make a sound," he said. "If you don't move, I'll leave. *Don't say a word!*"

He pulled up his pants and stared at her. It was the look a person would give a bad dog. As he arranged his clothes, she took a compass bearing on the shag rug and let his semen dribble out where she could find it later.

He walked toward the bedroom door. He was a

small man, about five eight and 150 pounds, but he seemed heavier, more dense than others his size.

"God bless you!" she called as he walked from the bedroom. It was almost involuntary, someone else's voice.

He charged back, waving the knife. "What?" he said. *My God*, she thought, why did I say that? He gave me a chance to live and I didn't have the sense to take it.

His dark eyes narrowed as he bent over her and said, *"Wh—what did you say?"*

She lowered her voice. "I said, 'God bless you.' I mean, I have no hard feelings. I mean, it's . . . I'm gonna be okay." She wanted him to know that he hadn't ruined her for life. She wanted to deny him his sick satisfaction.

He glowered down at her, then switched to a look of contempt, as though she were too pitiful to take up his time. With a shrug he walked out.

She waited, berating herself. Why did you open your mouth? *Why did you open your mouth?* Any minute he's coming back to kill you. You could have saved yourself, but—typical Ann—you had to have the last word. . . .

After a while she dared to look outside. The little red car was gone. She locked the doors and windows as she'd done three weeks before. She was careful not to smudge any possible fingerprints. Be careful now, she told herself. Don't walk on the spot on the rug. Get dressed. Go for help. Above all, preserve the evidence.

It dawned on her that she was naked. As she

dressed, she wondered why anyone would want to steal sex from a total stranger. What did he see in me? She sniffled softly to herself.

No one was home next door. She tried another house, then two more. It was early on a Tuesday afternoon; people were at work. Across the street her staccato knock was answered by a woman with two children at her skirt. "Please," Ann whispered, "can I talk to you alone? There's been . . . an incident. Across the street. I've just been raped. I need to call the police." Her practical side took over. "You may want to send your children to another room," she advised, "so they're not exposed to this."

She felt disembodied, almost as though she were hearing someone report a crime on TV. One preprogrammed sentence followed another. She wondered if she might be in the early stages of shock; her heartbeat was fluttery and she was shivering. Somehow she had to finish her job, summon professionals like her husband, put them on the trail before the angry man got too far away.

The two policemen followed her around the house, delicately dusting for prints with black-and-silver powder, cutting out the telltale patch of rug, photographing footprints and tire tracks, measuring every little thing. A neighbor arrived, gave Ann a hug, and asked, "Would you like me to pray with you?"

It was comforting, a long rambling prayer that asked God to keep her safe from evil, to help her put this outrage into perspective and not blame herself, to remind her that the Lord was the blessed controller of all things and she had to put her trust in him. Ann cried.

At headquarters, the detectives were compassionate, perhaps, she thought, because she was married to one of their brother officers. She realized that she still hadn't called Phil, but she didn't want to be distracted from her immediate task. She was the only person who could tell these investigators everything the rapist had touched and said, the only one who could describe his clothing and his car and assist them in making up a composite sketch. And it all had to be accomplished while the details were fresh in her mind.

Hours passed. At 3:18 P.M. she signed her name to a five-page handwritten statement and climbed into her blue Datsun for the twenty-minute drive back to the real estate agency. In her boss's glassed-in office she gave a report on her second open house. As she spoke, she felt herself beginning to lose control. She sobbed and shook; her knees trembled. She couldn't keep her legs from bouncing up and down. She heard a voice: "It's shock. Delayed shock."

A young agent walked in and asked, "What's wrong, Ann?"

Someone told him the story. Later she heard that he'd gone outside and thrown up.

iv

McDonald Smith drove his little red Fiat back to his office, shuffled some papers, and arrived home in time for dinner with Nan and the kids. He figured the blond agent had been his fiftieth victim, give or take a few. The number didn't matter. They were only women.

PART ONE

TWISTED

■

1950–1968

1

His paternal ancestors came from a hard-bitten part of Ohio known for moonshine, rolling hills, and played-out seams of coal that caught fire and burned underground for years. Neighbors described these particular Smiths as bright but unusual, a discreet way of putting it. Most of the family members seemed industrious and law-abiding, but there were a few who liked to spice up their dull lives.

Mac's father Calvin was born on a rock-strewn farm in northern Appalachia to a put-upon mother who always insisted on dressing at least one of her six sons in skirts to take the place of the daughter she never had. Her husband, Mac's grandfather, was a self-proclaimed psychic who claimed to be descended from George Washington's contemporary, Lord Fairfax.

As late as the 1970s, the family home in the hills still featured a two-seater outhouse, hand-pumped well water, a stash of corn liquor, legions of bugs, a pack of cringing mutts, and five or six dozen cannibalized cars slowly settling into the ground. By those late years, the lady of the house had fled and Mac's paternal grandfather had taken to sharing his bed with a series of rural women who seemed bewitched by his psychic powers, his single tooth, and his glass eye. That guy's sure *different*, they said.

One of the old man's sons, Mac's uncle Slim, grew up to become a hustler and card shark with reputed underworld connections. "Never worked a day," a kinsman noted proudly. Another uncle was shot to death in a case of mistaken identity. (It was said that at the instant of the shooting, Mac's psychic grandfather sprang from his chair and yelled, "They shot George!" Then he led authorities to the scene.) For months after the killing, gunmen cruised the Smith home, shouting out the windows of their souped-up cars, "We got the wrong goddamn Smith!" Muffled voices warned over the phone, "We'll hit Slim the next time." But they never did.

As a juvenile, Mac's father Calvin, oldest of the six brothers, served time for auto theft. Soon after his release from a boys' industrial school, he met and married Dove McDonald Cane, a soft, pretty, brown-haired child of fifteen. Dove's family history was less piquant than the bridegroom's, and her family was shorter-lived. Her mother married at fourteen, became a grandmother at twenty-nine (duly noted by a Columbus newspaper), and died of cancer at forty-two. Dove's father, Mac Smith's maternal grandfather, ran a country store. His grandchildren remembered him as a grouch who was seldom seen without a bottle of beer. When a four-year-old granddaughter asked him for candy, he told her, "If you want something, you're gonna pay for it." It was the kind of anthracite hardness that enabled the store to sur-

vive the depression of the 1930s in a region that
stayed poor in the best of times.

Calvin Smith, a good-looking boy with flashing
white teeth, hair the color of India ink, a quick
mind, and his father's appeal to the opposite sex,
was as thin as his child-bride was plump. (In later
years Dove's children spoke of the claustrophobia
they felt when she hugged them to her "giant
boobs," as one daughter described them.) Their
first child, named Walter and called "Brother," was
born just as Dove turned sixteen. Calvin Smith
treated the baby as an intrusion. He'd always demanded Dove's time and attention, and it seemed to
annoy him that he had to work to feed his family
when most teenagers were still out raising hell.

Like other members of the Smith clan, Calvin
was quick and bright. Dove had a ninth-grade education and a flair for math, but her husband's intelli-
gence seemed to go deeper and broader. He would
dawdle over a crossword puzzle at breakfast, and
when he left to go to work she would find every
square filled in. It didn't seem fair to Dove that such
a promising boy had to do manual labor for a living.
Who wouldn't be upset and frustrated? As a child
he'd planned to study law, but he'd had to quit
school in the sixth grade to help raise his five
younger brothers.

More and more, Dove found her husband's
finely chiseled face hidden behind the family Bible.
She'd been raised in a religious family, never
smoked, drank, or took the Lord's name in vain. But
Calvin out-Bibled the most pious. She wished he
would pay more attention to her and less to Ruth
and Esther.

■

Still in their teens, the Smiths moved into a run-down apartment near Dove's people in Columbus. Calvin refused to let her work, but his own paycheck didn't cover their needs. He kept dreaming up financial schemes, some practical, some beyond his reach. He sounded like a sawed-off Fred Flintstone, ranting about how much money he would make. But he also turned into the hardest working man Dove had ever known. He would make deliveries all day on his trucking job, eat on the fly, and return to a second job at night. Once he financed an antiquated cement mixer and started a short-lived business. On summer weekends he bought loads of fruit and vegetables at the wholesale market and hawked them on a street corner. It was a harsh life, unrelieved by vacation trips or other diversions. Then McDonald Joseph Smith came along.

2

Dove awoke from the twilight sleep in her room at the White Cross Hospital in Columbus and saw a nurse carrying a newborn child like a sack of feed. "Oh, look," she said in her round-voweled eastern Ohio accent, "they got that baby upside down." Then she discovered that the child was hers. Nearly forty years later, in her unending quest to figure out how seven pounds and six ounces of gurgling infant had grown into a hundred and fifty pounds of snarling criminal, she wondered if that early positioning might have sent too much blood to his head and affected his mind. She reckoned it was as good a theory as any.

Everything else about the infant seemed normal. "Mac" was physically intact, bright, and aware, a blond baby with an easy smile and placid disposition. Dove couldn't stop hugging the sweet-smelling package. She'd intended to breast-feed him, but the doctor vetoed the idea. Mac slurped his bottle and developed neither colic nor other disorders. At six months he was sleeping through the night.

Calvin Smith showed no intention of letting another brat impinge on his young life. When the infant needed changing or burping or hugging, Calvin sat stone faced in his chair. His animosity toward the two-year-old "Brother" seemed to increase, and Dove found herself overcompensating by paying more attention to Brother and less to the newborn.

Mac grew inward, a soft-voiced, contented child, capable of entertaining himself with a doll or a pacifier, sitting alone, hardly noticed, while Brother was drawn to his mother's breast and slapped silly by his father. Little Mac seemed at home with the situation.

Friends decided that the young couple hadn't been ready for the pressures of raising one child, let alone two. The Smiths battled over everything from muddy floors to overdone noodles. One day Dove tuned to a dance-music station instead of country and western, and Calvin stomped their little white radio to pieces. They argued over his harshness toward Brother and his coldness toward Mac and his preoccupation with the Bible and the time he spent with cronies. He seemed to view females as the enemy; he described her female relatives as "the vultures," certain others as "the weasels." Dove figured that some men just didn't like women—except in the kitchen and bedroom.

Cold and distant, he was also capable of jealous fits. When a big boorish fool made an unseemly comment to Dove at an amusement park, the five-feet-six-inch Calvin issued a challenge and ended up on the ground, his lip dripping blood. He wanted to fight on, but peacemakers held him down to keep him from being killed. Dove tried to figure him out.

He doesn't want me, she thought, but he'll risk his life trying to defend me from some jerk that isn't worth the price of turnips. What is Calvin's problem?

3

One day little Mac heard a scream and found his mother being dragged across the yard by her long brown hair. He helped Brother ram a lawn mower against their father's leg. Calvin Smith peered at his two sons as though they were strangers, then stalked away.

No one knew when his snits would erupt into violence. The family would be at the dinner table when—*crack!*—he would knock Brother off his chair for eating with his mouth open. One night he tied Dove up "to learn you a lesson." Brother heard the outcry and called police. When they arrived, Calvin threw his arms around his hysterical wife. "Well, now, Dovey," he said in his soft country voice, "you know I'd never do a thing to hurt you." After the cops left, he shoved her down the basement stairs, tore off her clothes, and beat her with a belt.

Living on the rim of the volcano, Mac learned how to please, how to avoid trouble and not offend, how to keep out of range. He seemed to skip past the predictable periods of rebellion—the terrible twos and sixes, the different periods of bonding and withdrawal. He did as he was told without whining or complaint. "A great kid," his mother called him. "A perfect little guy."

Mac's placid behavior gave Dove more time to spend on poor abused Brother. Mac idolized his older sibling, worked with him collecting newspapers and shoveling snow and mowing lawns, but he loved his father and mother, too, and he lived in fear of losing one or the other or both. Whenever his dad attacked Brother at the dinner table, Mac stared into his hashbrowns. If little Mac did something wrong, the father usually found a way to put the blame on Brother. "God damn you, boy," he would grunt as he slapped his older son's face, "You're s'pose to keep Mac outa trouble." Mac knew he should speak up, but he didn't dare.

Despite his wispy stature, Calvin Smith was sturdy and well coordinated, a natural athlete. For a while he coached junior football and basketball. One night Brother sank a long shot and ran back past the bench. "How's that?" he asked with a proud grin.

"Get back down the court!" his father muttered. Then he turned to Mac and said, "Ain't he one of the goofiest looking kids you ever seen?"

Mac thought, That crew cut makes Brother's ears stick out a little, but if he's goofy looking, what am I? Every boy on the bench heard what Dad said. I wonder if he says things like that about me.

But then his father took Mac on one of his delivery routes, dropping off packages and freight. Perched on the big front seat of the truck, the child was beside himself with excitement. That night his mother capped the perfect day by serving spaghetti. The men of the family went outside and engaged in a snowball fight, and his father picked Mac up and swung him around.

Not long afterward, Mac made a mistake while helping to bleed the brakes on the family car. "You cain't do nothin' right," his dad said. After that he seemed to return to his old policy of ignoring the boy. It didn't make Mac love him less. Everyone knew that Calvin had a hard time showing his feelings, except with his fists. The poor man wore himself thin for his family, twelve or fifteen hours a day, sometimes on weekends too. There were different kinds of love.

4

Three days after Mac's fifth birthday, his sister Maria was born, and Dove Smith had her hands full with the baby. The lessening of her attentions didn't bother Mac, nor did he feel jealous of the new arrival. He paraded his sister around on his thin shoulders and cooed at her like a new dad. He smiled and felt good when Maria snuggled against him. He no longer missed his mother's hugs and the billowing breasts that once had enveloped his face. For the rest of his childhood, he would be happiest in the company of Maria.

He soon discovered fascinating differences between them. The subject of sex was forbidden in the household; he'd picked up his first tidbits of information from yellowing old pornographic magazines stacked in a row garage behind the apartment building. At six he began experimenting with his cousins under the bedsheets. Mac and a neighbor boy played with each other off and on for a year and a half. But girls heated his blood. One day he was attempting to inspect his little sister when their mother walked in on them. "Just you wait till your father gits home," she said.

That night Calvin Smith led Mac into a back bedroom and whispered, "You didn't do nothin' wrong, son. You gotta learn about girls one way or another." He took his slipper off and winked. "We're just gonna let your mother think I'm whup-pin' ya," he said. He slapped the sole against his bony thigh while Mac pretended to cry.

Mac became well-versed in the uses of deception. At dinner he spat vegetables down the hot-air register when his mother was in the kitchen. One of his un-cles taught him how to pocket small items from the grocery store. Mac began to enjoy putting some-thing over; it was a challenge, an adventure. And there were seldom any consequences.

When he was still a small boy he fell into the habit of exaggerating, telling half-truths, sometimes lying outright. "Sorry I'm late, Mom. There was this gas explosion . . . I pulled this lady out. . . ."

Sometimes he lied to get attention: "I seen the governor today . . . a two-headed calf . . . a man eight foot tall. . . ." His mother tagged him a "pathological liar" and seemed amused. "Mac'll tell ya a lie just for fun," she told a friend. "He's slicker'n snot. You'd swear he's telling the truth."

It became the family joke: "Listen to Mac lie."

5

In 1961, when Mac was nine and his parents were in their mid-twenties, Dove bought her husband a cheap guitar. Calvin took the instrument on his truck runs and practiced on breaks. He rolled out of bed at three in the morning and rehearsed country and western songs about lovelorn men and triflin' women till it was time to leave for work. Later it seemed to the rest of the family that he'd gone from beginner to expert in about three days.

It wasn't long before he was singing and playing in bars, first for drinks and then for pay. His Bible gathered dust. Once in a while he came home wobbly. When a relative wrote from Los Angeles that there was work for short-haul truckers and plenty of C&W bars, he made a snap decision to pull up his Ohio roots and take his family west.

Mac didn't cry—he was proud that no one had ever seen him cry—but it hurt his ten-year-old heart to leave cousins and friends. He had to give away his collection of Spider-Man comic books—"too heavy to haul," his dad said. Nor was there room for his bike; Mac sold it to a friend on credit, and never collected.

.

The long drive west revived his spirits. He sprawled on pillows in the far back as the old Mercury station wagon creaked on its worn-out shocks. Sometimes his mother took the wheel and his dad picked at his guitar while the others sang along. Calvin Smith had always chided his children that they couldn't carry a tune in a bucket, but on this trip he taught them lyrics about a lost boy and two Indians who jumped in a lake and a whole songbook about bad women who done men wrong. For once, Mac felt close to someone besides his sister Maria.

6

After years of living poor, the Smiths settled into the warmth and sunshine of the downscale L.A. community of Wilmington, near San Pedro harbor. Economically they were as far from the snooty communities of Beverly Hills and Bel-Air as they'd been in Ohio, but all Californians shared the same lustrous weather and the same bougainvillea and hibiscus and night-blooming jasmine and other free and natural wonders. The sunny neighborhood warmed their bones and made them glad they'd fled Ohio's ice and snows. California had big open playgrounds and a beach that ran for a thousand miles. It seemed as though everyone drove customized cars or Beetles. In the evenings the Smiths sat on the porch of their furnished apartment and talked about getting rich. Their father assured them it wouldn't be long. He drove short hauls out of a Teamsters hiring hall for twelve and fifteen hours a day and never seemed to tire. He might have been short and slight, but a lifetime of hard work had made him uncommonly strong. On weekends he bought burlap sacks of potatoes from the wholesale market in downtown L.A., paid the kids two cents a bag to fill ten-pound bags, and sold the spuds on street corners.

Mac and Brother imitated their dad's industriousness by delivering the Long Beach *Press-Telegram* and the *Los Angeles Herald-Examiner*. On the side, Mac shined shoes on the San Pedro waterfront. Sometimes he hauled his papers out to anchored ships by water taxi and found himself invited to exotic meals. The merchant seamen liked the scrawny kid with the big smile and the snapping shoe rag, and soon he'd saved $170. He didn't object when his father borrowed his bankroll, but he wondered why the money was never mentioned again.

After a few months in Wilmington, Calvin Smith seemed to lose interest in his family except to smack Brother every now and then. Mac learned to accept his father's logic: If Brother was punished, Brother must be at fault. It wasn't fair, but neither was life.

When Calvin began concentrating his attention on his nighttime troubadouring, Dove stopped encouraging him in his music. He asked her to come with him to hear him perform, and she told him that when Christ returned to Earth she didn't want Him to find her in a saloon. They had the same conversation several times, sometimes at the tops of their voices, but she never yielded.

Mac stuck to his well-worn policy of noninvolvement, getting along by going along. His father made sporadic attempts to reshape Brother, but the younger son went unnoticed. Mac loved his dad but wouldn't have said so on pain of death; love wasn't a word that came easy to any of the Smiths. Anyway, Mac figured his dad had given up on him at birth.

Almost every year the Smiths moved, first to another apartment house in Wilmington, then to Torrance, to Harbor City, to Carson, to the outskirts of Redondo Beach, back to Carson, from one low-rent L.A. satellite to another. Mac seemed almost free of family authority, at peace with his exciting new world. He made up for the loss of his comic books by starting a collection of pennies. He bought roll after roll at the bank with his shoe-shining money, and by his twelfth birthday he'd collected every Lincoln penny except the rare 1909 SVDD and the 1914 D. Then he started collecting *Playboys*.

Within a few blocks of the apartment, street games were played incessantly, unimpeded by snow or storm or traffic. In races, Mac's pipe-stem legs churned like eggbeaters, and most of his competitors viewed him from behind. When teams were formed, he was selected before his older and bigger brother. He was a loyal teammate and made friends easily. Highly competitive, he emulated his father by concealing his emotions. He kept his grades up with hardly any effort.

No one in the family took much notice of him. The unexpected arrival of baby Lina put more demands on his mother's time. Once again there was no money for baby pictures, so the father hired a professional photographer, spread the proof sheets on the sunny porch, and rephotographed them with the family's ancient 8-mm. movie camera. Then he returned the proofs as unacceptable. Mac took note of his father's cleverness. Studio portraits for nothing!

Lina's birth drew Mac and little Maria even closer: two against the world. Sometimes they paid for their

7

Every summer the Smith family piled into the old Mercury station wagon for a two-week visit to the kinfolks in Ohio. Across desert, plains, and mountains, the parents fought with themselves and their children. To save money, they drove straight through, three days and nights with the children sleeping across one another's limbs, eating bread and bologna, afraid to ask for a drink. Their dad hated to lose a second's time. On a typical hot day, the mother said, "Calvin, let's buy the kids some pop."

"Pop just makes 'em thirsty," he said.

At Needles, California, the thermometer on a roadside building read 106. "All right, goddamn it," the father said, pulling into a small market, "I'll get 'em a drink."

He returned with a quart of buttermilk. "They're not gonna like that stuff," Dove warned.

Mac took a sip and turned red. Maria couldn't swallow a drop. Brother made a face and his father slapped it. "You damn kids," Calvin said. "There's not a goddamn thing wrong with buttermilk." He flung the carton out the window.

■

Each trip seemed to end at Dove's sister's house in Columbus at 3:00 A.M., where their uncle would come to the door with his hair mussed and a shotgun under his arm.

"Don't shoot," Calvin would say, and everyone would rush inside and talk till sunup.

After a few days the visitors would move in with the glass-eyed grandfather, then pass on to other relatives. The kids enjoyed playing with their cousins, but they learned to give their father a wide berth when he was on his old turf. With his brothers and friends he seemed more prickly than ever. The Smith males liked to pass a bottle around and make cracks about women.

At a restaurant counter in Columbus, Calvin accused Dove of flirting with the waiter. "You're just like all them other goddamn whores," he said. He mashed a hamburger in her face and dragged her outside.

"Don't!" the children heard her yell. "The police'll put you in jail!" No one asked why she didn't call the cops herself.

On one of the Ohio vacations Calvin's shady brother Slim taught Brother and Mac how to put on a heavy overcoat and steal from stores. The freebooting uncle also taught them how to stack a deck, deal seconds, and make crooked bets. His message was that there was plenty of money to be made off suckers and it sure beat working.

Mac went to a Thrifty Mart with a friend and dropped a deck of cards and a stack of poker chips in the pocket of his coat. Outside the door a security guard stopped him. Mac remembered his uncle's advice about staying cool and lifted his arms high. "If you want to," he said, "you can search me."

"No," the guard said. "That's okay."

With this success behind him, Mac began a life-long career of shoplifting. Every time he went to the supermarket, one of his favorite paperbacks stuck to his hands—Rex Stout, Agatha Christie, Mickey Spillane. At night he lost himself in his books. Pornography also had a stimulating effect, but the store clerks kept a closer eye on publications like *Hustler* and *Penthouse,* and sometimes he had to pay cash. He started a collection of stroke magazines, perfected the art of self-abuse, enjoyed a few circle jerks with his cousins and other boys, and began to think about undressing girls and bending them to his will.

8

To his teachers and friends Mac seemed happy, bright, well behaved, a contented boy. But as he grew toward his teen years, he saw himself as a nerdy kid, barely tolerated by others. He lied more than ever. There was a pattern of furtiveness about him that was inadvertently documented in the family's home movies. Everyone understood why his mother shied from the camera; she was touchy about her figure. But the rest of the family wondered why Mac always seemed to lower his head or cover his face when the filmmaking began.

He was the only one who knew about his feelings of shame and revulsion. It grossed him out to see his face in the bathroom mirror, let alone in home movies. He was convinced that his relatives and friends would drop him if they only knew him better.

At twelve he still wet his bed. Sometimes seven-year-old Maria crawled in with him, and there were nights when he drenched them both. He would lecture himself before he went to bed—"C'mon, you damn dummy, stay dry one night!" Then he would lose control again.

His parents acted as though he was using his enuresis to punish them. "You *know* you can do better than that, young man!'' his mother yelled as she collected the sheets. His father's sour face reminded him that he couldn't do anything right.

The adolescent Mac retreated into hot sexual fantasies, sometimes three or four times a week. But despite all the practice, he failed in his first attempt at intercourse. She was fifteen, the steady girlfriend of a buddy named Rudi O'Shay. Mac fondled her in the trees behind the schoolyard and spent himself on her jeans. He felt like taking a bus to Peru.

For a while, sports provided the excitement that he craved and the recognition that he wasn't getting at home. He drank chocolate milk and lifted weights to bulk up, then started hanging out at a nearby park that sponsored junior teams. He didn't get much heavier, barely a hundred pounds, but he had his father's speed and coordination. His best sport was baseball. In his first season as a second baseman he led his league in stolen bases, an accomplishment memorialized on the park's bulletin board. That winter he played center on an undefeated basketball team and broke a rookie scoring record.

The awards ceremony was a downer. His parents arrived ten minutes after he'd accepted the award for ''Best Sportsman.'' His mother said it was a nice trophy but it was time he was getting to bed.

9

Before Mac reached his thirteenth birthday, his mother came under the spell of a fundamentalist pastor. Up to then, no one had ordered the Smith children to attend church. At seven, back in Ohio, he'd heard one of his Bible-thumping aunts say that the only unforgivable sin was blasphemy of the Holy Spirit, and he'd gone out to the tomato patch and muttered, "God damn the Holy Spirit!" When nothing happened, he'd felt more relaxed on the subject.

But now his mother was issuing stern warnings about Satan, eternal fire, giant locusts and other beasts that would bite and sting and never let up. She didn't hesitate to back up her threats with force, lashing out with belts and harder objects. One night she came home from church full of excitement. "Our preacher is right," she declared. "He don't waste time talking peace on earth. His job is saving souls. And yours"—she fixed her gaze on Mac—*"yours isn't saved!"*

He decided that his mom didn't like him anymore and tried to win her back. He brought home a steady supply of love offerings—costume jewelry, flowers, gewgaws. He couldn't wait for Mother's Day or her birthday. And still she seemed to be slipping away. If it would impress her, he decided, he would dedicate himself to her new religion.

Night after night he listened as the stick-thin pinheaded pastor preached damnation and salvation in a thick southern drawl. Mac and the others twitched with shame. After one service, Dove led her son to a deacon who smelled of mints and had tufts of hair protruding from his nose. Mac listened attentively as the old man spelled out the ground rules for redemption. Dancing was forbidden. Smoking was a one-way ticket to Hell, even without inhaling. Pool cues were the Devil's tools and rock 'n' roll was his music. Card games were out, along with magazines; even the most pious publications distracted from the Scriptures. Movies were forbidden, even Bible films like *The Ten Commandments*. All sins were equal in the eyes of God. Drinking 3.2 beer was as grievous as murder because the body was the temple of God and one sip defiled it. Evil thoughts were the same as evil deeds. To imagine an act of fornication was to commit it, with eternal fire the automatic result.

But . . . there was an out. The worst offender, the lowest sinner, could be saved by God's grace and love. The deacon explained, "You can always go to the Lord for forgiveness, and I promise you it'll be granted. But not until you've accepted Jesus Christ as your personal savior."

Mac couldn't wait to unload his paperbacks. His mother fussed over him as he memorized passages from his new Bible. After a few weeks of study, he went forward at a Sunday night service, expecting to be blinded by an inner light. But nothing happened. I must've missed something, he said to himself.

He guessed it was just one more reminder that he couldn't do anything right. But he kept trying. One summer night Dove, Brother, Maria and Mac were baptized together in a tub behind the altar. He didn't feel as inspired as some members of the congregation, singing and wailing and yelling Hallelujahs, but at least the baptism qualified him for Heaven.

That summer the church's Bible class held a contest to increase attendance. Mac went from door to door to sign up his friends and neighbors. At the awards ceremony, his name was called and he walked onstage. The elongated pastor smiled and gave him a double handshake. A spotlight illuminated the first prize in the attendance contest: a green-and-white Schwinn bike with a chrome headlight, balloon tires, a buglelike horn that the preacher couldn't resist tweaking, and a pack strapped to the rear.

While the parishioners applauded, Mac wheeled his bike down the aisle and into the soupy warm California night. His mother suggested that they tie it to the top of the car, but his father said, "Son, you just ride on home. We'll follow."

For five miles, Mac pedaled in front of the old Mercury station wagon. Every few minutes his dad beeped his horn and Mac waved. It was the highest point of his life: Mac triumphant in the glare of headlights, doing something right. He was thirteen.

10

After he won the bike, the stuffy little apartment began to resound with daily and nightly prayer. Mother, daughter and sons prayed for new shoes and ice cream, for cooler weather, for better health, for Calvin Smith's salvation and their own. On New Year's Eve Dove and the children bobbed for apples in the church rec room and welcomed 1966 with an hour of prayer in the sanctuary.

Of course, there wasn't time for both church and sports. Mac loved playing baseball so much that he'd once talked his father into taking him to a game in Watts in the middle of the "Burn Baby Burn" riots. But at the first practice session of the new season, Dove collared him and took him home. "Salvation first, then play," she announced. Unless her children ran fevers of over 100 degrees, she required them to attend Bible Study on Wednesday nights, Boethia Club on Friday nights, Sunday School, church services, and choir practice. In summers a Bible class met four days a week.

The all-star second baseman missed another practice and then the opening game. He turned down an invitation to a teenage mixer because he didn't want the embarrassment of being hauled off the dance floor for Boethia Club. It was the era of long hair for boys, but his pop-up brush cut was already too long to suit the pastor and too short for his friends. He was becoming an outcast.

One Sunday the preacher refused to admit Maria to Sunday School in a dress that exposed her knees. When the outspoken child protested, he said, "Mrs. Smith, take that girl home and whup her—and get rid of that dress!" Mac tried to dissuade his mother, but she followed orders.

Mac began to backslide. His skill at lying came in handy. "I was on my way to church, but there was this big accident. Blood all over the place . . ." Ashamed, he tried to revive his faith by going forward at a Billy Graham Crusade, but again he felt nothing.

At a street bazaar in Long Beach, he spent his bus money on a picture of Jesus. "Where'd you steal it?" his mother asked. Mac thought, What's the use? When I tell the truth, she still thinks I'm lying. He was almost sorry he'd won the bike. Too much was expected of winners. For three years he'd been free to run the streets, and now his mother was turning him into a puppet. In the dark shadows of his room, he studied *Playboy* and cussed the name of God.

He didn't understand why his brother Walter tagged along to church like a suck. Dove fussed over her favorite son, but Calvin was still harsh with the boy. One night he administered a twenty-minute thrashing while the mother called through the locked door, "Calvin, please! Don't whup him on the head."

Mac talked his brother into staying late at a forbidden movie, and when they got home, their father was waiting up. "It's eleven o'clock," he said, grabbing Walter by the collar. "Where ya been?"

Before the boy could answer, Calvin knocked him out with a roundhouse punch. Mac started to explain that it wasn't Walter's fault, but held back. His brother was used to taking the blame.

A few nights later Mac delivered the *Press-Telegram* to an elderly patient at Harbor General Hospital. "Take a dime for yourself," the woman said, waving weakly toward a glass on the table. Mac took two dimes. On the way out of the hospital, it bothered him, but not enough to return the money.

The next night the woman's room was empty. At the nurses' station he was informed that she was dead. He knew what had happened. She'd learned about the stolen dime and died of shock. It was a disquieting realization. For months he'd been stealing coins from his father's produce stands to finance purchases of Twinkies and RC Cola, but he decided it was no longer worth the risk to his dad's life. At thirteen he still had a semblance of conscience.

11

On a cool night in mid-November 1965 Calvin Smith failed to come home from a gig. Dove swooped down on the country and western bar and was advised by the bouncer that he'd left with a bar-fly named Ruby who went around telling folks she was psychic. Calvin had met her in the alley out back; she'd been drinking whiskey with two bums.

Dove shook her head. Whatever her husband's faults, she explained, he didn't go for loose women. If he'd shown any interest in this creature, it was probably because she'd claimed to be psychic. His dad and granddad had written the book on that subject.

Dove sat up waiting. She wondered if Calvin's absence had anything to do with the fact that it was Walter's fifteenth birthday. She mulled over the information she'd gleaned at the bar. It made no sense. Some drunken slut drinking with two bums, and Calvin leaves with her? Maybe she is a witch. . . .

Two days went by before he phoned to report that he'd found the woman of his dreams and intended to marry her. Dove begged him to come home. She

was a one-man woman, and for all Calvin's orneri-
ness, she missed him. Besides, they were short on
food.

One support check arrived and bounced, then
another. When he'd been absent for two weeks,
Dove opened her last can of corn and ladled it onto
a potato. There'd been a few dollars around the
house, including Mac's stash from shining shoes,
but it had gone for baby food and formula for Lina,
still not a year old.

The winter holidays arrived, oddly stuffy and warm
for folks brought up in Ohio. Dove led her children
in prayer at the foot of her bed. "O Lord," she
wailed, "we pray Thee, return our daddy to the
home where he belongs. O Lord, save us from the
witch that has him in her clutch. . . ." By now she
was convinced that the Devil was to blame. What else
could explain Calvin's behavior?

Each night she and the children repeated their
prayers. She instructed them to make their voices
sound as pathetic as possible so the Lord would respond. When nothing happened, Dove told them to
have faith and patience. "The Lord answers *all*
prayers," she assured her kids. "Our prayers *will* be
answered."

Over the phone she begged her husband, ca-
joled, threatened to report him to the police. A
week before Christmas she told him that his children were starving, and the response was another
rubber check. When she called for emergency help,
the pastor and a deacon rushed over with a tree, a
ham, and a box of canned goods. The Salvation
Army brought a small tree and a frozen turkey. A

delegation from Mac's school contributed cash from their pockets and a tree. Suddenly the bereft little family had three Christmas trees and a kitchen stacked with food.

Dove beamed. "What's that teach you about prayer?" she asked. Mac had to admit he was impressed.

On Christmas Eve, mother and children attended services. When they returned to their apartment, the front door was unlocked and the kitchen light was on.

Dove started to read her husband's Christmas note aloud, then stopped. "You motherfucking lying bitch," she read to herself. "You said you had no food."

12

Mac tried to come to grips with his own personal loss. He couldn't believe that his father had left for good. It was true that he abused Walter and fought with Mom, but he'd never laid a hand on Mac, and he still called Maria his little princess, and he seemed to like baby Lina. He was just overworked, bulldogging trucks through L.A. traffic, loading and unloading in hundred-degree weather, peddling vegetables, doing odd jobs, picking his guitar for nickels and dimes. Mac thought, Dad's the hardest-working man on Earth. He wouldn't up and leave the people he loves for a barroom slut. He just caught the seven-year itch a few years late.

Dove refused to accept the loss. Others might think it was permanent, but she knew better. God was with *her*, not with some danged witch. She didn't bother to look for work. At twenty-eight, she had four young children and a ninth-grade education. She'd never even waited tables.

Well-meaning friends drifted in and out, patting the backs of her hands and casting anguished looks. The pastor knelt on the living room floor and led a delegation in prayer. Lately there'd been rumors that he'd been sharing his buggy-whip shape with some of his female parishioners, but Dove refused to listen to such gossip and silenced anyone who brought it up. The pastor was a man of the cloth, she insisted. It was blasphemy to question his private life.

For two months the family lived on handouts and the money the brothers brought home from paper routes and odd jobs. The landlord threatened eviction. Mac was sifting through his penny collection trying to decide which coins to sell when his mother stomped into the room and grabbed him by the hand. "Let's go," she said. "Me and Walter are gonna fetch your father."

"Dad's . . . coming home?" Mac asked.

"One way or another."

Her round face was pink, damp with sweat. Mac wondered what she had in mind. Did she think they could beat Dad up? Kidnap him? She was short, only five three, but she was heavier than her husband and knew how to fight. She'd whaled on every one of them at one time or another, and if her hands wouldn't do the job she didn't hesitate to grab a lamp or some other weapon. Mac imagined the scene at Ruby's place, the clawing and scratching, his mom shrieking, his dad cussing, the witch casting spells.

"I'm not going," Mac said. He didn't want to fight his father or any other man. Confrontation wasn't his style.

"Yes, you are," his mother insisted.

"Like hell I am," he said. It was the first time he'd defied his mom face-to-face.

Later he found out what happened:

Walter and his mother pulled up outside the witch's house and Dove honked the horn. Calvin appeared in his shirtsleeves, then ducked inside.

Dove yanked a jack handle from the trunk and smashed the front door. When Calvin appeared, she went for his throat. Walter stepped between his parents and Calvin knocked him down. While father and son rolled on the lawn, Dove hacked her husband's hands with a tire iron.

The fighters jumped up. Blood ran from Calvin's fingertips as he kicked Walter in the groin. By the time neighbors broke up the fight, the boy had to be taken to the hospital.

A few days later Calvin came home. Three months had passed since his walkout. "You see?" Dove told her children. "The Lord *always* answers prayers." It was her favorite message.

Her husband's hands were in splints. He explained that Ruby had put him under a spell and somehow the battle royal had broken it. He swore that he'd never intended to leave. Ruby was still casting incantations to get him back, but he promised that he was home for good.

13

Dove decided that the only safe move was to hie the whole family out of town. She'd always lived in fear of the supernatural; to her, Satan was real and so were witches. She reminded Calvin that three years before, they'd loaded their earthly goods into their station wagon and traveled from Ohio to California. The road went both ways. They could be halfway to Columbus before the witch knew they were gone.

Mac sold his paper route to his best friend, Rudi O'Shay. It hurt to leave, but his mother explained that the witch had left them no choice. Calvin welded a hitch on the Merc's rear bumper and attached a home-made trailer to carry furniture. The evening before they were to leave, he admitted that he felt a supernatural pull from Ruby and asked Dove to come downstairs with him while he changed the tires. "Ruby has this holt on me," he explained. He seemed to think that his wife's piety might serve as a shield.

They reached an uncle's house in two and a half days. Within a week they were in a bare bones apartment of their own. His father contracted to buy an old junker for his mother so she wouldn't feel so cooped up with the baby. He lined up some freelance trucking jobs and started playing guitar for ten dollars a night and tips.

Mac could see that his parents were harder than ever on each other, impatient, quick to take offense. Every conversation seemed to end with his dad walking out and his mom in tears. One night they began to rehash the California fight in front of the kids. Calvin asked what kind of a whoring bitch would break her husband's hands with a tire iron, and Dove asked what no-good fornicating sinner would kick his own son in the balls. And for what? So he could keep on living with a witch!

"Ruby's a *white* witch," the father insisted. "They's good witches and bad."

"There's *witches,* period!" his mother said, spitting out the words. "Witches have Satanic powers. The Scriptures don't mention good witches."

When Walter spoke up on his mother's behalf, his father kicked him. Then he stomped out the door and didn't come home till dawn.

A few nights later Mac and his father were driving crosstown when Calvin spoke in a strangled voice. "Son," he said, "I—uh—I—" Mac looked over and saw that his dad was crying.

He slid to the outer edge of the seat. He'd never seen his father cry and didn't like the feeling. He wished his dad would lose his temper, yell, curse, hit —anything but cry.

Mac stared out the window as they pulled up to his uncle's house. The two Smith brothers huddled for a while, and Mac saw his uncle hand over a wad of bills. He wondered what was up but didn't dare ask.

•

At noon the next day the family was driving in a rainstorm when Calvin announced that he needed cigarettes. The others waited in the blue station wagon while he disappeared into the downtown White Castle. Fifteen minutes later he hadn't returned, and Dove asked Mac to take a look.

"He's not there," the boy reported to his mother. "Uh . . . there's a back door."

Her face turned the color of chalk. She jumped from the car and ran inside. When she returned, tears mixed with the rain on her face. Her voice broke as she said, "That son of a bitch has run off!"

The White Castle was on a major thoroughfare; it would have been easy for Calvin to step onto a bus. But where would he go? "The witch has drawed him back," Dove said. "I'll bet my life."

She laid rubber driving away from the curb, and a motorcycle cop stopped her three blocks away. She was breathing so hard that she could barely speak. "My husband left me!" she gasped. "My kids is deserted!"

He examined her California driver's license and said, "Okay, lady. I just want you to be careful."

She pulled around a bus while the children checked out the passengers. They searched the bus station, the railroad terminal, the airport. It was a clean getaway. Mac sat in the backseat and tried not to cry.

That night the maternal relatives came over, consoling Dove and trashing Calvin the way he'd always trashed them. Mac felt as though they were pulling out his insides. He couldn't believe that his dad would do him this way. He *loved* his father. It wasn't fair.

Little Maria and her mother bawled out loud and kept the baby awake. Maria confessed that she'd accidentally walked in on Dad while he was sitting on the toilet and he must have run away because of the embarrassment. Walter insisted that it didn't matter why he'd left; they were lucky he was gone. In their bedroom that night he told Mac, "Dad's no good. Any man who would drag us across the country and leave us in this dump—"

"Maybe he hasn't left," Mac interrupted.

"Bullshit."

"Maybe he was hit by a car."

But in his heart Mac knew better. He hadn't told anyone about the crying scene with his father the night before—it seemed so private. Now he knew that his dad had been trying to warn him, trying to give him a chance to brace himself, *him alone.* He should have talked his dad into staying with the family, promised him that they'd all get jobs so he wouldn't have to work so hard. Over and over he said to himself, If you'd just said a few words, Dad never would've left. It was the same old story. He never did anything right.

14

For two months the family squatted at an aunt's home in a seedy part of Columbus. When Dove got word that Calvin and his witch were living in Carson, a suburb east of Torrance, she sold the blue station wagon and hustled the children back to California by Trailways bus. She rented an apartment not far from her husband's love nest, and the battle resumed.

Calvin passed word that his children should be permitted to move freely between the two households, but Dove vetoed the idea. "You're livin' in *sin*!" she hissed into the phone. "Get right with Jesus, Calvin Smith!"

Mac felt whipsawed. He missed his dad terribly. So did Maria. They plotted together but realized they were helpless. Mac was barely thirteen, Maria seven. They knew what the authorities did to runaways.

Neither parent budged. One afternoon when Dove was sick in bed, Calvin sneaked in and tried to steal the baby. Dove ran him off.

Food was scarcer than ever. Dove's telephone pleas brought a routine response from her husband: "Lemme see my kids and I'll pay up." She dubbed

Ruby's place "the household of Satan" and refused to yield.

By July of 1966, Mac hadn't seen his dad in three months. "Mom, please," he begged his mother in the yard, "can't I just go over and say hello?"

"That man deserted us," she said, hands on her wide hips. "Why'd you want to visit a man that lives with a witch?"

"He's my dad," Mac said.

"He's the Devil."

Mac blanched. Half the preaching at his church was about the power of the Devil. The word made him shiver.

It was a blistering day and he still had papers to deliver at the hospital. "Mom," he said, "why can't I live with Dad for a few months and then come back?"

"*What?*" Her eyes widened and she slapped his face hard. Without thinking, he slapped her back, then took off running. He heard her yelling, "Mac. *Mac!*"

He knew he was in bad trouble. He ran the mile to his father's place and Ruby welcomed him. He phoned home and told Maria he was gone for good. When she cried, he said, "Maybe you can come over here and visit."

Dove complained to the police, but when they learned that the runaway had taken refuge in his natural father's home, they told her it was a civil matter.

Mac was content. He was with his dad.

15

It wasn't long before the boy realized that Ruby was more slattern than witch. She was well-worn and showed it, especially around her narrow eyes. From the beginning she tried to convert Mac to her peculiar ways. At first he told himself that if she meant so much to his dad, she must be a special person. She was certainly warmer than his mom, though she could be just as mean. She hated housework; Mac was so ashamed of the dust and filth and dirty dishes that he didn't even think of inviting friends.

Ruby put him right to work. He washed, cleaned house, ironed, cooked, bathed her three-year-old kid and put him to bed. She constantly bad-mouthed his family. "Your mother's a whore," she proclaimed one morning as he took a break from his chores. "Didja know that?"

Mac blinked. "No," he said.

"She run around on your dad."

He thought he understood what Ruby was doing and tried not to blame her. All she knew about Mom was what she'd been told by Dad, and Dad had always been insanely jealous. Mac knew his mother's faults, but a woman who spent every minute doing for her family and praying to God didn't have much time for a secret sex life. Besides, if she was involved

with other men, she wouldn't have allowed herself
to get so fat.

One day Ruby piped up, "Your mother never took
to you, did you know that?"

"Huh?"

"If you think she gave a shit about you, ask her
to show you your baby pictures."

"We were too poor," he explained.

"She coulda stepped in a booth and got three
pictures of you for a dollar. Was she *that* poor?"

Lying in bed that night, Mac tried to remember.
He'd seen baby pictures of Walter and Maria and a
set of Lina on 8-mm. film, but he'd never seen one
of himself. It made him wonder.

On a dry dusty evening when his father was at work,
Ruby informed him that his mother was currently
sleeping with the preacher. When Mac didn't react,
she added that Dove had also gone to bed with
Mac's best friend, Rudi O'Shay, as well as a few deliv-
erymen and the electrician.

Mac listened without comment. The wilder the
charges, the more confused he felt. He remembered
what his mother had called Ruby. Witch. Satan's dis-
ciple. Devil. Blasphemer. Home wrecker. *Slut.* Why
were these two women so hateful toward each other?
Were all women like that?

The next night Ruby left Mac alone with her
three-year-old son and went off to a bar to watch his
dad sing and play guitar. The child climbed into his
lap and Mac felt himself getting hard. He gave the

little boy a cookie for licking his penis and another for taking it in his mouth ''like your baby bottle.''

After a while, Mac went into the bathroom and masturbated. The boy didn't seem troubled, but Mac felt bad. The kid might tell.

16

A month after he'd moved in with Ruby and his dad, Mac was lured back home by a beguiling call from Maria. When he stepped inside, Walter and Rudi O'Shay popped out of the shadows and grabbed him.

"Into the bedroom," he heard his mother say. Her voice was cold.

Mac struggled, but Walter held him down and Rudi put a knee in his back.

His mother ushered in the preacher's wife, a stern woman with pale rose lips and colorless eyes like her husband's. Her face looked dusted with flour. Mac watched as she removed a floppy straw hat and laid it on a chair.

"Lord," the woman prayed, her arms outstretched toward the low ceiling, "we ask that thou removest the demons from our loved one. O Lord, our Mac is possessed of the Devil. O Lord, come into this room and free our beloved son from Satan's evil spell." She pronounced it "spay-ell."

The reedy voice rose and fell as the pastor's wife waved her bony hands over his body. "In the name of Jesus," she chanted, "come out of this child. *In the name of Jeee-sus . . .*"

Mac realized he was the beneficiary of an exorcism. "O Lord," he heard, "an *eee*-vil spirit made this poor boy leave his mumma." The woman sang a few lines of a hymn and began babbling in words he couldn't understand.

"Cut it out!" Mac yelled. He hated to be pinned. There were no demons in him. It wasn't *eee*-vil to want to live with your dad. He kept trying to break loose, but Walter held him in a hammerlock.

At last he stopped resisting. His muscles were sore and tired. "I, uh—I feel better," he said weakly. "Honest, I think I'm okay now."

"Praise Jesus!" his mother yelped.

He hadn't done his nightly paper route, and it was late. Walter and Rudi rode shotgun as he picked up the stack of Long Beach *Independent*s in the lobby of the hospital and asked if the two boys would help with his deliveries. "The patients hate it when I'm late," he said.

"You won't run off?" his brother said, squeezing his arm till it hurt.

"No, no!" Mac promised. He wished he could strangle them both.

They divvied up the newspapers and headed for separate floors. As soon as they disappeared, Mac ran out the front door and made his way to his dad's. He vowed to come back and punish his brother and Rudi. But somehow he lost the urge, along with his paper route.

17

A month before his fourteenth birthday Mac was hitchhiking home from a friend's house in Redondo Beach. A middle-aged man picked him up and passed him a pint of Southern Comfort. Mac had tasted corn liquor with his cousins and sipped beer with Rudi O'Shay, but this drink went down like pop. "Thanks," he said, and took another swig.

Before long he was drunk and they were parked. A mouth nuzzled his jeans.

The man let him out a block from home. He was two hours late, but Ruby and his father were asleep. He turned off his light and stared out his window. I'm a queer, he thought. I enjoyed that! God damn, I'm a gay homosexual.

The next day he rehashed the experience in his mind. I was drunk, he rationalized. I didn't know what the hell the guy was doing till he was half done, and by then it didn't matter whether he was a man, woman or dog. It could have happened to anybody. *I'm as much a man as anybody.* . . . He comforted himself with the thought.

18

In November his father confided that he was taking Ruby to Ohio for good. He said it was the only way they could escape his mother. Dove had taken to following Calvin's truck and raising a ruckus when he performed. "Things is hard enough, son," his dad explained. "Folks in Columbus are into country music. I'm not gonna be part of the rat race anymore. I'm all wore out punching somebody else's clock." Mac was welcome to come along.

The boy thought about it but declined. He was tired of doing housework and listening to Ruby's sewer mouth, and two thousand miles were too many to put between himself and his little sister Maria. There were times when he even missed his mother. Dove could be hard to take, no doubt about that, but she meant well. And she was . . . his mom.

"I'll come visit you, Dad," he promised.

At the parting, Ruby kissed him on the lips. He started to shake hands with his father, but both held back at the last second. Mac wanted to tell his dad that he loved him, but he held back on that, too. He waved till their old car was out of sight. He hoped Ruby liked buttermilk.

∎

He hadn't lived with his mother for four months. A while ago, Maria had told him over the phone that Mom had fallen apart when the divorce papers were filed; she sat around the apartment wiping her eyes and clutching her Bible. Mac wondered what awaited him on his return. More tracts? More church? He'd passed his fourteenth birthday; he was semi-emancipated. He and his mother would have to work out some ground rules.

He expected a small homecoming ceremony, with Maria performing one of her whirling dervish dances and Walter giving him a brotherly slap on the back and the baby cooing and giggling in his face. Maybe Mom would fix his favorite meal: spaghetti, fries on the side, Jell-O and marshmallows for dessert.

But when he arrived, his little sisters were playing with a baby-sitter and Walter was out. His mom and a friend named Sue Robinson were in the bedroom preparing for a double date. Dove seemed flustered when she saw him. She explained that the date was Sue's brainstorm and she was just going along to be sociable.

Mac tried not to stare. His mom had lost weight, but her breasts still strained her flowered dress. Her bare legs curved upward from an open-toed pair of heels. She was wearing eye shadow and lipstick. And she'd bleached her hair!

He tried to reason with himself. Why the hell should she sit home with a bunch of brats? She was thirty-two years old, good-looking, unattached. She hadn't walked out on anybody or deserted her kids. What was the harm in dating?

After the others went to bed, he slumped in the

living room chair and leafed through his secret collection of *Playboys*. He thought, Why did she have to dress like that? Why put all that crap on her face and peroxide her hair? Is she trying to get laid?

He wondered if some of the nasty stories had been true. No—of course not. Ruby was just a bitch with a mean mouth. But the idea gnawed at him. He felt irked on his father's behalf, and then on his own. His mother still had four children to raise. She belonged at home.

He slipped into her bedroom. The night-light shone on the picture of Jesus that he'd bought at the bazaar in Long Beach. The family Bible lay on the floor next to the bed; the last thing she did every night was read the Scriptures. He wondered what passage she would read tonight. Maybe a little something on fornication?

He was still awake when he heard the women come in. They were giggling. They sounded stupid.

The next morning he asked to see his baby pictures. "We didn't take none," his mother said. The makeup was gone; she looked the same as ever except for her blond hair.

Mac asked, "Why not?"

"You wouldn't let the photographer get near you. You were two months old and threw a conniption fit. Just cried and carried on! 'Okay,' I said, 'we'll try later.' And then—I dunno. We run outa money, I guess."

As the days went by, Dove constantly reproved him for the weeks he'd spent under the witch's roof. When Maria mentioned that she wished she could take the bus to Ohio and visit her dad, Dove slapped her and sent her to her room. Mac sneaked in and stroked her hair. "Don't worry, Maria," he whispered. "Mom doesn't mean it."

The eight-year-old child replied, "That's just the trouble, Mac. She *does*!"

Dove insisted that Mac cleanse his soul of the witch's contamination by spending extra time at church. Satan and salvation were always on her mind. She dragged him to an exorcism ceremony, and he could almost smell the fires of hell as he listened to the leader: "Demon, I demand with the blood of Christ that you leave this body!" The exorcist's head turned and his eyes followed the invisible demon as it scrambled toward the exit. "Get out in the name of Gawd!" the leader shrieked. Then he slammed the door and pressed his body against it while Mac and his mom joined in a chorus of Hallelujahs. Another soul saved. . . .

The boy found the ceremony too scary for comfort. He confided his fears to Maria, and the two of them sat trembling in the darkened living room past midnight, staring at the shadows where the demons dwelt.

Sometimes he wished he could return to the playgrounds and the gyms, but at fourteen he had no time for sports. His mother had sold everything that was convertible to cash, including Mac's penny collection. The brothers attended school half days so they could work in the afternoons, but their combined incomes barely covered the rent. When the cupboards were empty, Dove sent Mac to the market with food stamps. He cringed when the checker set aside a pack of Marlboros and said, "This item isn't allowed." He felt the other customers' eyes boring into him as he left the store with his handouts.

He remembered when he'd worked on the church's food drive for the needy. Now the Smiths were the needy. Every week the sharp-faced pastor and one of the deacons drove up in a rattly old station wagon and unloaded canned corn, chili, rice—the staples of the poor. Before they left, they handed each child a religious tract. The charity was supposed to be anonymous, but everyone in the church knew who was on the dole.

Mac hated to show his face at services, but his mother continued to hold her children to the same old schedule—"God watches the rich *and* the poor," she warned. She seemed to think that a kid could go to school and deliver papers and shine shoes and mow lawns and still have the time and the energy to attend five or six church meetings a week.

When Mac balked, she locked him in his room. Then she went out on dates. He squirmed in his bed, wondering what she was up to. Sometimes he relieved his pain with his hand.

19

An eviction notice arrived, and the family moved to an Afro-Hispanic neighborhood. Mac was reduced to wearing Walter's old jeans, three sizes too big and holed in the knees. In the cruel world of junior high school fashion, his two-year-old clothes made him the class dork.

He took an afternoon job as the janitor's assistant, a double embarrassment because fellow students could see him cleaning toilets and scrubbing floors. At night he shined shoes on the waterfront and ran errands for hospital patients. His grades slipped. His friend Rudi O'Shay turned him on to diet pills to keep him awake.

Mac thought Rudi was cool. He was a latchkey kid; his father was a bookie, his mother a secretary; both were alcoholics. Even Dove liked Rudi. Quiet and bright, he was the neighborhood "instigator." He was more mature than Mac, an inch taller, the only boy in the neighborhood who was a better athlete. At seventeen Rudi was an experienced gambler and hustler. He knew tricks and scams reminiscent of Uncle Slim in Columbus.

The friends experimented with LSD, and in the middle of his third trip, Mac heard a voice: "It's a hard life, and then you die. Why bother?" He woke up terrified and vowed not to touch the stuff again.

Speed, pot, and beer proved safer and cheaper. Face flushed from Coors and uppers, he stumbled into a children's pageant at church and hollered, "Thash my sister! *Right up there!* THASH MY Maria!" A deacon threw him out.

When his mother got home, Mac was in bed. She pummeled him awake. "What're you on?" she demanded.

"Mom, please, *Mom!*" he yelped. She hit him with a small hard fist, but he refused to confess. He passed out and didn't know what had happened till he saw his bruised face in the morning.

For a few weeks his mother let up on him. He decided it was her way of apologizing. When she told him that her friend Sue Robinson wanted to treat them to a movie in Long Beach, he was puzzled but pleased. Why would Mom defy the church rules about movies? He'd never heard of *I Am Curious (Yellow)*, but any film sounded interesting.

A few minutes after the picture began, he thought, Somebody has made a mistake. Why aren't we walking out? He wondered what his mother and Sue were thinking. They'd paid $3.50 a ticket to see a display of perversion that made his stroke magazines seem as tame as the L.A. *Times*. He wondered if Sue Robinson behaved like the Swedes on the screen. His mom's presence made him unbearably tense.

Driving back home, the two women chatted away as though nothing had happened. Mac thought, Maybe Mom *is* sleeping with the preacher;

maybe that's why the church sends over so much food; maybe that's why we can go to movies now. Maybe she slept with other guys, too. Maybe . . .

His thoughts turned to other women: the witch, a slob who fornicated with his father; Rudi's girlfriend, out chasing dick the first time he turned his back; the women of *Playboy* and *Penthouse* and *Hustler* showing their pink. A bunch of sluts. Was there one decent female in the world? Yeah: Maria. And little Lina. But they were kids. He wouldn't give a bent 1975 penny for the rest, including his mom.

For weeks he couldn't get his bearings. Black was white, up was down. He wanted an explanation from Dove, but subjects like pornie films weren't discussed in their house. He went to bed confused and angry.

One night she bawled him out for leaving late for Bible Study. "And make sure you stay till the end!" she yelled. "I hear you been sneakin' off."

He barely listened as the preacher rumbled through the same old shit: All sins were equal; sinful thoughts were the same as sinful deeds; if you coveted a woman, it was the same as if you'd done it with her. . . .

He thought, Is it a sin to watch a movie where a half-naked woman opens her mouth and gropes for a man's crotch? Is that as evil in the eyes of God as . . . doing it? Where does that leave my mom?

When he came home, she was waiting up, a deck of cards in her hands. "I found these in your drawer," she said, ripping them in halves, one by one. "You know what the preacher calls these. Satan's calling cards."

"The preacher has something to say about dirty movies, too," he blurted out.

"That movie was Sue's idea," she said as she walked out of the room. "I . . . didn't know."

I'll bet you didn't, he said to himself. I'll bet you didn't know you bleached your goddamn hair, either.

A week later Sue Robinson deposited her two children at the Smith apartment while she went shopping with Dove for high-heeled shoes. Sue's daughter was twelve, her son seven. As Mac entertained them, he felt an urge to take down their pants. When they acted reluctant, he intimidated them with voice and manner, then rubbed himself against the girl's bare stomach. It felt dangerous and exciting. He warned them not to tell.

Sprawled across his bed that night, he couldn't contain his excitement. He imagined his favorite high school cheerleader in her short-short skirts as he dragged her under the grandstands and screwed her till she begged for mercy.

It became his favorite fantasy.

Soon he realized that lying had become more than just a game; it was a survival tool, an absolute necessity. If he didn't lie, he wouldn't be able to do *anything*. So it was his mom's fault, he figured, not his.

He was pleased to find that dishonesty no longer troubled his conscience or his pride. What the hell, everybody lied; he hardly knew a kid who didn't. The biggest lies were the easiest to float. If he was caught, he fell back on impassioned denials. It was a variation of his uncle's old advice on what to do when caught shoplifting. Brazen things out. Act innocent. It worked.

When he came home after smoking pot with Rudi, his mother said, "You weren't at church."

"Yes, I was," he insisted.

"I talked to the counselor. You weren't there."

"I was in the back. I guess he didn't see me."

"He stood at the door hisself. You didn't come out."

"I must've been in the bathroom."

"What was the lesson?"

"Sinful thoughts." It was a safe guess. "Stuff like that."

"You're a dang liar!"

"Listen, Mom, I'll get you a note if it'll make you happy."

As usual, the subject was forgotten by the next day. Mac's lies were a family tradition.

20

Brother Walter scored a permanent source of "whites" and set about getting revenge for the beatings his father had given him for Mac's misdeeds. Maria dashed around her battling brothers, rained punches on Walter's back, yelled, "Leave my Mac alone. *Hit me instead!*" There were times when Walter obliged. It deepened her bonds with Mac, but it left them both black and blue.

Whenever their mother was gone, Walter went on the attack. Dove refused to believe it was happening; she'd always sided with Walter. Her favorite son was now seventeen, and she still gave him the benefit of every doubt. When he pitched Mac through a picture window and slashed the webbing of his thumb, leaving a permanent scar, he explained that it was all Mac's fault. Dove warned Mac to stop antagonizing his big brother.

At the dinner table Dove caught Walter chewing with his mouth open.

"Walter, we may be poor folks," she said, "but good manners don't cost a penny."

Mother and son had a hot argument that ended with Walter threatening to punch her out. After that, everything seemed to change between them.

Walter stepped up his usage of whites, and the dinner table became a war zone. Dove refused to relax her rules. As long as her children lived under her roof, they would be clean, polite and obedient—and they *would not chew with their mouths open!* High on bennies, Walter swung at her and put his fist through the wall, then punched several more holes for good measure.

To the annoyance of both brothers, their mother continued her habit of pawing through their personal possessions and entering their rooms without knocking. "We're not little kids," Walter reminded her.

Mac piped up, "We got no privacy."

A few nights later she held something up and asked, "Walter, what was this doing in the lining of your jacket?" He grabbed the pill from her hand and stormed out the door.

Later that night Mac heard a scream from his mother's bedroom. He rushed in and found Walter standing over her with a lamp in his hand. She was gripping the side of her head with bloodstained knuckles.

Maria called the police but Dove refused to let them in. "It was all a mistake," she said calmly. She explained that she'd accidentally hit her son with a lamp, but he wasn't hurt. The cops left.

A week later Walter moved out. At fifteen, Mac was now the man of the house. Proud of his new authority, he brought home gifts for everyone, but Dove barely seemed to notice. She'd started to date regularly, two or three times a week. She was into clothes and fashion and stupid things like eyeliner and blusher. She did a makeover on her figure and looked as curvy as a pornie star. It was enough to make him sick. His mom was thirty-three; she'd been married and had four children, and she still had two little girls to raise. Why didn't she set an example? Women in her position had no business dating at all.

21

Rudi O'Shay was working the graveyard shift at a fast-food restaurant, and he talked the manager into offering a job to his good friend Mac. The pay was $1.25 an hour.

"Walter's left home," Mac complained. "I can't support my family on that."

Rudi said, "Trust me." The company underpaid its employees, he explained, but there were ways to get even. The most popular technique was to short-change customers, but it was important to keep track of the sales because the cash register and the stock had to balance at the end of each shift. Rudi pointed out that fries were inventoried by the bag and apple turnovers by the serving; the trick was to serve fries in turnover bags. The conspirators served milk shakes in pop containers and pocketed the difference. When the place was empty, the junior man collected containers from the trash bins and rinsed them for reuse. The various techniques were good for five or ten dollars per man per night. Rudi said that every shift was in on it and the company was too stupid to catch on.

The thievery was a nice perk, but Mac was finding it hard to punch a time clock and work indoors.

Whenever he arrived home, his mom harangued him about church and school. There were times when she seemed sorry he was alive. He decided that she must have detected some flaw that he wasn't aware of himself—a wimpiness, perhaps, or undersized *cojones*. He still worried about the night he'd drunk the Southern Comfort. A real man would have resisted, drunk or not.

After three months of night work, he still wasn't netting enough to meet his total needs. The schoolgirls teased Maria about her frumpy clothes. Lina was five, big enough to notice that she wasn't allowed to buy ice cream from the truck like the other girls. Sometimes the family went two or three nights in a row without a substantial dinner. His mother had always served big meals, but now they were eating soggy macaroni with a faint dusting of parmesan, Sloppy Joes divided four ways, shrimp casseroles minus the shrimp. When Dove bought flank steak or chicken or pot roast, she made it stretch till it grossed them out. Sometimes she threatened to phone the church for more free canned goods. Mac felt as though he was letting her down.

He looked for more income. One job had never been enough for his father, but then Calvin Smith hadn't had to go to high school at the same time. Mac thought about quitting, but his IQ was 120 and he still had hopes of becoming a scientist. This dismal life couldn't last forever.

22

Then the police caught Mac and Rudi trying to hot-wire a borrowed 1952 Cadillac after they'd lost the key. The two boys were jailed for investigation at 10:00 P.M. and released six hours later, much to their disappointment. They thought of it as a lark, a learning experience, and wished they could have stayed to sample the breakfast. They recounted their adventure to friends and families, sometimes with fictitious details about the murderer in the next cell and the guard who'd threatened to break their kneecaps. Calvin Smith, himself a graduate of a juvenile facility, told Mac over the phone from Columbus, "It's a goddamn shame they didn't keep you a week or two. Then you mighta learnt something."

A notice on the fast-food restaurant's bulletin board instructed employees to be on the lookout for two black males who'd robbed one of the branches at gunpoint. Rudi's eyes twinkled at the news. "I got a feeling, pardner," he told Mac. "Them dudes are gonna strike again."

Three months later, while Dove Smith was visiting in Ohio, Rudi emptied the restaurant's cash register and Mac stuffed the money in a sack. They reported the "robbery" to police, complete with descriptions of the two black gunmen.

With his two-hundred-dollar share, Mac bought a big wreath of yellow carnations, his mother's favorite, and lettered a gold sign, "WELCOME HOME MOM!" When Dove walked in, a new TV was tuned to a religious program. "And I want you to pick out a living room suite," Mac said. "I'll make the payments."

Dove seemed pleased. Later it seemed odd to him and Maria that she didn't ask where he got the money.

Rudi decided that their next financial caper would require firepower. Mac didn't balk. He'd admired Rudi on the athletic field and admired him even more now that they were playing for keeps. Rudi was a cool, ballsy guy, just what Mac wanted to be.

So he went home and said, "I'd feel better if you had a gun, Mom. Things are getting bad in this neighborhood."

She protested and he insisted. They went to a K mart and bought a Saturday night special in her name. She hid it in the back of her closet and he liberated it the next morning. He'd just turned sixteen.

The banditos headed for a fast-food restaurant on Western Avenue, ten miles from where they worked. Rudi steered his old car into the drive-through lane, ordered hamburgers and fries, and told the kid at the window, "We got a gun."

Mac showed the pistol and tucked it back into his belt. "Put the money in a sack," Rudi ordered in a low voice. "The cash drawer *and* the safe."

They sped away like characters in a movie. Mac felt a rush; he'd never been in such *control*. He couldn't wait to rob again.

A month later they hit the same place, then followed up at another restaurant in the chain, a few miles away. For the first time in his life, Mac had plenty of cash. He brought home a cassette player for his mother and a bouquet of pink carnations. And he made a down payment on an old Buick so she wouldn't have to bum rides from her friends.

At Christmastime, he bought a handsome jacket for a pretty neighbor named Jennifer and received a soap-on-a-rope in return. When he told his mother about the exchange of gifts, she blew up. "Why, she's sayin' you stink! I can't believe this! You spent all your money on that li'l girl and all she can say is you *stink*? Oh, Mac, you must feel so bad."

On their Christmas visits around the neighborhood, Dove repeated the story. "Can you believe it, that silly goof spent every cent he had on that jacket. . . ." Mac told her that she didn't understand; he was *happy* about his gift; the girl didn't have much money, etc. But his mom made him feel like a fool.

Mac asked Maria, "Why is she doing this to me?" It was the same question that Maria had often asked him.

"She's just being mean," Maria explained. But Mac put it down to his mother's tendency to misunderstand, to get things a little wrong. He preferred that explanation.

23

On New Year's Eve Dove dragged the family to early prayer meeting in the church sanctuary. Back home by 10:00 P.M., Mac sneaked out to attend a forbidden dance. When he returned five hours later, the apartment was dark. He opened his bedroom window inch by inch and crawled inside. His mother slammed into him fingernails first, threw everything she could get her hands on, and put a deep gash in his arm.

After Dove left for her next date in a cloud of cologne, Mac sat in the living room popping brews and leafing through a dirty comic book. He was thinking his usual thoughts. *What's Mom doing right now? Is she taking her pants down for some guy?* He couldn't think about it and he couldn't *not* think about it.

Sonia the cat jumped into his lap, and he stroked her warm soft fur. When she started purring, he slid his fingertip between her hind legs. Sonia squirmed, but he held her in a tight grip and pushed his finger inside. He knew he was acting weird, kinky, but it was exciting. And who would ever find out? His mother wouldn't be home till after midnight and the girls were asleep in their room.

He opened his jeans and tried to make the nervous cat lick him. After he masturbated, his troubles seemed to fade, and he dozed off.

He enjoyed a few more sessions with Sonia before his eye caught the housing project's newest occupant, a green-eyed redhead named Nancy McCullough. On their second date the seventeen-year-old girl confided that she was safe; she'd taken birth control pills for three years. Her father lived in the East and her mother worked nights at an aircraft plant. If Mac was interested, they could meet at her place.

Nancy seemed sent from heaven to relieve his sexual agonies. On his nights off from the fast-food joint, he tiptoed down the hall to visit her before sneaking back to get up for school. Soon the two of them were going steady. For the first time Mac discerned a connection between sex and love. He was surprised to find that he loved Nancy even when they weren't doing it. He even told her so, sputtering over phrases that he'd thought he would never say. He introduced her to Rudi and his other friends as his fiancée and started saving for a ring. His father had married at sixteen, his mother at fifteen, and his grandmother at fourteen. It was a family tradition. What difference did age make? At sixteen he was already supporting a family. He couldn't imagine a life without Nancy. In his heart they were married already.

One midnight he knocked at his lover's apartment and no one answered. In the morning, Nancy's mother told him, "She's gonna be gone for a while."

"Gone? Where?"

"Uh—just gone."

He figured she'd decided to visit her father. But why the hell hadn't she said something? And why was her mother acting so smirky and cute?

Three days later the love of his life returned from Las Vegas wearing Rudi O'Shay's wedding ring. Mac congratulated them both.

For a month he was in a haze. He ran the fast-food restaurant's cash register like a robot, barely comprehending the numbers. He cut classes at school and moped around the park. In her childish way, Maria tried to console him. His mother seemed to understand that he was hurting and laid off him for a while. He looked in a mirror for clues to his failure. A kid looked back, a child, five and a half feet tall and as wide as a knife blade. Rudi was nearly nineteen now, a jock, a *man*. Rudi did things right. No wonder he'd got the girl.

After a while, Mac realized that Nancy was just a woman, no more, no less. He'd been a fool to expect otherwise. There wasn't a trustworthy female on earth. His dad called them "bimbos," "broads," "bitches" and worse, and he was right. They were put on earth to break balls.

Mac wasn't surprised when Nancy suggested a one-night stand a few weeks after her wedding. It took him a long time to get around to asking why she'd dumped him. "Oh, Mac," she said, stroking his balls, "you can't even *drive*!"

24

The fast-food bandits continued to strike in L.A. and Orange County. Mac learned to drive and began serving as wheelman. He could hardly stand the excitement. He'd sleepwalked through most of his life, but this was the real thing. He felt neither misgivings nor shame about his victims. "Nothing personal," he would say with an easy smile. "We're not gonna hurt you. Just gimme the money." The biggest one-night take was $845, the lowest $350. He kept his mother swimming in carnations. On date nights she often pinned one to her clothes. It made Mac feel a little better to know she was taking a remembrance.

Shortly after he turned seventeen, the two-man crime team decided to hit the fast-food joint on Western Avenue, scene of their earliest robbery. Mac was driving the first car he'd ever owned, a '67 Le Mans that he'd spray-painted robin's-egg blue. This time the windowman gave up a bag of money without waiting for instructions.

As Mac drove away, he heard a ping. "He's shooting!" Rudi yelled. Mac floored the pedal.

In a darkened parking lot they found a puckered hole in a rear fender. Mac felt jumpy. Through a dozen holdups, it hadn't occurred to him that someone might try to pierce his skull with a bullet. He drove the car to Palos Verdes and pushed it off a cliff.

Three days later, he was arrested. Police had found the bullet-dimpled car and traced its ownership.

At a preliminary hearing Dove testified that he was the best son a lonely mother could ask, the sole support of his family. Her sobs filled the room.

The preacher and his wife described him as an honest lad who knew his Bible and hadn't missed services in six years.

In his own behalf, Mac told the judge the same story that he'd already rehearsed on his mother: the robberies were Rudi's idea. He'd just gone along for the ride.

The judge glared and said, "I don't have much sympathy for young punks like you, but for your mother's sake I'm leaving this in the hands of the juvenile authorities."

Mac was sentenced to six months in a juvenile home. The place was run like a seminary. Cigarettes were forbidden, so his mother smuggled them past the guards inside licorice sticks. He appreciated her contempt for the rules and her refusal to blame him for the crimes. His mom had her faults, but she was there when she was needed.

After two months as a model inmate, Mac was released in her custody. Mother and son were required to attend weekly group therapy sessions with a dozen sullen kids and their parents. His mother spoke up at the first meeting. "It was my fault," she admitted. "Himself and I, we never worked things out."

Privately she warned Mac that he'd better get right with God before he was smitten down on the golden streets. He knew what that meant. "Mom," he said, "I'm not goin' to church five times a week."

She folded her arms across her pouter-pigeon chest. "If you live in *my* house," she said, "you'll go."

He was in her custody and had no choice. At his first session of Bible Study, the lesson was from Romans: "The goodness of God leadeth thee to redemption." He was sure his mother had requested the topic. He heard a buzz as he took his seat. Everyone knew he was a convicted robber. He felt conspicuous and ashamed.

Dove arranged a social evening with two of the church's brightest stars, young marrieds in their early twenties. Mac hadn't been in their tract house fifteen minutes before husband and wife fell to their knees and asked the Lord to forgive their new friend. He felt like a junkyard dog going through retraining. After a dinner discussion about redemption, punch was served and everyone watched a TV showing of *It's a Mad, Mad, Mad, Mad World*. Mac respected the good Christians for their intentions, but he knew he would never be able to connect with them or anyone like them. He was different now.

25

With his life of crime interrupted, money grew tight again. The girls were growing and needed clothes. His mother stayed home in the daytime and dated at night, still shopping for a husband. Mac landed a minimum wage job in a warehouse, humping boxes of audio cassettes from midnight till 8:30 A.M. If he drove straight from work to school, he arrived in time for his second class, senior biology. The subject was important to him, but he could hardly stay awake. His final grade was *F*.

Mac was shocked. Without half trying, he'd always maintained a *B* average. This was his first failure since cursive, and that had been in the second grade.

Rudi was still serving a two-year sentence and couldn't provide his customary relief of 'ludes and reds, so Mac drowned his frustrations in beer. He wandered into church reeking of mints, stumbled around the warehouse all night, and nodded out in the school parking lot. Sometimes he wondered if his drinking was worth the candle, but nothing else was happening in his life and he was getting too old to play games or collect pennies. He spent a lot of time masturbating. It was the easiest way to relieve his sexual tensions.

·

In a lucid moment he realized that his college ambitions had been naïve from the beginning. What was he but a runt version of the Willie Nelson wanna-be back in Columbus waiting to be discovered? Mac no longer saw his dad as an undiscovered genius but as an ordinary man with just enough musical talent to hold the attention of drunks. Why, he couldn't even read music. For the first time, Mac realized the truth about the Smith males. They were dreamers, bull-shitters, long on mouth and short on performance. What a joke his plans had been.

When a classmate informed him that there were good jobs available to kids who quit school before the horde poured out in June, he stopped attending class. He consoled himself that nobody could work a full shift every night and maintain enough standing to graduate. He went to work on a catering truck.

After one week he found the job boring and began looking around for excuses to stay home and drink beer. He told the caterer that his dad's new baby had died and he needed two days off. A few days later he called half-drunk and said he'd run over a child. The next day he said that he had to visit the victim in the hospital, and the third day he said he had to attend her funeral. His mother repeated the stories to her friends. "That Mac," she said. "He's got the durndest imagination."

During a summer vacation Maria spent a week in Columbus with her father and Ruby, and when she returned, Mac said he would like to make the trip himself. Dove called them both ungrateful scum. "Why'd you want to go back *there*?" she asked. She reminded them that their father was married to a Satanic slut. "Why would you want to live under the same roof with a drunken witch that stole a man from his wife and four children? A man that *don't even go to church*?"

Mac barely listened. She was talking about a man who'd never raised a hand to him. His *dad*.

26

A first cousin, Peggy Smith, arrived from Columbus on a visit, and Mac blinked when he saw her. He remembered Peg as a sulky adolescent, gawky as a foal. Now she moved with a dancer's grace and looked like a finalist for Miss Ohio. Mac couldn't imagine that such a dazzling creature would give him the time of day, but to his surprise she seemed interested. The two of them stuffed Maria in the trunk as a chaperone and drove to the drive-in theater. A few nights later they went alone, and Mac was even more surprised to find that Peggy was willing to go as far as he wanted.

Soon the teenagers were in love. Every morning he awoke with a smile. He took a new interest in his job. He wasn't just getting by anymore; he was planning his life with Peg.

On a warm summer night he learned that she was three weeks late. Mac held her tight and told her not to worry; it was nature's way. Hadn't they already talked about getting married?

When he broke the news to his mother, Dove was strangely quiet.

Mac came home from work a few days later to find Peggy gone. "She's took off," his mother said. "For good."

"Took off? *Where?*"

"She didn't say."

No matter how much he begged, his mother claimed that she knew nothing. A letter to Peggy's old address in Ohio was returned. Long-distance calls to the uncles and cousins produced lies and doubletalk.

It was two weeks before his mother admitted that she and Peggy's parents had conferred by long-distance phone and decided on an abortion. Peg's father had hauled her off to a doctor in New York City, then ordered her never to see Mac again.

Mac said, "What about our baby? Why didn't you ask us what *we* wanted to do, Mom?"

"You're kids," Dove answered. She held up her hand to show that the subject was closed.

Mac threatened to find Peggy and marry her. His mother warned that she could have him jailed if he left the state. He stayed in his room, popped pills for three days, and lost his job.

After he came down from his high, he saw that his life had turned into a chaos of conflicting allegiances. He loved his mother but couldn't stand her. He loved his father but couldn't be with him. He loved Peggy but couldn't be with her either. He loved Maria but couldn't stick around to protect her much longer. If only Mom would butt out and let them breathe. Her rules made no sense; she was so damned *inconsistent*. For years she preached that abortion was cold-blooded murder; then she helped deliver Peggy to the knife. One minute she was smearing on a pound of makeup, or escorting her sons to a pornie movie, or smuggling cigarettes into the juvenile home, and the next minute she was preaching the Ten Commandments and the sanctity of marriage and the evils of drink. To impress his probation officer, Mac continued to accompany her to church, but he couldn't relate to her rules or her God or to her.

One summer night he came home late from smoking pot with some beaners. His mother had been out with Ray, an older man who'd become her steady, and she was waiting up. "Where ya been?" she demanded.

"Playing chess," he said smoothly. "With Carl."

"Carl's been lookin' for ya," his mother said. "He called five minutes ago."

As always, Mac refused to admit he'd lied. "I don't care *what* you say," he snapped. "Carl just dropped me off."

His mom wouldn't drop the subject, and he finally told her that jail was preferable to living in this crazy house and being forced to spend half his life in church listening to a minister who screwed his female parishioners. When Dove threw a lamp, he ran to his bedroom and locked the door. He knew only one consolation after scenes like this. He took out his girlie magazines and fantasized banging one of the sluts.

The next day he asked to be returned to jail. His probation officer turned down the request but conceded that it might be better if he moved away from Dove, provided he honored the conditions of his probation, including group therapy.

∎

Mac and another juvenile offender took a small apartment a month after his eighteenth birthday. He'd barely moved in when his mother phoned to say that she'd decided to marry Ray. Mac felt weak in the knees. Well, he thought, you've done it again, Mom. Betrayed your own kids.

He'd always known she was man-hunting, but he'd tried not to think about it. He wondered if the two of them were sleeping together now that they'd made the commitment. Maybe that's why she'd started fattening up again. "Don't expect me at the wedding," he announced.

He'd never had much to say at group therapy, but he looked forward to the next meeting. Seated alongside his mother, he announced that she was about to make another stupid mistake.

Dove piped up, "He means I'm getting married. Him and myself don't agree about this."

Some of the others smiled at her approvingly. "Mom's already *been* married," Mac argued. "She's already had her life and she don't need to get married again." His voice cracked with intensity.

"He just wants to be man of the house," his mother said.

When he refused to alter his position, Mac heard himself called everything from a chauvinist to a moron. After a while, he fell silent. You dumb son of a bitch, he said to himself. See what you get for opening up?

He had to drive his mother home, and on the way he listened as she bragged about Ray's income and bank account. "I don't want any of his goddamn money," Mac said.

"Mac!"

"And I want my living room furniture back."
He only wished he could make her return all the
flowers and other stuff.

He dropped her off and drove toward his new
apartment. When he was a block away, he noticed a
fire engine pulling away from the curb. He ran upstairs and found his door blocked. A marshal explained that a young man had nodded out on the
couch while smoking. He let Mac look around inside. There was nothing left but charcoal.

It was 1:00 A.M. and Mac realized he had no
place to go but his mother's apartment, nine miles
away. His car wouldn't start and he didn't have the
bus fare. He trudged through the night and arrived
as the sun was coming up at 6:30. Dove welcomed
him home.

27

He sold his orange Chevy for $200 to buy new work clothes. He added a swing shift job at Wacker Chemical to his graveyard shift job at a gas station, hitchhiking from one place of business to the other. On a night off his brother arrived to show off his new Pontiac Bonneville. Walter was twenty now, married, a struggling salesman, showing signs of overcoming his childhood. Their home situation had placed the brothers at odds for most of their lives, but Mac had always admired Walter and kept in touch.

A light mist was falling as Mac took the Bonneville's wheel for a test drive. He was cruising along a boulevard at about twenty miles an hour when a car passed him on the right, splattering water and obscuring his vision. Too late, he spotted pedestrians in the Vermont Avenue crosswalk ahead. He braked hard, went into a skid, and bowled over two men.

Paramedics reported that one of the victims had a broken leg; the other was bruised. A traffic cop wrote a ticket for failing to yield to pedestrians. Mac was still upset when he went home and told Maria what had happened. "Jeez," he said, "it was a new car."

28

Maria and little Lina were happy with their new apartment and their new stepfather, but the sight of the middle-aged newlyweds turned Mac's stomach. Almost forty years old and kissing in broad daylight! He wondered where their tongues were.

His beer drinking had escalated to almost a case a day. He knew it was excessive but didn't care. Beer was something to look forward to. What else was happening in his life? It was a good high—and cheap.

A rare letter arrived from his dad on a day when Mac was too drunk to make out the handwriting. " 'My home is yours,' " Maria read aloud. " 'You kids know I've always wanted you here. . . .' "

Mac popped another brew. He remembered his dad strumming his guitar and wailing something about a night rider waiting for a train. They'd been separated for almost five years, and the passage of time had refurbished his dad's image. Mac thought, What a great guy! Never made me go to church, never hit me, never wolfed at me when I stayed out late. He was a little rough on Walter, but didn't he deserve it? Look how mean Walter was to Mom, knocking her down and drawing blood. Dad just spotted Walter's sadistic side before anyone else.

Mac's thoughts turned to the snowball fight in Columbus and the way his dad had hugged him and spun him around. He remembered the family sing-alongs on the trips to Ohio and the five-mile ride on his new Schwinn after he'd won the prize at church. He thought, Mom wanted to stow my bike on the roof. Jesus Christ, I just won first prize! Wouldn't you think she'd want everybody to see? Nope, not Mom.

He decided to make another new start, this time in Columbus. He arranged to have his probation terminated two months early for good behavior. He promised his mother that if he didn't find work in Ohio, he would return home. She didn't fuss and scream. He guessed the newlywed had something else on her mind.

He walked all over south Columbus before he located his father's mobile home, in the corner of a seedy trailer park. The trailer was on cinder blocks and marked by a sign, WARNING! ATTACK DOGS! THIS MEANS YOU!

His dad was working and Ruby was attending to their two little kids and her son, the one Mac had fondled in California. The boy gave no sign that he remembered the incident and Mac vowed not to let history repeat. He also knew that he couldn't always be sure of his behavior. It was like fooling around with the cat; you did it, and the next day you couldn't imagine having done it and swore you'd never do it again—and then you'd do it again. He suspected that booze and lack of self-control were part of the explanation, but he knew there was more to it than that. Plenty of people drank, but they didn't finger cats or talk a little boy into . . . whatever. He didn't want to think about it.

Ruby and his father were living dirt poor; a housing project would have been a step up. No wonder Dad never sends money, Mac said to himself. They barely got enough to eat.

Ruby's housekeeping was worse than ever. In Mac's first letter home he told Maria that if someone walked in and dumped a sack of garbage on the floor, it would have been an improvement. What a contrast to their mother's neatness!

But at least there was a little warmth and humanity. Ruby was a plain-looking woman, not in the same league with Mac's slimmed-down mom, but Ruby was Dad's choice and that meant her looks didn't matter. Mac himself had never had an ugly girlfriend and damn few plain ones. Nancy and Peggy were gorgeous, and Jennifer of the soap-on-a-rope incident made guys turn and stare. He'd never had trouble getting good-looking women into bed. His problem was how to keep them there.

In Columbus, the prospects looked slim. He had no income, one change of jeans, and a round-the-clock craving for beer. In sober moments he realized that he was probably an alcoholic like his grandfather and would have to do something about it . . . eventually. But the fun-loving Ruby kept providing him with brew and bourbon and making him feel at home. She assigned him the threadbare couch and a thin greasy blanket. It was a hot summer and he slept in his shorts.

■

Instead of looking for work in the daytime, he found himself sitting around drinking and listening to Ruby's nonstop chatter. "Demons?" she would say. "Sure they's demons." She told how she'd warned Calvin that Satan had infiltrated a certain bar, and sure enough, when Calvin arrived for his gig, "a black velvet silhouette of the Devil was the first thing he seen."

"What'd Dad do?" Mac asked, his dark eyes wide.

"What'd he do? *He split, man!* What would you of done?"

She asked to read his cards. Oh, God, he thought, this card-reading shit comes straight from the Devil! His mother had warned him about Satanic tricks like this.

Ruby exposed the six of diamonds and said it signified a bright future, but only if he stayed away from California. "Don't go back to that whorin' mother of yours," Ruby warned. "Did I tell ya she screwed your preacher? And your pal Rudi?"

"Yeah," Mac said, sinking a shot glass full of bourbon into his glass of beer. "You tol' me."

"You don't believe me?" she asked in a challenging tone.

"Yeah, I believe ya." He thought, Why argue? I'm a guest here. And he halfway *did* believe her. His mom was a woman, wasn't she?

29

At close range it didn't take Mac long to learn that every report about Ruby's odd behavior had been understated. She fashioned altars and topped them with birthday candles laid out in weird patterns. She made effigies of her enemies from corncobs and newspapers and stabbed them with pins. She spieled out gibberish that was even crazier than the babbling that he'd heard at exorcisms. She asked him to write questions on scraps of paper and then held them to her forehead like Johnny Carson on TV. Most of the time her answers seemed to make sense; if they didn't, she always had an explanation—the vibes were bad, the moon was on a cusp, she'd misunderstood the question, etc. She said she'd once done an occult act at nightclubs in Vegas and other big towns, taking challenges from the floor. No one had ever stumped her.

Seated in the litter of the dark living room, Mac's three-year-old half brother at her feet, Ruby spun tale after tale in the cadences of a voodoo storyteller. "A jealous woman stole one of my ceramic dolls and took it clear to East Chicago. That doll don't move one inch that I don't know where it's at and what it's doin'. The woman throwed it in the bottom of a dumpster and it crawled to the top.

And it yelled in this itty-bitty voice, 'Ruby. *Ruby!*' I drove five hunnert miles on the turnpike and fetched it back. That doll knew *everything* that went on in my house. Why, it turned its head so it could see! You'd put it over the mantelpiece at night and in the morning it'd be starin' atcha from the commode.''

Ruby was now twenty-eight, ten years older than Mac. She hadn't changed much. She was as short as his father, flat chested, cylindrical, plain of face and figure. And *lazy*. Her favorite position was lolling on a broken couch that she'd draped with a tablecloth to cover the stains and cigarette burns. Mac picked rubble off the floor, washed stacks of dishes, and took out the garbage and trash. Sometimes he rubbed the sleeve of his shirt across a window so he could see the sun while he swigged his beer and bourbon. He bagged moldy food from far corners of the refrigerator and carried it to the dumpster. Ruby never helped. One night when they were alone, he opened a can of chili and heated it on the two-place propane stove. The kids went to bed and they had a quiet dinner together. From then on she seemed to expect him to cook. What the hell, he figured. I'm living here rent free. I owe her something.

Most of the time he stayed semidrunk, but not so zonked that he didn't think about sex. One evening when Calvin was trucking, Ruby poured a couple of bourbon boilermakers and stepped into the bedroom. After five or ten minutes she reappeared in a cloud of cheap perfume. Her thin gown hung open, revealing small breasts and a bony chest. Instead of covering up, she giggled and poured more drinks. After a while she led him to the bed.

When they were finished, she warned, ''Don't tell your father.''

Mac sobered up and realized that their secret would never keep. He thought, She'll get drunk and confess, or she'll use it to hurt Dad in an argument. That was the way women were. He thought, Maybe Dad'll wake up someday and dump this crazy bitch. Then him and me can talk man to man. He suspected they wouldn't find much disagreement.

A week later Ruby took him to bed again. He realized that she didn't intend to stop. And as long as she kept providing the booze and the bed, neither did he.

He found it harder to talk to his dad, not that they'd ever had much to say to each other. Mac didn't doubt that his father loved him, but he also knew that Calvin Smith didn't share himself, didn't reveal his thoughts or his emotions. And since Mac was much the same way, they usually sat together like father-and-son zombies. He wondered how long his secret would keep.

30

A winter storm coated the trailer court with ice, and cold air seeped through leaks in the corrugated sheet metal walls. Mac's sneakers were soaked from trips to the store for Marlboros and beer. He had no winter jacket. The place wasn't big enough for three adults and three kids; his back was rubbed raw from a broken spring in his sleeping-couch. The single deck of cards was sticky and warped from hundreds of games of solitaire. He was tired of housekeeping and baby-sitting and wondering if he'd made a mistake leaving California. At least it was warm there. He missed Maria and little Lina; sometimes he even missed his mother. She was settled into her new marriage by now, and his sisters wrote how lucky they were to have a great guy like Ray for a stepfather. Mac thought, A great guy wouldn't have married my mom in the first place.

Late one morning he bummed bus fare from Ruby and rode downtown in a cold rain to pick through the Goodwill clothes rack. He turned into an army recruiting office and talked to a ramrod-straight GI with shiny medals and three stripes. The sergeant handed him a fistful of literature and an application. Under "Education," Mac wrote, "Four

years H.S." Had he ever been arrested? "No," he
wrote. He was in the army.

Three months later he was as fed up with Fort Knox
as he'd been with his father's trailer court in Columbus. He wondered how a loner like himself had ever
been suckered into joining an outfit that treated human beings like slaves. Life with his mother had
been more inspiring, even with all the church sessions. He requested a meeting with his company
commander. "Sir," he said, "I lied to the recruiter.
I served time in California for robbery." In a few
days he was hitching toward the setting sun on Interstate 84.

PART TWO

ACTING OUT

■

1969–1980

31

Mac Smith turned nineteen in a one-room apartment back in Torrance, and no one threw him a party. In the year he'd been away, things had changed. His pal Rudi had served his sentence for the fast-food stickups and returned to prison for driveaway gas theft. Mac's old sex partners were nowhere to be found; it still pissed him off that his first woman had double-crossed him by marrying Rudi and his second had aborted his child (and now he heard through the family grapevine that she was in a penitentiary back east). He checked on the lovely Jennifer of the soap-on-a-rope incident, and learned she'd married a salesman.

The new stepfather was as good a guy as advertised, but Mac still hadn't come to grips with his mother's marriage. He winced every time he heard a sound from their bedroom. He visited from time to time, but only to see Maria and Lina.

His life settled into shades of gray. By day he worked in a factory and by night he drank beer and popped pills. The most exciting woman in his life remained his fantasy cheerleader. Through the years he'd gone from having sex with her to taking her by force, from acts of lust to acts of terror and control.

"Drop those pants, slut!" he would say. "Down, pig. *Now!*" He would take her from the back, the front, in her hand, in her mouth, every way imaginable. Her eyes bugged open and she pleaded for mercy.

The more he fantasized, the less interest he took in conventional sex. A line from his favorite song played in his head: "You're my puppet girl. . . ." He thought about finding a real-life cheerleader and dragging her under the grandstands, but he'd sworn he would never return to jail.

He read in a magazine that most rapes were unreported because the victims were humiliated, ashamed, dehumanized. Sex crimes were epidemic; in the United States a rape was attempted every three and a half minutes; police couldn't keep up. On a national average, he learned, fewer than 10 percent of all rapes resulted in arrests, let alone convictions. One of every forty rapes resulted in jail time.

Encouraged by the numbers, he began scouting his old high school neighborhood. He assured himself that he didn't intend to rape; he just wanted to toy with the idea.

It was ten o'clock at night when he spotted the girl leaving the gym. She was small and pretty, about the same age as his cheerleader. He waited for a lull in the traffic and grabbed her from behind. He was in such a frenzy that he raised her to his thin shoulders like a weightlifter and hauled her thirty yards to a construction area next to the parking lot.

Everything she did made him hotter. She took orders, pleaded for her life, cried, shut up on command, didn't resist when he yanked down her shorts. He rammed into her body and felt himself going soft. "I'm sorry," he mumbled. "Oh, my God, I'm really sorry."

He ran home and double-locked his apartment door. He was sure that the cops would arrive any minute. What a dork he'd been! He might as well have left his calling card. He was a familiar figure in the neighborhood and he'd made no attempt to disguise his looks or his voice. Why, the girl might have been one of his old schoolmates!

When he began to think more calmly, he realized that he was an amateur at rape just as he'd been an amateur at robbery. He promised himself to go straight.

Nothing appeared in the papers the next day or the next. He thought, God damn, she didn't report me! Those magazine articles were right.

As his fears diminished, the urge returned. He went from feeling sorry for his victim to realizing how lucky she'd been to encounter him instead of some mean son of a bitch. She hadn't been hurt. What was she doing cruising a dark street at night in shorts? Her tears hadn't meant a thing. Women turned tears off and on.

32

For months he reverted to his fantasies, substituting the girl in the parking lot for his cheerleader. The unforgiving rapist showed no mercy and never failed to get off. He told himself, This isn't bad. I can live with this.

But while he was working at his boring job in the factory, he kept flashing back to what he'd learned in high school math about odds. If only one rape in nine was reported, a guy could rape four or five times and still be an even money bet to get away with it. And he could improve his odds by selecting victims who wouldn't tell—hookers, runaways, dopeheads. He thought out a final refinement: to rape in such a degrading, disgusting, humiliating way that the victim wouldn't be able to talk about it.

He spent weeks perfecting the act in his head. Of course he would never follow his script, but it was a hell of a stimulant for beating off. He was sure he'd learned his lesson.

Four months after the incident with the schoolgirl, he got high on 'ludes and offered a ride to a woman of about forty. As she was about to enter her darkened house, he flung her under a pepper tree and threatened to kill her if she made a sound. He'd barely pulled down his pants before he realized he was going to fail again. As he sped away, he wondered if it was the beer or the pills.

In his apartment, he repeated the same pattern of emotions: terror first, then apprehensiveness and shame, then anger at himself for losing control and risking ten years behind bars.

Once again he monitored the newspapers and the news programs. By the fourth day he was sure that his crime hadn't been reported. He asked himself, *Why was that stupid woman hitchhiking at night?*

He sharpened a screwdriver as an intimidator. After three more tentative attacks, he finally got off during a rape in Redondo Beach. It was the rush of his life, better than beer and bourbon, better than whites, better than any sex he'd known. Doing it *to* a woman was ten times hotter than doing it *with* one.

Not one of the incidents was mentioned in the media. He figured that each rape shortened the odds against him, but what if he moved out of state for a while? Wouldn't that improve his prospects? A smart operator could deal himself a whole new hand simply by moving to another jurisdiction.

In late 1973, just after his twenty-first birthday, he headed back east.

33

Maria was unhappy. Months had passed without a word from her dear brother Mac, and then he phoned to say he'd returned to Dad and Ruby. Maria felt defenseless, betrayed. How could she cope with her mom alone?

Then her father phoned with the surprise of the year: Mac had married. It took her a few minutes to comprehend. "Mac?" she blurted out. *"Married? Uh, what's she like?"*

"She's okay," her dad replied. "Divorced, two kids of her own. She's a friend of Ruby's."

"How'd Mac meet her?" Maria insisted. She was twitching with curiosity. She loved Mac so much; she hoped he'd found someone he deserved.

"He gave her a ride home," her father said. "Next thing we know, they're hitched."

"What's her name?"

"Nan."

"How old is she?"

"She's, uh—older."

Maria thought, Mac needs a steadying influence after what he's been through. Maybe this is a turning point. Oh, Lord, I hope so! . . .

.

It took three days to wangle permission to visit Columbus. At the bus station, Dove instructed her sixteen-year-old daughter, "Phone me every day, hear? And remember—you're there to see blood kin *and nobody else*!"

Calvin and Ruby had moved into a low-rent apartment, but Maria found that their habits hadn't changed. They were selling Amway and using the living room as a demo and storage area. The place was a sty.

"Ruby, aren't you afraid of fire?" Maria chided her stepmother.

"Why bother?" Ruby said nonchalantly. "It's just gonna get messy again."

Maria couldn't wait to meet Nan. She pictured Mac's wife as a tiny blonde or redhead, cute as a ladybug, a perfect match for her own cute brother. One thing about Mac, he always hung with good-looking women.

Mac and his new wife were scheduled to come to dinner, and Maria set to work with a scrub brush. She was on her hands and knees in the kitchen when a tall, busty woman sauntered past and disappeared into the bathroom. Ruby appeared and asked, "Well, whattaya think?" she asked.

"About what?" Maria asked.

"About *what*? About your brother's wife."

"*That woman*? How old is she?"

"Oh, thirty-five, thirty-six."

Maria smiled as though pleased at Mac's choice. He was twenty-one, and if he married an older woman—well, he must've had good reason.

But even after spending an evening with the

newlyweds, Maria couldn't make sense of the marriage. Nan was nice but ordinary, and she was burdened with a couple of kids of her own. Two or three times during the dinner she corrected Mac like a stern parent. Hadn't he had enough of that?

Maria thought about enrolling in a Columbus high school. Her mother didn't need her now that she had her new husband Ray. The couple had moved out of the projects and into a two-bedroom apartment in Torrance. It was a warm, pleasant place, landscaped with palms and ice plant, but Maria had felt like an intruder. She was constantly being shunted off to church or sent to her room like a child.

Her dad advised his "princess" to remain in Ohio. Ruby agreed. Maria could take care of the kids and the house, and Ruby could get a job. The money was needed.

Maria broke the news by phone and wasn't surprised when her mother blew up. Calvin told her not to worry; there were about eight state lines between them and California, and Dove could kiss their ass.

The Columbus police arrived at 1:00 A.M. with a warrant for "Maria Smith." Her father and Ruby were out on a gig. The cops recommended that Maria dress and pack. She didn't quite hear the charges— something like "alienation of home."

She felt claustrophobic as the padded van rumbled through the streets. The police allowed her one phone call. She didn't know Mac's number, and her father still wasn't home. She spent the first night in a holding cell with whores and drunks. On the second evening a matron announced, "Your mama's here."

A female cop escorted her to a car parked outside the jail. A familiar round face appeared in the front passenger's seat next to a driver. "Let's go," Dove snapped.

Back home in California again, her mother showed Maria a court order that gave her the same power over her teenage daughter that she'd once had over her son. Dove screened all phone calls, in and out. When Calvin phoned to ask where in the goddamn hell his daughter was, Dove hung up. She refused to allow Maria or little sister Lina to take a call from Mac. She talked to him herself and told him that Maria was where she wanted to be, in the warm embrace of a good Christian family. "She's had enough of witches and stewbums," Dove spat into the phone.

One day the phone rang while Dove was out, and Maria was thrilled to hear Mac's voice. In tearful bursts and gulps she told him what was happening. He seemed more disgusted than angry.

"That's just Mom being Mom," he explained. How many times had he consoled her with those same words? *Mom being Mom:* the story of their lives. He assured Maria that she was big enough to be on her own. He told her he would drive out from Columbus and pick her up on a street corner.

"Oh, Mac," she said, trying not to cry, "Mom would just send the cops again."

"It's up to you, Maria," Mac said. "Dad and me know how to hide you."

She thought of the whores in the holding cell and the ride in the padded van. Her dad might have a hiding place, but where? Under the floorboards? On her toothless grandpa's farm with the outhouse and the junked cars? Her mom had the law on her side. What was a sixteen-year-old kid against the cops?

She thanked her brother and said no. "How's Mom treating you?" he asked.

"Like shit."

"Don't worry. Ruby put a curse on her." He sounded serious.

34

A few weeks later Mac showed up in Torrance with his wife Nan, his two stepkids, and a dog. He walked into the apartment and asked his mother, "Can we camp here till we can find a place?" Maria was thrilled. She was under his protection again.

Ray was working the midnight shift, enabling Mac and his new wife Nan to use the master bedroom till morning. There were kids atop kids, dogs being used for pillows, chairs pulled together for beds, sleeping bags scattered like throw rugs. Miraculously, Nan and Dove got along well from the start. Maria wasn't surprised; the two older women were only three years apart.

Mac got a job in a paint plant and began putting in overtime. When Nan complained, he made matters worse by hanging out in beer joints. Everyone in the family wondered why she didn't lay down the law; she was three inches taller than Mac and seemed to intimidate him. But instead they slashed at each other with words. Mac charged armloads of candy and pop and chips on her overdrawn credit card, then played Big Daddy around the house. Sometimes he wandered in with two or three half-drunk buddies, handed out beers like a big shot, and ordered Nan to serve dinner. That was sure to set her off.

Maria tried to make sense of the scenario. It looked as though Mac was playing Bad Kid to Nan's Mean Mom. She wondered if he was trying to relive his childhood. Who would want to repeat those miserable years? As much as she enjoyed her brother's company, it was a relief when he moved his new family out.

35

In March of 1975, when Mac Smith was twenty-two and living in an apartment in Redondo, he finished playing in a pickup baseball game just after dark and drove to the corner of Hawthorne and Torrance boulevards. A White Front store had gone out of business and there was seldom anyone in the big parking lot. As he waited in the shadows, a grandmotherly woman came into sight. When she was in the middle of the lot, he sprinted across the asphalt and grabbed her from behind.

"Please," the woman cried. "Don't do this!"

He tore at her clothes, then shoved her to the pavement and tried to rape her. After a few seconds he muttered, "Oh, fuck, this isn't gonna work."

He explained to Nan that he'd been out looking for a part for the car. When the police arrived, he insisted that he'd been home all evening. They marched him outside and showed him that the hood of his car was still warm. He blamed the afternoon sun. One of the cops informed him that a passerby had witnessed the attack and made a note of his license number.

Mac stuck to his denial. What an outrage that an innocent person could be dragged from his own home! He was a happily married man. Why would he need to attack some old bag?

He was placed under arrest for attempted rape.

Dove's anguish turned to anger at the police when Mac swore over the phone that he was innocent. "They got the wrong car and the wrong face," he explained. "Some damn rapist is out there driving a car like mine."

His mother set about saving her innocent son. She studied the parking lot for clues, then canvassed the busy neighborhood for the look-alike car. She walked miles in shopping centers and malls searching faces for Mac's double. She figured she'd been as tough as anyone on her son, and the good Lord knew he was steeped in sin, but what kind of mother would let her own flesh and blood go to jail for another's crime?

Walter was of little faith. "I think Mac's sick," the older brother confided to Maria. "We've got to get him some medical attention."

Just before the trial in downtown L.A., Mac asked Walter to lie for him on the stand. "It's my word against theirs," he told his big brother. "And I've got a police record. Just say you left the baseball field and followed me home because I'd been having trouble with my car."

Walter refused. Perjury was a penitentiary offense.

For a while the trial seemed to go Mac's way. The elderly victim's eyesight was weak; she wasn't sure she could identify him. She stuttered and had a hard time recalling his exact threats. But the couple who'd witnessed the rape were convincing, and Mac was found guilty on a reduced charge of third-degree assault, a misdemeanor. The judge sentenced him to six months in the county jail.

On the way out of the courtroom, Maria intercepted the nosy couple and asked how they could live with themselves. They walked away fast.

36

Mac served four months. His wife Nan was waiting for him when he got out, and the old bickering resumed. After so many months in a cell, he found the domestic routine more boring than ever and looked for every excuse to get out of the house.

About a year after his release, he picked up Maria for a quick visit to their father in Las Vegas. It appeared that Calvin and his wife hadn't found much more work in Nevada than they'd found in Ohio. Ruby brought out the tarot cards and predicted that someone in the family would come into "a lot of money."

When she turned over a card for Mac, her eyes opened wide. "You've got to get out of California," she warned him. "I mean *now!*" She looked scared.

"Why?" he asked.

"If you don't leave, mister, I see you spending a major part of your life in prison."

On the six-hour drive back to L.A., Mac said he hated to leave the West Coast. "Washington state would be good," he mused. "Somewhere around Seattle." Then he added, "Not far from the Canadian border."

•

Two months later Nan announced that she was pregnant with their first child. Mac responded by quitting his job and loading the car for a long trip. There wasn't enough room for his *Playboy* collection; Maria stashed four boxes of magazines for him. He annoyed Nan by maxing out her credit cards for toys and games for the long drive up I–5. He said that he wanted her and his two stepchildren to enjoy healthy restaurant meals—no bologna sandwiches and buttermilk for Mac Smith's family.

Just before they headed north on overloaded shock absorbers, Maria took her brother aside. "Mac," she said, trying not to cry, "why are you doing this?"

He frowned. "I thought you knew," he said. "It's 'cause Ruby saw what she saw."

"You believe . . . a witch?"

"I can't take the chance."

"But Mac, if you haven't done anything wrong, how could you go to prison?"

"I already went to jail for something I didn't do. Once is enough." Maria guessed it made sense.

37

The Smiths found a small rental house in Lynnwood, a leafy middle-class suburb just north of Seattle, and Mac went to work making cablevision hook-
ups. A daughter was born, and then a son. With two
stepchildren under the same roof, he now had six
mouths to feed. He took every part-time job he
could find but still came up short. Nan was on his
case harder than ever.

"She did not like my drinking," Mac explained
later, "and I wouldn't talk to her. I had to hide
things from her and I was distant. I manipulated her
for sex by telling her it was her responsibility as a
wife. She didn't want to be involved with me sexually
after I was gone eighteen hours a day and drinking."

He loved his wife and children and realized what a
disaster it would be if he were caught raping again.
He worked out a system to improve the odds. He
decided that a rapist should have booze on his
breath so he could argue later that his judgment
had been impaired. But he couldn't let himself get
drunk—that could lead to mistakes. And from now
on he would be more selective about his victims—no
more grannies on street corners. He planned to re-

double his concentration on loose and easy women, worthless pigs who would turn off a jury. And if his victim fought, he would quit. It was a useful litmus test: If she didn't resist, she was probably looking for it. Hookers were the ideal target. They were already peddling their asses; he would only be stealing their time.

Fortified by his methodical new approach, he returned to his career of rape after a year of inactivity. By sticking to his plan, he held mistakes to a minimum. One came in 1976, when he was twenty-four and still living in Lynnwood. Another nosy passerby jotted down his license number and the county prosecutor charged him with the rape of a fourteen-year-old runaway. But the case was dropped when the frightened victim left the state. Mac was so relieved that he phoned the arresting officer and gushed, ''I know I have a problem. I'm gonna get some professional help.''

The cop told him how to reach a priest who specialized in helping sex offenders. Mac dialed the number but hung up. He hadn't set foot inside a church since leaving home, and he hated to return now. After a few more days he realized that he didn't need therapy. All he had to do was tighten up his act.

38

He lost another job. There weren't many openings for unskilled laborers, and he was forced to take work in the freezer room of a meat-packing plant in Renton, just south of Seattle. It was scut work on the graveyard shift; nightwork was beginning to seem like a family curse.

On a warm day in June 1977, four months before his twenty-fifth birthday, he left the plant at 9:00 A.M. and joined three of his fellow packers at a nearby tavern. At noon he downed his last beer and stepped into the bright sunlight to head home in his little red Fiat.

A chubby girl in a tight-fitting green dress accepted his offer of a ride and said she was going to Payless Drugs to buy a birthday present for her brother. They exchanged names. "Jill" looked like a teenaged whore and had a vocabulary to match.

In the parking lot she said, "See ya around." Her whole body twitched as she walked. That told Mac all he needed to know about her character.

He tried to remember how long it had been since he'd had any. Nan was working as a secretary and usually "too tired." He hadn't got off in weeks, hadn't raped in months. Too bad he'd told this whore his name.

On the other hand . . . the world was full of Macs. And rape was still the safest crime. His victim list was approaching forty now and he was beginning to feel uncatchable. He wished this bitch hadn't had such a good look at the Fiat, but women didn't know dick about foreign cars. He'd raped several in this one and hadn't been reported.

He walked into the cavernous store and found Jill picking through cassette tapes. She said she had to meet her boyfriend at the Sheraton Inn.

"Fine," he said. "I'll drive ya."

In the car she rattled on about rock singers and songs. She admired his eight-track cassette player, and he asked what she thought of the Jackson Five. "Too fucking great," she replied. He went out of his way to agree.

She seemed eager to see her boyfriend. "What're you guys gonna do at the Sheraton?" Mac asked.

"Nothin' special. Have a few drinks." The boyfriend had to be back at work in an hour, she explained. He was just out of prison for raping two teenagers at rifle point. She gave Mac a sly glance, as though to say she was getting plenty, and something stirred in his crotch.

It was 1:00 P.M., the sun was high and bright, and he tried to think of a secluded spot. He drove past Sears, turned down a gravel road, and told her that he had to pick up his brother's kids and take them to work. "No," he corrected himself. "Not to work. To *school.*"

He steered around a bearded old man out for a walk, turned into a one-lane dirt road, and backed the car into a brushy area behind the back wall of his plant. The nearest house was three hundred feet away.

He told her that she could have it easy or hard. "Please, no!" she begged.

He grabbed her by the throat and said, "You can either fuck me or suck me." She began pulling at her pants. This was the best part: taking control.

He was shocked to find whip marks on her body. "My, uh—my boyfriend," she explained.

"You like it that way?"

"With him, yeah."

He thought, What a freak! When he was finished he wiped himself off with his T-shirt and ordered her out. "Sit right there and look toward the woods," he ordered her. "If you turn around I'll come back and hurt you."

The victim informed local police that she'd been raped and sodomized by a vicious little man with a scar in the webbing of his left thumb. He was twenty-five or twenty-six, about five eight, medium build, straight blondish red hair to his ears, a thin moustache, and a small penis. He was well groomed and his body was clean. Even though the temperature was in the mid-seventies, he'd worn thermal underwear. The interior of his car was immaculate. The horn button on the steering wheel bore the letters FIAT. When he'd bent her backward over the seat, she'd memorized the number on a metal ID plate. It was 2049046.

The Renton police chief assigned Detective Don Dashnea and six other officers. Rape wasn't an everyday crime in the suburban community, and a man who would attack in broad daylight had to be considered dangerous.

The ID number was traced to the meat packing company's credit union and thence to Mac J. Smith. Less than forty-eight hours after the rape, two uniformed officers waited near the employees' door of the plant. At 8:55 A.M., a bearded man in a dark blue jogging jacket came out and drove off in a little red car. The officers signaled him to stop, handcuffed him, and placed him under arrest for rape. "That's a pretty serious charge," he said. He seemed cool.

In a long career, Detective Don Dashnea couldn't remember a more personable felony suspect. The kid confirmed his identity and signed a Miranda waiver. He admitted that the victim's version of the incident was roughly accurate. He insisted, however, that Jill had wanted it as much as he had. Driving toward the Payless, she'd complained about "this fucking heat." Would a decent girl have talked like that? Then she'd hiked up her skirt and used it to fan her face, revealing that she wore no underwear. And once they started, she turned out to be kinky as hell. She wouldn't let him kiss her but elected to "blow him" instead. Then she offered her ass. What was a guy to think? She'd already told him she was into S–M and showed her scars. He admitted that he should have backed off, but he'd drunk two pitchers of beer and his judgment was clouded.

Dashnea's report of the interview concluded: "The suspect related to Reporting Officer that he really does not believe any of this would have happened had he not been drinking. The suspect confided to R/O that he believes he has a drinking problem, and that he and his wife have discussed this possibility several times, indicating that their relationship is a bit strained as a result of his drinking."

After three days in jail, the likable rapist was released on his own recognizance "in order to work at his present employment."

Thirty-four pages of documentation, including Mac Smith's unsigned "confession," were delivered to the King County prosecutor's office in Seattle. An aggressive deputy named Mary Kay Barbieri reviewed the file, interviewed the victim, and suggested charges of first-degree rape. Her supervisor vetoed the recommendation with a notation that the case was a loser.

Barbieri asked him to reconsider. She'd learned that Smith had been convicted of an assault in California and involved in another in Washington. A former schoolteacher, she was well aware of the dismal arithmetic of rape enforcement and suspected that this particular sicko had been active for years.

Her supervisor agreed, but he pointed out that Mac Smith's guilt or innocence wouldn't be decided by two crime-wise prosecutors but by ordinary people with ordinary prejudices. The jurors were sure to compare the soft-spoken defendant to the tough-talking victim and send the poor guy home with a pat on the back, especially after they heard defense testimony about her jailbird boyfriend and his whip. It wasn't fair and it wasn't just, but it was reality.

With reluctance, Barbieri dictated the final report:

The victim's story and the suspect's story do not differ in any significant detail. The defense is consent.

Both the victim and the suspect say that the victim told the suspect that she liked pain with her sex. In fact, the victim says that the defendant was taken aback when he saw whip marks on her body (put there by her boyfriend).

In a case where everything depends on the victim's credibility, these statements are too damaging when the sole issue to be litigated is consent.

The charges were dropped.

39

After his latest close call, Mac decided to turn his life around one more time. He enrolled in a real estate course and landed a job as an agent in Kent, a town south of Seattle. By his twenty-sixth birthday in 1978, he'd worked his way up to sales manager, second in command to the broker. He plowed some of his commissions back into the business and soon became part owner.

A new agent named Mike Drake found Smith to be an amiable companion. Mac bought his share of beer and minded his own business. When barroom fights broke out, he slipped away. "One thing I liked about him," Drake said later. "His personality didn't change when he drank." They bowled together and became best friends. It seemed to Drake that Smith had only one problem: "His balls were bigger than his brains." He liked to go to a strippers' bar near the airport and bullshit the women. Any old lie would do. He had a short affair with a real estate saleswoman twice his age and then put the moves on a kid in her teens. Mike thought about warning her away, but Mac seemed to read his mind. "Whatever you do," Mac instructed his friend, "don't let on that I'm married. I really *want* this one."

Drake figured the poor guy mustn't be getting much at home. Anybody could see that the Smith marriage was in trouble. There were problems with the teenage stepdaughter, who hated Mac's guts. His wife Nan pushed him around and he took it. She bawled him out in front of the whole staff, and he just stood there with a hangdog look.

One day Mac showed Mike a newspaper picture of a suspected rapist. "I wonder if I should shave off my beard," he said, "because, ya know, I look a lot like that guy."

Drake put it down as another aimless remark. Where women and sex were involved, Mac didn't always make sense.

Another real estate friend invited the Smiths to Sunday services and dinner. Mac seemed interested in the church doctrine until Nan said in a cold voice, "You don't want to become an Episcopalian."

That seemed to end the matter. The friend thought, Why doesn't Mac think for himself? A grown man doesn't need a mother. . . . But no one heard Mac complain.

At the peak of his newfound financial success, he moved his family into a bigger house in a rural community called Black Diamond. He contracted to buy 4.6 acres on a lake in the shadow of the Cascades and started short-platting the property for resale. His brother Walter was well on his way to a successful sales career, and Mac boasted to his friends that this generation of Smiths was different. "Up to now," he said, "our folks never had much chance."

Then the bottom fell out of the real estate market. Within six months the office was running at half staff. The dazed survivors played Monopoly, perused the newspapers, and raced each other to answer the phone. As sales manager, Mac tried to whip up enthusiasm, but it was no use.

He seemed to take the hard times personally. "It doesn't matter what I try," he confided to Mike Drake. "I can't seem to do anything right."

He showed another agent a flyer advertising motivational tapes. "See?" he said. "This guy's a year younger than me and he owns twelve real estate offices. A millionaire! It makes ya feel like a failure."

When mortgage rates reached 17 percent, Mac and his family had to give up the house in Black Diamond and move to their Lake Sawyer plot—two adults, two small children and Nan's two teenagers crowded into a cramped mobile home. Mac's colleagues began to suspect that he was altering petty cash slips to provide himself with pocket money. He was involved in a few shady transactions, and an incriminating file disappeared from his desk.

Then Mac arrived at the office smelling of smoke and broke the news that his trailer had just burned down. The firemen hadn't been able to save a thing. With glistening eyes, he described how it felt to stand with his crying son and watch everything they owned go up in flames. Fortunately, he said, he'd just taken out fire insurance.

■

The family moved into a furnished house in an unstylish neighborhood. Friends noticed that some of the Smiths' most valued possessions began popping up, including a coveted painting of horses, edged in gold on a black background. How had such items survived the blaze?

Fire department files listed the cause as a defective toaster.

40

By the spring of 1980 Mac was twenty-seven, broke, and desperate. Nan's salary as a secretary provided the skimpy cuisine of the poor: rice, beans, wieners, and occasional hamburgers that were mostly suet and Helper. She insisted on handling the money and refused to advance him a few bucks for beer or pot. He no longer visited his favorite bar, the one where the strippers stretched out their G-strings for tips.

At the office he went through the motions. No one came to his open houses, not even brokers. His life turned into a dreary succession of empty days. *Boring.* The odd rape was all that held his interest. He sought young hitchhikers and whores as his victims, although there was beginning to be a sameness about them.

He attended a few competitive open houses and ended up feeling ashamed for the agents—they came at him like sharks in a feeding frenzy till they learned he was in real estate himself. Then they exchanged horror stories. At an open house in south Seattle, a female agent sounded so happy to see him that he halfway suspected she was putting the moves on him. "Oh, God," she gushed, "a live human *body*! I've been alone in this dump for five hours."

It gave him an idea.

41

His first open house assault didn't work out. The agent looked like a class act: hair in a bun, understated makeup, slender body sheathed in a suede cloth suit set off by pearls. But when he flashed his knife, she wouldn't stop yelling.

He forced her to the rug and she grabbed the blade of his knife.

"Let go!" he ordered. *"Let go!"*

She held tighter. He didn't know what to do. This goddamn woman was crazy; her eyeballs were rolling in their sockets. If he yanked the knife too hard, he would slice her hand. He'd been threatening women for years and never cut one. One nick could double his sentence; it was the difference between attempted and aggravated rape. Plus—he wasn't into blood.

He squeezed her wrist till her veins stood out. The weapon fell to her skirt. "If you say a word about this," he said, "you're dead."

All the way home he cursed himself for changing his M.O. Now he faced a familiar task: monitoring newspapers and news shows. This hysterical nut case was bound to call the police; she wasn't a hitchhiker or juvenile delinquent or off-duty whore, and she'd done nothing to be ashamed of.

But he didn't hear a word. It was an enlightening experience. Bimbos and kids weren't the only females who didn't report rape. A guy could develop a taste for women in pearls.

He found another open house ad in the morning *Post-Intelligencer* and drove the twenty-five miles from his office in Kent to the address in Everett. The two communities were separated by the sprawling mass of Seattle and about six different suburbs. He would rape once in this new jurisdiction and never return. It was the latest refinement in his technique.

He waited in his car till the agent was alone. She asked him to sign her log, and he scribbled the first name that came to mind: Mike Drake. She introduced herself as Ann Carmichael. She seemed unsure of herself, vulnerable. He liked them that way.

As she led him through the rooms, he looked her up and down. She was tall, blond, and *built*. When she couldn't squeeze into a convenient crawl space over the garage, he asked if she had a tape measure and jumped her when she was in the closet on her hands and knees.

At home, he shaved his beard and moustache and turned on the TV news. Once again the media appeared to be into lighter stuff. He'd noticed that the Seattle press paid little attention to crime and hardly any to rape. The cops seemed busy with murders and bank robberies and traffic tickets.

He liked the idea of escalating to a better class of female—neater, healthier, less likely to give him one of the cruds that were going around. Who wanted to go through life scratching and putting on salve? Every time he thought of some of the dogs he'd raped, he wanted to throw up. His mother had taught him to be clean.

42

On a misty summer afternoon two months after the Carmichael rape, he drove to a new development called Park Mar North, just south of the Everett city limits. It was hard to find the open house in all the curves and cul-de-sacs and spurs. When he finally located the place, a good-looking saleswoman introduced herself as Paula and explained that the sample house wasn't for sale. But the one on Lot 23 was available and she would be glad to show it. He couldn't believe his luck. Was this bitch asking for it or what?

As they strolled the arc of the street making friends, he told her his name was Mike Edson, he worked at Techtron and his wife at Boeing, and they lived in Maple Valley. He said they'd already qualified for a VA mortgage and had $15,000 to work with.

He barely listened as she showed him the first floor. In the master bedroom she pointed out the deep walk-in closet. "Just what I've been looking for," he observed.

He waited till she started measuring and then pulled out his pocketknife. "Do everything I tell you and you won't get hurt," he said.

"Why are you doing this?" she asked. "What did I do wrong?"

"Nothing. I'll give you till I count to ten to take your clothes off."

She was trembling so hard that she didn't get the first button undone till he reached the count of six. He pointed the knife at her throat. When she was half-undressed, she asked, "What about your wife, Mike?"

Jesus Christ, he thought, she's into family counseling. He told her to shut up and quit bawling.

"Please," she begged, "put down the knife." He laid it on the shelf and ordered her to her knees. He stripped to his white bikini shorts with the pink flowers and looked out the window. The only car in sight was his Fiat.

He ran her through most of his fantasy positions. It was great to have another puppet girl. But she wouldn't shut up and it was taking away his edge.

"You're not making me feel good," she whined. She kept griping and wheedling even when he was licking her. After a while he gave up and left.

He thumbed through the Everett *Herald* and the Seattle papers and watched a couple of local news shows. He realized that he'd been getting lax about monitoring the media; he'd been raping for eight years now and never drawn a line of media attention. He tried to imagine the reaction if he'd committed the same number of murders or even bank robberies. He would be top news from San Diego to the Canadian border! The way things were going, he could rape for the rest of his life. He could rape his way to the old folks' home!

On Saturday, June 28, 1980, seven days after the Park Mar incident, his eye caught a one-column headline on page 11 of the *Seattle Times:* "Man sought in rapes of saleswomen." He read:

> Everett police and Snohomish County deputy sheriffs say the same man has been linked to rapes of two real-estate saleswomen.
> Both women were raped at knife point while showing the man a vacant house. One rape occurred April 15 and the other June 21, one just inside the city limit and the other just south of Everett.
> The man is described as in his late 20s or early 30s, 145 to 150 pounds and about 5 feet 7 inches to 5 feet 10 inches. The man was driving a small, red foreign-made car.

Mac was unnerved by the accuracy of the description and also by the fact that the Everett P.D. and the Snohomish County deputies appeared to be working together on the cases. What made them so certain that "the same man" committed both rapes? —he'd been clean-shaven at one and bearded at the other. It showed that the cops weren't completely stupid. If other police agencies began pooling information, someone was bound to notice that a serial rapist had been working around Seattle for four or five years.

He decided it was time to abandon the open

house technique and stay away from Everett. Not that he intended to quit raping. It was the only time he felt whole, worthwhile. He thought back on the fast-food stickups with Rudi. When he'd pulled out that gun, he felt alive. The rest of the time he was going through the motions.

Even though he couldn't afford to make the change, he replaced the Fiat with a blue Ford Fiesta hatchback. He let his beard and moustache grow back in a slightly different style and returned to cruising for teenyboppers, runaways, and whores. There'd never been a shortage.

43

About the time of his twenty-eighth birthday in the fall of 1980, Mac stumbled on a perfect setting for his activities. He'd always been drawn to the "Sea-Tac Strip," a few miles of motels and hotels catering to businessmen and travelers in search of good times. There were fast-food restaurants, strip joints, car lots, massage parlors and other establishments along the four-lane highway that adjoined the Seattle-Tacoma Airport. Whores of both sexes ran up to cars and showed as much skin as the law and the weather allowed, and wild young women stood on street corners with their skirts hitched up and their thumbs in the air.

It was easy enough to get them into his car, but —where could he rape them? The Strip never shut down. Green-and-white cars from the King County Sheriff's Department eased by in second gear, sometimes joined by the black-on-black cars of the Port of Seattle Police Department and the all-white cruisers of the State Highway Patrol. If this was a high-crime area, it was also a high-enforcement area. No place for a rapist . . .

Idly reconnoitering, Mac drove west from the neon glare toward the southern perimeter of Sea-Tac Airport. He followed a narrow dirt road past a sign advising that the area was under annexation proceedings by the Port Authority. He drove through a line of Douglas firs and found himself in an exurban ghost town. It looked as though a death ray had zapped the community. Houses sagged toward the ground or were reduced to a wall or a slab. Ornamental trees and rhododendrons bordered abandoned homesites. Wild ivy propped up unpruned fruit trees and covered sagging fences and trellises.

A jet passed overhead with a whistle and a roar. Its landing lights blinded him when he looked up. The scene put him in mind of a war movie.

He stopped the Fiesta next to a bare fireplace set in a pile of bricks from its own collapsed chimney. The aircraft noise faded and was replaced by barely discernible chirrings: bugs, he figured, maybe squirrels or raccoons. Nothing could be heard from the busy Sea-Tac Strip, up the long hill six blocks away.

This was the place.

The girl was hitchhiking south on the Strip. It was two o'clock on Monday afternoon, October 6, 1980, three and a half months since he'd decided to return to down-scale victims. He'd just finished showing a house and was still in his working outfit: tan sports coat, brown tie, blue dress pants, and expertly shined loafers. His brown vinyl case was on the backseat.

The girl climbed into his metallic blue Fiesta. He drove south toward Tacoma, then made a right turn off the highway. He explained that he had to drop something off at his brother's.

As they drove down the hill on South 208th Street, she launched into the story of her life. He nodded and grinned and sympathized. She was fourteen and was just returning home after running away. She ran away so often that her folks didn't bother to come after her.

He told himself that she was probably into juvenile hooking, maybe supporting a habit or a pimp. Whores were already screwing their brains out, so what the hell difference did it make if he grabbed some for free? He could hear himself explaining this to a judge some day; he figured it would be good for a lighter sentence, if not an acquittal. Why should society care about women who lowered their pants for a living?

He turned off the main road, drove into the woods and pulled into a dirt driveway near the airport's southern boundary. "This sure is a funny place to meet your brother," the girl said in a quavery voice.

He showed his pocketknife and made her undress. When he was finished, he instructed her to walk into the woods and not look back.

Six nights later the old restlessness returned. His encores were usually spaced at longer intervals, but Nan was threatening to kick him out and he was too antsy to hang around their crummy little house. He thought, Here I am, all dressed up in my cream-colored Sunday suit and vest, and every credit card in my wallet is maxed out. It was raining, and he couldn't even afford to drop into a strip joint. In the Sea-Tac clip joints, money ruled. If you had the bread, every woman in the place would fuck you and suck you and run you a foot race. If you were broke, they figured you'd just fallen off the watermelon truck.

He cruised the Strip aimlessly. The rain on his windshield turned the bright lights to blobs and fuzzy lines. He hadn't planned to rape or not to rape. As he passed the Sandstone Motel at South 200th, he swore he saw a movie star reflected in the glow. He braked and backed up. She was Lauren Bacall minus forty years—tall, slender, about seventeen, with lank brown hair and race-horse legs and an expensive-looking fall coat. "Hi!" he called out. "Where ya headed?"

"Tacoma," she said. She didn't seem all that interested.

"Hey, great!" he said. "That's where I'm goin'."

She sat quietly as he drove south on the highway, then made the same quick turn onto 208th that he'd made six days before. This time he varied his story. His sister lived nearby and he had to pick her up, he said. He'd been trying to talk her into moving to a nicer neighborhood.

His new tires hissed on the wet pavement as he turned on Twenty-second Avenue South, drove several blocks through the deepening woods, then aimed the car down an abandoned driveway. The girl gave a wheezy little gasp and said, "I want to get out."

He stopped at a fence post almost hidden by blackberry runners. When he warned her that he had a knife, she started a high-speed rap, claiming she'd just stuck up a store and the cops were on her tail. "Sure," he said. What an imagination!

She said she was having her period, then added she had VD. "Sure," he repeated. They always had a story.

When she begged him not to hurt her, he waved the knife and said, "Baby, all I'm gonna do is rape you. If you do what I say, I won't hurt you."

It was a bitch of a job to reach across her and lower the back of the passenger seat. Instead of a lever, the Fiesta had a knurled knob that cranked the seat back inch by inch. When he finally got it down, he ran her through his entire repertoire, quick and hard. Then he ordered her to stand in front of his car till he backed out. He drove through the dripping branches and headed home for dinner.

PART THREE

JUSTICE
DENIED

■

1980–1981

44

The old man thought he heard a sound, but his hearing wasn't much better than his eyesight and he didn't bother to drag his tired bones out of the squeaky rocker. Paul Liston's small house with the oddly canted walls was the last building left standing on this shallow hillside—they'd carry him off in a pine box before he'd sell to those damn Sea-Tac lawyers—and in twenty years he'd become accustomed to certain noises: jet planes reducing their power and landing, wind in old fences, the battle cries of feral cats. He hated to see his furry friends hurt one another. He was dying himself, but happy that he'd eked out another twenty-four hours.

"SUN OCT 12," he noted in his journal in his squiggly hand. "Day of rest at house. Fine TV fare: *The 6th Commandment*—very realistic. *Moonlite Bay*—Doris Day at best. Abbott & Costello rampage. *The Universe*. Costeau & dolphins."

He was beginning to make another entry when he heard crying and a pounding on his door. A woman was out there. He had no neighbors and was reluctant to open up. At seventy, a fellow had to be careful, especially here in the woods where the only law was a bunch of glorified security guards called the Port of Seattle police.

The hammering kept up. After a couple of minutes he opened the door on a rain-soaked young woman. She stumbled inside so agitated that he couldn't understand her words. She flopped into a worn-out chair in front of the woodburning stove, waved her arms, and sobbed.

"What's the matter?" Liston asked. *"What happened?"*

She muttered something about a knife. Her nose started to run and he handed her a handkerchief. She kept on jabbering.

He couldn't remember when he'd ever seen such a frightened woman. She slumped into the chair and peered at him through crabbed fingers. He wondered why anyone would be afraid of a broken-down carpenter with cancer eating at his stomach.

He caught a few more phrases: "I've been raped," then "I need help." Her words were so muffled that he wasn't sure he'd heard right. If she'd been raped, she sure didn't look it. Her clothes were neat and she wasn't dirty.

"What's your name?" he asked.

"Celia," she mumbled. "Celia Dalton."

"Do you want me to call the police?" he asked. The child nodded.

A Port of Seattle police dispatcher logged the old man's call at 7:22 P.M.

45

In his home thirty miles north in the neat Seattle suburb of Bothell, Detective Corporal Ronald Parker was watching the National League playoff when the message came in from headquarters. There'd been a rape, and he was on call. An alcoholic and former shipfitter, he was thirty-five, a big man with a thick body, two inches over six feet, in his second year as a detective. He asked the dispatcher to notify the State Patrol that his southbound 1978 Chrysler Cordoba would be exceeding the speed limit on Interstate 5. It was an extra power stroke, a privilege of uniform and rank.

He reached Port police headquarters at Sea-Tac Airport in forty-five minutes, perused the preliminary report in the dispatch office, loaded his Polaroid camera, and arrived at the crime scene a few minutes after nine. A clump of Port officers busied themselves in the dark. He followed a weed-choked driveway by flashlight and stepped on the foundation of a demolished house. He spotted a tire track in the soft humus, but there didn't seem to be much else in the way of clues. He assigned a few chores and oversaw the preservation of evidence. A female officer would drive the victim to the scene and then to the hospital in Seattle.

Back in his office, Parker scanned the paperwork. The Dalton girl had been raped in a late-model royal blue compact with bucket seats that were covered in velveteen or velour. She'd spotted a temporary license glued to the rear window and thought the number contained several sixes and sevens. A gewgaw had dangled from the rearview mirror—maybe a necklace or garter. She described her assailant as a six-foot bearded maniac with shoulder-length light brown hair, a cream-colored suit and vest, maybe a green shirt. In the course of the questioning, she mentioned that one of her girlfriends had recently been raped in the same woods by a man in a blue car, but the crime hadn't been reported.

It was after 11:00 P.M. before the heavyset detective had time to search for the rape car. It seemed logical that if the perpetrator knew his way around the labyrinthine roads of the condemned land south of the airport, he might be from the Sea-Tac neighborhood.

The office was almost empty and Parker looked around for a partner. Patrol Officer Jose Santiago had just gone off duty and changed to civilian clothes, but the young officer volunteered to help out. Together they checked the parking lots at the Vance Hotel, My Place Tavern, Red Lion Inn, and the Hyatt House, all close to the spot where Celia Dalton had been picked up. Not one car bore the temporary license placard that was issued to new vehicles by the state's Department of Licensing.

By midnight the drizzle had weakened to an occasional drip. The two cops continued searching on their own time because, as Parker explained later, "it was an interesting case. I'd never been involved in a case like that before." In nine years on the airport job, he'd spent most of his time chasing illegally parked cars off the passenger loading ramp. It had been only a few years since he and the other Port policemen had received their county-wide commissions, enabling them to make arrests off Port property. Some still went unarmed.

At ten minutes before 1:00 A.M., the busy investigators spotted a white temporary license pasted in the rear window of a shiny new car parked outside the Raintree Lounge on the Sea-Tac Strip. They perked up when they noticed that the number was 661–677. They walked around the blue Chevy Chevette, peering through the windows. Sure enough, it had bucket seats, though they seemed to be covered with some kind of plastic, not velour or velveteen. A Playboy air freshener hung from the rearview mirror. They made a radio check and learned that the car had recently been sold by Good Chevrolet. Of course there were no outstanding wants or warrants.

The two officers checked inside the Raintree, saw no one in a cream-colored suit, and went back outside to sit on the suspicious car from a parking place in the shadows.

Twenty minutes went by before a bearded young man with blondish brown hair emerged with a young woman. He seemed to fit the suspect's description except that the rapist had been taller and worn different clothes.

The unmarked Port police car followed a block behind as the blue Chevette pulled onto the Sea-Tac

Strip and headed south, then made a U-turn into a convenience store. The officers radioed for assistance. It was possible that the rapist had picked up another victim and was en route to a double dip. Parker and Santiago were excited. Most cops worked a lifetime without working an on-view rape.

Heading south again, the Chevette eased toward the curb lane as though to make a right turn at South 208th Street, the same route taken by the rapist. The trailing car and a backup unit slowed. It wouldn't do to spoil things now.

But the blue car returned to the number one lane and continued south. The cops closed in. Somehow, they figured, the guy had made them; they had to stop him before he rabbited and they became involved in a high-speed chase.

46

"I wasn't speeding," Steve Gary Titus remarked to his housemate as he steered the new company car into the rear of a Puget Sound Bank branch. "I don't know why they're pulling us over."

A uniformed officer leaned into the window and asked for his driver's license.

"I left it home," Titus explained. "I spilled some coffee on my other pants and I had to go back to change. I must've forgot my wallet."

When he stepped into the blue glow of the flashing lights, Titus was surprised to see two police cars: one marked and one unmarked. He asked, "What's wrong?"

"Tell ya in a minute," a loud voice answered. "Walk over this way."

Titus walked toward the unmarked car. Someone asked, "Where do you work?"

"Yegen Seafoods. We're the franchisee for Ivar's Seafood Bars."

"How old are you?"

He looked to see if Mona was close enough to hear. "Uh—twenty-nine," he answered.

A burly plainclothesman asked if he owned a cream-colored suit. No, he said. He didn't own any suits.

"Where ya been tonight?"

"With my fiancée," he explained, beckoning toward Mona. She was standing to one side, being questioned by a uniformed cop. Their voices didn't carry.

"Doing what?"

He explained that they'd gone to the discotheque at the Doubletree Inn but found it closed, tried out a disco called Maxi's but hated the '40s-style music, and finally hit the Raintree about 12:30. They'd danced, had a couple of drinks, and now they were on their way home to the Comstock Apartments in Kent. "Why?" Titus asked.

"There's been a rape," the detective answered. "The perpetrator had a beard and a car like yours and a cream-colored suit."

"What time did it happen?" Titus asked.

The plainclothesman ignored the question. Titus knew about setups and false prosecutions from watching TV shows like *60 Minutes,* but he wasn't concerned. From the time he'd arrived at his father's fifty-eighth birthday party that afternoon, he could account for every minute of his day and night. *With* witnesses. His total life of crime had consisted of smoking some weed and driving too fast, but that didn't seem to be the issue tonight. This stop was some kind of screwy mistake. But what the hell, he was still feeling good from that last pop at the bar. The cops were only doing their job.

"Is it okay if we search your car?" one of them asked.

"Sure," Titus said. "Go ahead."

They seemed interested in the tires and wheel wells, with their customary rainy-weather mix of street dirt and pine needles from his heavily land-scaped apartment complex. The big plainclothes-man confided, "I'm not gonna arrest you because your tire tracks don't match." But he wondered if Steve would mind following them to headquarters and having his picture taken for the record.

"Sure," Titus said. "Why not?"

On the ten-minute drive, he joked with Mona and she joked back. What a story they'd tell in the morning!

Everyone seemed in a friendly mood as they walked into the Port of Seattle police headquarters on the second floor of the Sea-Tac terminal. Titus took one of the uniformed officers aside and whispered, "I'm thirty-one, not twenty-nine. I don't want my girl-friend to know." He was touchy about their age dif-ference. Mona had just turned twenty-one and looked about fifteen. There would be plenty of time to tell her the truth after the wedding.

A cop shot a half-dozen Polaroid pictures in front view and profile. Steve found the procedure so amusing that he couldn't stop smiling.

"Okay," the big detective said, "you folks can go now." He seemed to be running the show.

In his chirpy voice, Steve said, "Hey, can me and her have our picture taken together?"

The photographer snapped one off for a sou-venir.

In the parking lot, they interrupted a policeman who was photographing the Chevette inside and out. They watched as he bent to take close-ups of the tires. Steve didn't mind. The car was his latest perk as a district supervisor in charge of a hundred employees at seven seafood bars. He'd taken delivery two days before.

The couple reached Steve's apartment on the Kent-Kangley Road at 2:30. Before they went to bed, Mona took another look at the Polaroid shot and let out a snort. "Look," she said, "Bonnie and Clyde." They fell asleep in the general good mood of the evening.

47

Lights burned late at the Port police office. A Red Lion Inn waitress had volunteered that she'd last seen her good friend Celia Dalton in the coffee shop at 7:00 P.M.; Celia had said she intended to hitchhike home to Tacoma. Twenty-two minutes later, the first report of the rape incident had reached the dispatch office. Whatever else could be said about the perpetrator, he didn't waste any time.

By midnight a half-dozen officers were involved in the investigation. An ambitious chief had promised to whip his assortment of meter maids, baggage inspectors and gate monitors into a professional police department, and the time was right for a legitimate bust, the splashier the better. A few months earlier, the airport cops had enhanced their record of buffoonery by charging an innocent young railroad worker with raping a parking garage cashier. In the middle of a belated lie detector test, the "victim" broke into a sweat, stood up with a dazed look, and said, "I'm terribly sorry. I think this was all a dream." Charges were dropped.

But tonight's suspect looked good, despite his typical protestations. The officers realized that their chief would tolerate no more amateurish strokes. At 2:30 in the morning, someone discovered that a serious mistake had already been made: The rapist's tire tracks were turning to mush in the rain and they hadn't been cast or photographed. Detective Corporal Parker sped to the scene with another officer and snapped pictures. He already knew from visual examination that the tracks didn't match Titus's, but such discrepancies could be addressed later. Other vehicles might have used the driveway since the rape. Everything else about the case pointed straight to the bearded little guy from the fish bars.

Around 3:00 A.M., Parker napped at his desk for a few minutes, then returned to his work. He could catch up on his sleep after the facts were nailed down and the evidence sent to the prosecutor's office. His own reputation was in need of even more upgrading than the department's. The former ship-fitter had a long history of personal violence, and he'd been in trouble with his superiors for offenses ranging from insubordination to drunkenness to false arrest to womanizing on the job. Back home in Bothell he'd narrowly escaped arrest for pulling a gun on his cancer-stricken wife and then trying to strangle her. His superiors had recently ordered him to use some of his sick time for psychiatric counseling. He took pride in his badge and his gun and his standing as a law officer, and he swore he would never return to his backbreaking job on the docks. This rape case could be his ticket back to respectability.

By 10:00 A.M. he'd prepared a photo montage consisting of five stock mug shots plus the fresh pictures of Titus. Following standard procedure, the subjects had generally similar features and were shown in full face and profile. But Titus's paired pictures, in the upper right corner of the array, were the only ones in which the subject showed a smile and the only ones in which the profile and full-face shots were unseparated by a black line. The Titus pictures were also a third smaller than the others and were bound to stand out.

Parker rushed the montage to Celia Dalton's mother's home in Tacoma, where the victim was recovering from the incident of the night before. He informed Celia in advance that her assailant was one of the six men pictured; all she had to do was pick him out.

Celia fingered the cardboard folder for almost five minutes before making a selection. Then she pointed to Titus and said, "This one is the closest one. It has to be this one."

She also volunteered more information. Her rapist hadn't smoked. He'd told her his sister's name was Liz. He'd worn a belt and dark tan cord pants. His weapon was black and silver; it could have been a knife or a long-handled screwdriver.

Parker and Officer Diane Lathrop left the Dalton house and returned to headquarters to prepare an arrest warrant.

An hour before noon on October 14, 1980, two days after the rape, a three-man team of airport cops pulled into the Yegen fish company headquarters in Tukwila, a suburban town south of Seattle, and presented a warrant for the arrest of Steve Gary Titus for the crime of rape. They were advised that he was on his supervisorial rounds, probably at Ivar's Seafood Bar in the Northgate Mall, about fifteen miles north on I–5. The cops couldn't find their man at Northgate and returned to the Yegen office on Industry Drive to wait him out.

When Titus pulled in at 1:10, Parker advised him that he was under arrest and read him his rights. A tow truck was called, the company car was impounded as evidence, and the prisoner was frisked and handcuffed.

In the detectives' office at Port police headquarters, Titus repeated his claim of innocence. He didn't seem angry and he didn't request a lawyer. A police notation described him as "cooperative."

He patiently traced the events of the rape day, starting with his 3:15 arrival with his son Kenny at the birthday party in nearby Riverton Heights, two miles north of Sea-Tac. At 6:10 his parents promised to drive little Kenny home to his mother and Titus had left the party for his apartment, arriving about 6:30. He phoned his fellow employee Kurt Schaefer in the same building complex, and Schaefer arrived at his door ten or fifteen minutes later. At 7:00 P.M. Titus called his fiancée Mona in Tacoma, where she worked as a waitress at Denny's. He reminded his interrogators that it was a long-distance call and would appear on his next billing. He said he arranged to pick up Mona when she finished work at 10:00. Then he and Schaefer talked business till the TV premiere of *Superman* at 8:00 P.M. Titus left for Denny's at ten minutes after nine. He and Mona returned to the apartment so he could change his coffee-stained pants; then they'd gone dancing. He'd already told the rest.

Neither Parker nor his partner, Patrol Officer

Robert Jensen, took notes. The Titus statement
wasn't tape-recorded, typed, or signed, nor did either of the officers prepare a report while their
memories were fresh, standard police procedure. It
was as though the exculpatory session hadn't taken
place. No plans were made to interview the senior
Tituses, little Kenny, Mona Imholt, Kurt Schaefer, or
any of the alibi witnesses.

At 4:45 P.M., Detective Parker booked Steve Titus
into the King County Jail in Seattle on suspicion.
The victim had been abducted and threatened with
a weapon, qualifying the offense as rape in the first
degree. The possible penalty was twenty years.

48

Mona almost fell over when Steve finally convinced her that he was really in jail and it wasn't another joke. Steve Titus a *rapist*? What a joke! She'd known him for five months, and rapist was the last thing he could be. He wasn't even all that interested in sex. Mainly he was an overgrown kid, the most carefree man she'd ever met. He loved to party and trusted the *world*. She thought, *Maybe that's the problem.*

It had taken them two weeks to fall in love. He was short and compact like her, with blue eyes, fair skin, wavy light brown hair, and a perfect heart-shaped face. On their first date in June, they ended up in a hysterical beer fight. He liked to borrow a bunch of kids—his own son Kenny, who lived with his ex-wife, and Mona's two kids, who lived with her ex-husband—and drive them to an amusement park to ride bumper cars and eat till they groaned. Sometimes they played cards all night—Uno, gin, blackjack—or took turns on his Atari till she nodded out on the couch to the sound of the beeps and chirps.

She'd never been much of a drinker; one day he got her high on a double strawberry margarita and then insisted that she join him for an eight-hour raft ride on the tumultuous Snoqualmie River. When she lost her paddle and fell in, he pulled her out. "Hey," he said, "are we having fun or what?"

From the beginning Mona admired his constancy, his evenness. There were no hidden personalities, no horned monsters who emerged when he drank. He was always the same bubbly dude. Her first husband had been a father figure, serious to the point of grim, but Steve wasn't afraid to play the clown, to look silly at his own expense, provided it got a laugh. His dancing was pure 1965. She nicknamed his clunky, arm-flapping style "The Titus." He liked to dance to a fast song called "Funkytown" but could never keep up. Other dancers stopped to watch. She told him he looked like the San Diego Chicken imitating Mick Jagger.

Whatever they did, he listened to her, treated her like an equal, seemed to value her judgment. They made compromises and talked things out. Every day they phoned each other's answering machines and left moony songs instead of messages:

". . . So much in love, so hurt without you . . ."

She remembered how surprised she'd been when the cops had started giving her the third degree. "Were you with this individual tonight? Starting when? Do you have witnesses? . . ." She'd asked them two or three times what was going on, and they'd fobbed her off. When she'd found out that they were on the trail of a rapist, she was relieved.

They'd lived together since a month before the arrest. She soon realized how lucky he'd been to work his way up to a supervisor's salary, $2,000 a month, in three short years. He could roll numbers through his head like a human calculator, but he never knew his own bank balance. "I got enough to cover it," he would explain as he dashed off a check.

He was convivial to a fault. He gorged his friends with food and drink. If one of his guests parked himself for the night in front of the Atari, Steve kept running in and out of the kitchen with beer and dip. He had a bartender's personality; his animosities never showed. The only exception was his ex-wife. The two of them had screaming fights about child support payments and the custody of eleven-year-old Kenny, sometimes in front of the child. To Mona, it seemed like poor parenting, and she told him so. But some feuds went to the bone. It was out of character for Steve to dislike another person as much as he disliked Phyllis.

His other minuses hardly showed. He chain-smoked Marlboros, but so did she. He'd smoked pot in the past but had cut way down, especially now that his and her children frequently visited the apartment. He had a weird hangup about his age. At first he told her he was twenty-five, then inched it up to twenty-eight. Another employee told her that he was thirty-one. "It was like who cares?" Mona explained to a friend. "But it's a big deal to him. He wants to be forever young."

They planned a June wedding. And now it was the middle of October and he was in jail, charged with a repulsive crime. Mona knew about rape. A man had attacked her when she was eighteen and broken her nose. She'd been so distraught when police asked for the rapist's description that all she could say was, "He's black." She still saw that face in nightmares. Now the man she loved was charged with something as bad or worse. It had to be a goof-up.

49

In the fading home market of 1981, Mac Smith's half interest in the little Kent real estate agency was depreciating fast. The office had listings but no customers, accounts payable but none receivable, and a negative cash flow. There wasn't even a petty cash fund that could be tapped for beer money. When his friend Mike Drake bailed out to sell home security systems, Mac joined him. The new job didn't pay much, but it kept the pals in brew.

One month to the day after he'd attacked the Lauren Bacall look-alike, Mac got drunk, ran a red light in nearby Renton, and was broadsided by another car. His little blue Ford Fiesta, two months off the showroom floor, was carted away in pieces. His only satisfaction was that no rape victim would ever connect him to it.

After a frustrating month of hitching rides, he talked a bargain-basement agency into renting him a six-year-old Chevrolet Nova. The car was due back in two weeks, but Mac regarded the transaction as semipermanent, good till they caught him. To keep the guzzler in fuel, he practiced the art of the drive-away gas theft, filling up at Jiffy Marts and 7–Elevens and speeding away. It wasn't the real estate biz, but it was survival.

50

Kent Patrolman Bill Ross was working a case on his own time when a $5 driveaway theft was reported at the Super Seven Gas Station. Ross thought, *What the hell, I'm only a few blocks away.* To the eager young cop, chippy cases deserved the same attention as any other. A guy who would cheat a gas station clerk would commit worse crimes. Besides, Ross was young and craved action.

The Kent chief of police had disbanded his detective bureau and upgraded his patrol officers' responsibilities. The first car dispatched to a crime scene was responsible for handling the case to the end, including the preparation of final reports for the prosecutor. Of course, you were also expected to pick up road litter, chase stray dogs, and write speeders. The new policy made for an overworked department, but there were no complaints from Ross. He was thirty-one, a boyish-looking six-footer in his Photogray glasses, calm and unruffled, a Vietnam veteran who'd taken a four-year degree in law enforcement and wanted to be Columbo or Popeye Doyle when he grew up. Barely in his second year on the small department, he'd already handled an on-view homicide and a seventeen-man biker rumble, complete with knives and chains.

Now he flipped on his roof lights, rushed to the scene—and missed the perp by seconds. Inside the overheated cashier's booth, he pulled out his legal-size pad and interviewed one highly pissed-off cashier. She said the thief was a mousy-looking dude, not too tall, with a moustache and a beard, driving a clunky green Chevy, license number OJK930.

Ross ran the number and found it was registered to a rental agency on the Sea-Tac Strip. The place was closed. He'd just climbed back in his patrol car when the radio beeped three times and the dispatcher yelped, *"Officer shot!"* He hit his lights and siren.

The cop's bulletproof vest had been dented by a shotgun blast and his radio blown off his gun belt, but he was barely scratched. The first officer-shooting in Kent history was Bill Ross's case all the way. But the driveaway theft stuck in his mind as unfinished business, and on his next day off he returned to the auto rental agency and learned that the green Chevy had been rented to "McDonald J. Smith, DOB 9–14–52." The car was a month overdue. The face and vitals provided by the Department of Licensing matched the description of the hairy-faced thief given by the gas station clerk. Ross glued the driver's license picture and five others on a photo laydown and hand-carried them to the Super Seven.

The clerk couldn't make a match. Every cop knew that license pictures weren't worth a damn. Scratch one bust, Ross griped to himself. All that time wasted. . . .

51

In the Port of Seattle Police office a few miles away, Detective Ronald Parker was doggedly building the case that could save his career. Lately he'd been running into one aggravation after another. Sometimes it seemed as though the Washington State Crime Lab and the Port police were on different teams, one trying to convict the rapist and the other trying to cut him loose. Eighteen fingerprints had been lifted from Titus's car; the three or four good ones didn't come close to matching the exemplars of Titus or the victim. Semen tests were branded "inconclusive." Loose fibers from the Titus car didn't match clothes worn by the victim, and fibers from the victim's clothes matched neither Titus's car nor his clothing. The crime lab reported that fabric impressions in the car hadn't been made by Celia Dalton's jeans, blue sweater, or orange jacket. A facial hair found on her sweater was "dissimilar" to a sample taken from Titus. The tire tracks came from Michelin XZXs, standard on some compact cars but not the Chevette. No knife or screwdriver turned up, nor was there any sign of the brown legal-size folder that Celia Dalton had noticed on the rapist's back-seat, only a big metal display case that hadn't been reported by the distraught woman. No "necklace or garter" hung from Titus's rearview mirror, only the Playboy air freshener. And worst of all, every verifiable time check corroborated the rapist's alibi. Phone company records confirmed that he'd made a two-minute phone call to his girlfriend at exactly seven o'clock. Shirlee Watson, the Red Lion waitress, said she'd been chatting with her friend Celia then, just before Celia crossed the street to stick out her thumb. And twenty-two minutes later, Paul Liston's call for emergency help had been logged at the dispatch office.

A less motivated investigator might have given up, but Parker refused. He wasted no time checking out information that refuted his theory of the case. When alibi evidence turned up, he simply kept it to himself. He was encouraged by several bits of information provided by his colleagues. Patrol Officer Jose Santiago made an unassigned visit to the rape scene and reported:

> Walked around the area of the actual crime and found fresh cigarette butts on the ground (fresh: not waterlogged like the rest I found in the area). I checked them out and one of the butts had Marlboro on it. Reporting officer noticed the day before that the suspect (Mr. Titus) smoked the same brand. R/O saw the pack of cigarettes in the suspect's vehicle along with a black-looking felt pen. R/O put the butts into evidence for examination.

In her various statements, Celia Dalton had reported that her rapist hadn't smoked that night, but

Parker and his superiors knew that rape victims were seldom good observers. There were women who'd claimed that white rapists were black and vice versa, women who were attacked by tall men and described them as short; the list of oddities was unending. The unreliability of rape victims' observations was one reason that the crime was so hard to investigate and prosecute. Celia certainly proved the point. Hardly a word she said pointed to the rapist Titus, except, of course, her identification of him in a deeply flawed montage.

Parker drove the young victim to Steve's Highline Towing and showed her Titus's Chevette. Yes, she said, that was the car. The seat was covered with plastic instead of the velveteen she'd originally mentioned, but who expected the poor kid to get every last detail right?

Parker continued to withhold information, not only from the defense but from his nominal superior, Deputy Prosecutor Mary Kay Barbieri. The former high school English teacher, who'd once tried to bring Mac Smith to trial, had been placed in charge of a newly formed Special Assault Unit that handled sex crime cases exclusively. In a preliminary evaluation of the Titus material, she noted, "From the reports it seems like a good case up to this point."

But she took note of one defect. At the bottom of her note, she scribbled, "Bad montage! MKB." King County Superior Court Judge Frank D. Howard quickly eliminated the problem for the prosecutors. At a preliminary hearing, he ruled that Ronald Parker's defective montage was admissible.

52

By this time Titus had been forced to take the matter seriously and engage a lawyer—young Thomas Hillier II, hired by the family partly because he was highly recommended and partly because his hourly rate fell within their limited means. David Titus, the father, was a disabled war veteran living on a pension, and Steve's French-born mother Jacqueline worked as a waitress. Titus himself had accumulated no savings and had hardly any borrowing capacity.

From the beginning, Tom Hillier viewed Titus as an unlikely rape suspect—clean-cut, no record, good family, happy love life, and a stubborn insistence on his innocence. The facts of the case plus logic and common sense backed him all the way. It was comforting to Hillier to realize that he was defending an innocent man, not an everyday situation in the life of a defense attorney.

If there was a problem, it was the new Steve Titus. Mona Imholt reported that she hardly knew her fiancé anymore. Party time was over; in the words of the old jazz song, he'd lost his smile, changed his style. Hillier couldn't remember a defendant who seemed so personally devastated. The extreme reaction was one more sign of innocence, of course, but not necessarily the best persona to bring into court. Jurors preferred calm, sincere defendants and tended to distrust the hysterical and the righteous.

Titus wasted hours of consultation time raving about the corrupt system and "those crooks on the Port police." He continually demanded that Hillier explain how a perfectly innocent man could be officially charged with rape in the United States of America in 1981. From their first strategy session to their last, his main preoccupation was the justice system as exemplified by Ronald Parker and his cohorts.

As trial approached, Hillier began to run out of patience. "Look, Steve," he said after they'd gone over the same ground one more time, "they have the victim's ID of you and your car. They have the temporary license plate, the Marlboro cigarette thing. They have you going home and changing your pants. They have a bunch of circumstantial stuff."

"But it's all bullshit!"

"Fuck, Steve!" Hillier exploded. "You've been charged. *Now let's talk about the case!*"

But certain key elements were proving elusive. Hillier phoned the Port police every few days, demanding all available information including the exculpatory. Where were the semen reports? The fiber and fingerprint test results? The tire studies and the witness statements? Hillier heard rumors that some of the prosecution witnesses were changing their timetables. Well, then, where were their revised statements? Under courtroom discovery rules, he was entitled to see every item the prosecution planned to introduce.

He soon came to realize that the main stone-waller was the chief investigator himself. Over the phone, an affable Ron Parker would say, "You'll have all that stuff tomorrow, counselor." But the mails kept coming up empty.

One day Parker phoned and said, "If we don't find any physical evidence from our tests, Mr. Hill-ier, we're gonna dump the case. I'm not convinced that Steve did it. I'll never forget how cooperative he was that night. So . . . cheerful."

Hillier thought, The guy's beginning to sound reasonable. But later he wondered if Parker was try-ing to lull him to sleep, and if so, why. The young attorney knew about cops who shaded their testi-mony if they were sure they had the guilty party. But he'd never met a lawman who would make an all-out attempt to railroad the innocent.

Weeks passed and the crucial evidence wasn't forthcoming. Hillier decided to deal directly with the prosecutor's office.

His law firm had gone up against Mary Kay Bar-bieri in the past, and he knew her reputation. Her Special Assault Unit had turned into the shock troops of the local women's movement, slashing into the backlog of sex crime prosecutions. Even her loudest detractors had to admit that she performed a public service. If the balance was beginning to swing toward victims' rights and away from the rights of rape defendants, most offenders had it coming. Everyone agreed that the tough new ap-proach was an improvement on the days when one rape in forty produced a jail sentence.

Tom Hillier was convinced that behind Barbieri's Joan of Arc image, she believed in justice. He laid out all his cards. His argument was not merely that his client was the victim of several coincidences, but that no jury would convict on such flimsy evidence; King County and the Special Assault Unit would be wasting the taxpayers' money. And while they were trying to convict an innocent man, a dangerous rapist was on the loose.

Barbieri recalled later, "I respected Tom Hillier, and when an esteemed member of the bar says regularly and earnestly that you've charged the wrong person, you've got to take him seriously. But in the end, I said, 'Tom, we have more than enough evidence to make a case. My office can't make the decision that Titus didn't do it. That's up to a judge or jury.' "

She reminded Hillier that she'd been involved in dozens of felony prosecutions, "and you've always got victims who get things wrong. You've always got friends and relatives with alibis. And you've always got inconsistencies and oddities and contradictions. That's what juries are for, to sort those things out." She refused to drop the charges.

Barbieri assigned Deputy Prosecutor Christopher Washington to handle the case in court. He was a prosecutorial version of Hillier—young, bright, handsome, popular with female jurors, a skilled courtroom warrior. Both adversaries were reckoned by their peers to have brilliant futures, perhaps even end up on the bench.

Together they fashioned what appeared to be a fair pretrial agreement: Titus would take a lie detector test; if he passed, the charges would be dropped; if he failed, the case would proceed to trial.

Both sides agreed on polygraphist Dewey Gillespie, a former Seattle policeman known locally as "the dean of lie detector examiners." He was also known as a compassionate man with a conscience. With Gillespie at the controls, there would be no unseemly argument about the results.

Steve Titus had three days to stew. In his newly developing state of paranoia, he managed to convince himself that Ronald Parker and Dewey Gillespie were in cahoots. He imagined Parker telling the polygrapher, "Do us a favor. *Fail Titus.*"

At the outset of the test, Gillespie was impressed by his subject's calm. But when the tough questions began, the delicately balanced needles skittered across the register.

"It was a textbook case," Gillespie observed. "You could send the Titus charts to any operator in the country and he would conclude the same thing." The suspect had lied flagrantly.

The Port police were exuberant. Titus was dirty! The next step would be up to a jury.

53

A few weeks later, at four o'clock on a blustery winter afternoon, Joanie Kay Finley, a twenty-one-year-old woman who looked and acted much younger, was walking up a hill in Kent when a green Chevrolet pulled in front of her on the shoulder. It was almost dark at latitude 48 degrees N. "Excuse me," a pleasant voice called out. "Can you tell me how to get to the East Hill?"

Joanie was reluctant to talk—she had a history of being abused and misused by males, and her mother had warned her about strangers. She peeked at the driver. The bearded young man didn't seem threatening. Besides, there were other cars around.

She told him he was headed in the wrong direction. As she turned to point him toward Kent, the car door opened and something jabbed against her back. "Get in or I'll hurt you," he said in that same calm voice.

As they sped in the direction of the airport, he told her that his name was Mike and he had to stop at a friend's house.

"I don't want to go there," she insisted.

"Well, you're going anyway," he said.

When he stopped at a traffic light at the Sea-Tac

Strip, Joanie Kay tried to jump out, but the door was locked.

The man drove west to a woodsy area south of the Sea-Tac Airport and parked the car in a clearing where a house had once stood. A plane passed so low that she could smell the jet fuel. She blinked as the landing lights flashed across the treetops.

The man threw her purse and pack into the backseat and held a knife to her throat. "Take your pants down," he said, "and suck me off."

The softness of his voice gave her courage. "I don't want to do none of that," she protested. "I got a boyfriend. I'm supposed to be at his house right now."

The knife pressed against her skin. "Do it!" he said.

After she took him in her mouth, he tried to pull down the sleeves of her blouse, but they were too tight. He yanked his pants down and told her to get on her hands and knees. "No!" she said. "I don't want to do none of these weird things."

She held out her engagement ring for emphasis. He slapped her hand aside and pressed against her from the rear. As he snapped out his instructions, his voice turned coarse and deep. She thought, Why is he so mad at me? I never done nothing to him. By the time he was finished, she was sure she was going to be killed. I better do something, she told herself. I don't want to die.

Before she could decide what to do, he reached into the backseat, retrieved her things, and opened the door on her side. "Walk behind the car," he ordered her. "Don't turn around or nothin'." He sounded like a killer on TV.

She clutched her clothes as the headlights came on. The car began to move and her mood switched from fear to anger. *What a terrible thing to do! That dirty little man should be caught. I don't want him doing this to nobody else. . . .*

She wondered what he would do if she violated his instructions. He would have to back up, get out, and chase her on foot. She'd be fifty yards into the trees before he could even get started.

She turned her head and deliberately stared at the car, about twelve feet away. It was just turning into the lane. She caught part of the green-and-white license plate: OJK9.

She brushed her clothes with her hands and stumbled out of the woods to 208th Street. It was six blocks uphill to the neon-lighted Strip. Rush hour traffic streamed by. She hoped no one stopped; she felt dirty.

On the bus ride to her boyfriend's house, she kept repeating to herself, *OJK, OJK* . . . In school she'd had trouble with memory, but this was easy. JK was part of her initials.

Her boyfriend called the police.

54

Kent Patrolman Bill Ross, still vaguely annoyed at himself after a driveaway thief named McDonald J. Smith had slipped through his hands, walked into a sheriff's substation on routine business and paused to study the three-by-five-card file of unsolved felonies. He read the rundown on the Joanie Kay Finley rape and something tugged at his memory. He read it again and stopped at the license plate letters: OJK. He checked his pocket notebook and confirmed that they were the same letters reported in the gasoline theft.

He phoned the information to the assigned officer, Fae Brooks of the King County Sheriff's Police, a detective who specialized in sex cases.

A few days later Brooks called back to confirm that Smith was a rapist; he'd been handled twice in King County and had a California record.

Like the gas station clerk before her, Joanie Kay Finley was unable to identify Smith from a Department of Licensing mug shot. The victim of a two-year-old rape case was also shown the picture and made a positive ID, but she flatly refused to testify.

Patrolman Bill Ross thought about all the times

police had a criminal dead to rights and couldn't lift a finger, couldn't even bring him in for questioning. One particular asshole was certainly running in luck.

55

Unaware of his close call, Mac Smith decided that the green Chevrolet wasn't producing the results he wanted. It seemed that good-looking women were turned off by men driving junkers. What he needed was a twenty-four-valve smogbelcher off the show-room floor.

He donned his vested cream suit, walked into a Ford agency, flashed his old business cards, and drove off in a black-on-black 1981 Mustang with a convertible T-roof, four on the floor, reclining bucket seats, a digital clock, and mirrors molded into both sides. The first thing he did when he got home was cancel the insurance that the seller had required before making the deal.

Mac looked forward to interesting times. What hot young runaway wouldn't jump out of her go-go boots to climb into *this* car? He planned his next excursion to the airport woods.

56

One month after the Joanie Kay Finley rape and two days before the Steve Titus trial was scheduled to begin, Ronald Parker finally got around to writing up a report on his personal interview with Titus four and a half months earlier. The detective's reconstruction of the conversation came close to making Titus a rapist out of his own mouth. Included with the newspeak version was a fictitious description of the route Titus claimed to have followed from his parents' home to his apartment, showing that he'd driven past the spot where Celia Dalton was picked up.

Attached to the report was a timetable that purported to be officially computed by Parker's stopwatch, a touch of investigative precision. The detective wrote that Titus had told him he arrived at his apartment, eight miles from the rape scene, at 6:55 P.M.; in fact, Titus had arrived at 6:30 and had said so from the beginning. The effect of the jiggered timetables was to show that the accused man had had ample time to rape and then rush home to establish an alibi.

After filing the bogus report, Parker set about working his way around another problem: the nonmatching tire tracks. On the first day of trial in

Seattle, while the jury was being selected, he picked up Celia Dalton at her home thirty-five miles south in Tacoma and chauffeured her to the rape site at sundown. Yes, she said after several broad hints, Mr. Parker was absolutely right. Back on that awful night in October, she'd pointed out the wrong tracks! She said she was sorry she'd caused so much trouble, but she'd been under pressure at the time.

Deputy Prosecutor Chris Washington and his supervisor, Mary Kay Barbieri, accepted the last-minute information at face value. It certainly improved the case against Titus. "I thought, 'Good!' " Barbieri recalled later. "It never occurred to me that Celia was making it up."

57

Their opponent, Tom Hillier, was worried. It was a
legal cliché that anything could happen in trial.
Were innocent people ever convicted? Of course.
That was one reason he'd gravitated to criminal law.

Hillier had put most of his energy into trying to
keep Steve Titus from being tried, but he couldn't
get the state to budge. The Port cops were acting as
though they'd caught Charles Manson and the prosecutors were acting as though they couldn't take a
chance on letting the monster loose.

Hillier spent three days and nights reviewing the latest evidence belatedly supplied by Ronald Parker
and his sidekicks. As usual, it was incomplete, but
maybe that would work to Titus's benefit. The reports were so thin and contradictory that he
couldn't imagine a jury bringing in a guilty verdict.

He thought about the judge assigned to the
case. Charles V. Johnson was black and green. At
fifty-two, the former Arkansan was in his second
month on the Superior Court bench after eleven
years in Municipal Court trying traffic cases and
other misdemeanors. Everything about the tall, dig-
nified Johnson bespoke unpretentious competence;
he was one of the few Seattle judges who sometimes

called attorneys "lawyers," and he frequently used the expression, "I don't know." But this would be his first big trial.

The volcanic Titus remained a problem. Hillier drilled his client on the facts of courtroom life. "Look, Steve," he said, "you can't be uptight on the stand. You've got to make the jury relate to you. You've got to make 'em *like* you."

"What about the facts?" Titus sputtered. "What about the law? That's all that should matter."

"Look, Steve, this isn't *Perry Mason*. This is a real trial. We've got to create an atmosphere of nonhostility, of affection. I want the jury to think, 'Gee, what a nice guy.' It's psychodrama, Steve, and we've gotta live with it."

For a time the mellowing process seemed to be working. Titus showed flashes of the pleasant young man he'd been, even went out for a beer with Hillier and exchanged a few jokes. But the last-minute arrival of Ronald Parker's revisionist report on the original Titus interview undid every bit of progress.

"Goddamn, Tom!" Titus raged, stomping around the lawyer's office. "This son of a bitch is outright lying!" He shook the report in the air. "I didn't say *any* of this! He's changed my route, he's changed the whole goddamn time frame. *And he's quoting me on the changes!* Tom, that's, that's—he's the one who should be on trial!"

"First let's win this case," Hillier suggested calmly. "Then we'll decide what to do about Ronald Parker."

■

With jury selection well under way, it was too late to ask for a continuance, and maybe even inadvisable; it would only give the Port police more time to re-write history. To Hillier, the best course seemed to be to blow the prosecution out of the water with facts, evidence, and a warm cuddly defendant. Titus, still red-faced and breathing hard, promised to do his best.

58

As he stood before the bench, Christopher Washington looked like the model of the TV prosecutor. His black hair gleamed under the fluorescent lights. In contrast to Hillier's dark tweeds, his navy blue suit provided a dress-for-success look that he carried off with ease and dignity. His voice was sincere and strong.

But his opening statement described a surprisingly weak case. He seemed to be trying to precondition the bright, upscale jury to accept inconsistent statements, contradictory timetables, and vague testimony—and still convict the defendant. Celia Dalton, he noted, "can't remember the exact license in the back" and "doesn't even recall exactly what was said." She "can't be sure of time. . . ." Another prosecution witness, Paul Liston, had given two different times, 7:00 and 7:30 P.M., for the victim's arrival at his door. Detective Ronald Parker had photographed a tire track, "thinking it might be important," but as it turned out "it is no value in this case. . . ." And Officer Parker also reported seeing a vinyl book with a brown cover and a silver-tipped pen in Titus's car, but "unfortunately these were not seized." Washington admitted that fingerprints were found but none matched victim *or* de-

fendant. Hairs and fibers were also "of no value."
Celia Dalton hadn't been asked to turn over the
rape clothing till a month after the incident; by
then, they "had been washed and were of no
value."

Hillier held his own opener to a minimum and sat
back to listen to the state's first witness, Celia's
friend Shirlee Watson. The Red Lion waitress was
firmly on record as having last spoken to Celia at
7:00 P.M., the exact moment when Titus had been at
home making a phone call, but now she revised
Celia's departure time to no later than 6:20.

Celia took the stand herself and rolled back the
pickup time to 6:30. The two close friends had been
driven to the courthouse that morning by Ronald
Parker, but they denied that the case had been discussed on the way.

The turning point of the trial came early. Chris
Washington asked Celia if she saw her rapist in the
courtroom. "Yes," she answered.

Q. —Can you indicate, first of all, where he
is?
A. —Right there.
Q. —Seated at the counsel table?
A. —Yes . . .
Q. —At this time, I would ask the witness to
come down off the stand and indicate the dis-
tance Celia Dalton was from the defendant.

Tom Hillier didn't understand what Washington was getting at. What distance? When? During the rape? Wouldn't the physical distance between the parties have to be *zero*? What the hell was the prosecutor trying to prove? The woman had already identified his client from the witness stand. What purpose could be served by getting into his face?

Hillier jumped up and objected, and Washington responded, "Your Honor, I believe the prosecution is entitled to demonstrate for the jury the distance Ms. Dalton was from the defendant, so as to demonstrate her ability and opportunity she had to observe."

MR. HILLIER—Can she testify to that without demonstration?

JUDGE JOHNSON—She can, but there is nothing improper about her taking a position that would be the approximate distance that she was from him.

MR. WASHINGTON—That is the purpose of this request, Your Honor.

JUDGE JOHNSON—She may so take up that position, if you wish.

Hillier was baffled. He thought, Am I the only person in this courtroom too stupid to understand what Washington means by the "distance that she was from him"? The prosecutor seemed to understand and so did judge and witness.

Chris Washington, his line of questioning validated, pushed ahead. "Ms. Dalton," he said, "I want you to walk and stop when you get as close as you were.'' His face took on a sympathetic look as he added, ''That is *hard*. Look at the person, look at the defendant. Is this the person that picked you up that evening?''

Hillier considered objecting again, but Celia Dalton was already headed toward the defense table with the prosecutor walking alongside. Her hesitant steps and tortured body language dramatized her fear of approaching the evil presence. She managed to squeeze out a ''Yes'' before her face twisted in pain and she broke out in sobs.

Hillier called out, ''Excuse me! May we discharge the jury? I'd like to approach the bench.''

The judge hesitated. A female juror dabbed at her eyes. The clerk looked shocked and the bailiff frowned. The loudest noise came from Celia Dalton, sobbing into her hands.

''Have the witness seated in the witness chair,'' the judge ordered. ''Both of you may come right up here.''

At the bench, Hillier struggled to stay cool. ''If it please the court, Your Honor,'' he began, picking each word with care, ''the witness in this case, I anticipate, is going to testify that she was raped by an individual who she has identified for the record is my client. I don't think it takes much common sense to assume that when one is being sexually assaulted by another that they are as close as two people can possibly be together. Now to have to graphically demonstrate that in front of a jury shows an utter disregard for the feelings of this young woman. . . . It is to the detriment of this young man that this demonstration is allowed to be recorded in the presence of the jury. . . .'' He labeled Washington's

maneuver "prejudicial," "a cheap prosecutorial tac-
tic at best," and moved for a mistrial.

Judge Johnson denied the motion.

The tear-stained witness testified for hours. Hillier
had already decided not to risk antagonizing the
jury by attacking her on cross-examination—she *had*
been raped and thus was a sympathetic figure. His
gentle questioning failed to shake her story. At the
end he asked what made her identify Titus as her
rapist.

"Because," she said, "I know it is him."

After the Celia Dalton blowup, the rest of the four-
day trial seemed anticlimactic to everyone in the
courtroom. The prosecution's chief investigator laid
out his case coolly and methodically, with substantia-
tion from colleagues. Ronald Parker was well spoken
and assured, with a robust, mellow voice and a direct manner. He came across as a highly impartial
professional with nothing to prove. He made some
of his points with charts and maps. He seemed to be
taking pains not to prejudice the jury against Titus;
he was the only member of the Port police chase
teams who didn't claim that Titus had exceeded the
speed limit the night of the stop. It was a nice touch
of fairness, well noticed in the courtroom.

Hillier retaliated with his own array of witnesses, but
since they were largely unschooled in courtroom
psychology and confined to the literal truth, they
often appeared ineffective. Steve's asthmatic father,
David, a dour man, seemed as annoyed as his son by
the proceedings. In contrast to the precise time-

tables of the prosecution witnesses, his testimony was often vague and shapeless, of limited use to the defense.

> Q. —Do you recall what time it was that Steve arrived [at the birthday party]?
> A. —. . . I don't remember. I don't recall. He didn't get to stay very long, let's put it that way. I don't know.

And later:

> Q. —Do you recall when Steve left that evening?
> A. —Yes. I was watching the six o'clock news.
> Q. —How long had it been on?
> A. —Oh, just a short time, I think.
> Q. —Did Steve leave during that news?
> A. —Yes.
> Q. —Assuming the six o'clock news came on at six o'clock, approximately what time was it that you recall Steve left your house?
> A. —Oh, I couldn't say. I don't know for sure. I would be guessing.
> Q. —Was it past six-thirty?
> A. —I don't think so. It was getting dusk, I think. Yes, it was getting dark.

Jacqueline Titus testified in a lilting French accent that she couldn't remember her son's time of arrival at the party, but it might have been around three or three fifteen. She said he'd left at five or ten minutes after six; she knew because she'd glanced at the clock.

When her short appearance was over, she joined her husband in seats near the front. The senior Tituses seemed to cast an air of righteousness over the courtroom. In contrast to the relaxed Port cops in their crisp uniforms and highly shined shoes and badges, the parents were dressed simply and came across as American Gothic suburbanites, ill at ease and stiff.

Steve's older brother, Alan, wore the same aggrieved look as he stepped to the stand and took the oath. "Alan," Hillier asked him, "do you understand what the nature of this case is?"

"I understand the nature," he replied crisply, "but I don't understand why this is happening."

Washington objected and the judge ordered the jury to disregard the second part of the answer. Hillier had to admonish his own witness: "Okay, just answer my questions."

After testimony about a birthday photo the mother had snapped, Alan Titus was asked if he recalled what time his brother had left their father's party.

A. —Yes. I was watching the six o'clock news and I had asked Steve—he'd just gotten his new car, and that was the first time I saw it, that evening, and I wanted a ride in it.

MR. WASHINGTON—I'll object. It's not responsive to the question that was asked, Your Honor.

JUDGE JOHNSON—Sustained.

Q. (BY MR. HILLIER)—Okay. Do you recall approximately what time it was that he left?

A. —It was shortly after the start of the six o'clock news.

Q. —And how is it that you remember that?

A. —I invested in some investments that, with the Iranian hostage situation, I am very concerned as to what's happening in the news, and I always watch the world news at six o'clock.

Steve's friend Kurt Schaefer took the stand and backed up the alibi timetable, and so did Mona Imholt; both stood their ground under tough cross-examination. Telephone records confirmed the most crucial aspect of Mona's testimony: the 7:00 P.M. phone call from Steve.

When the trial recessed for the weekend on the afternoon of Friday, February 27, most observers figured that the defense might be a little ahead.

On Monday morning the defendant took the witness stand and seemed to forget every lesson that Tom Hillier had pounded into him. It was almost a repeat of his self-destruction in the lie detector test. Under Hillier's friendly examination, Titus was intense and tight-lipped; answering Washington, he was snappy and pugnacious. He twisted his fingers, sweated conspicuously, and looked ready to explode. His subtext came across with the subtlety of blows from an ax: the Port police weren't merely mistaken; they were *lying*. It was a big gulp to ask a jury to swallow.

When he stepped off the stand just before 3:00 P.M., everyone agreed that he'd lost his earlier advantage. The verdict was up for grabs.

59

Mona sat on the stone steps and tried to control her breathing. The jury had been out an hour, a puzzlement to her. She'd anticipated instant justice and strawberry margaritas all around. She'd expected to dance "The Titus" till the bars closed.

Steve disengaged from a hallway conference and slumped alongside her. His face looked blotchy and red. Lately he'd been developing high blood pressure.

"Honey," he said, "I've got something to tell ya."

He looked stricken. My God, she thought, the jury must have come in while I was in the ladies' room. They must have found him guilty.

He said, "It's about . . . uh . . ." He took a deep breath. "It's about . . . my age."

"Your age?" He made it sound like the end of the world.

"I'm, uh—thirty-one."

Her sigh filled the stairwell. "Oh, God, Steve," she said, hugging him hard, "I think I can live with that." She couldn't bear to tell him that she'd known from the beginning.

She looked into his light blue eyes and thought, How sad, how pathetic. Not even his own silliness made him smile anymore.

60

In its stuffy room, the jury went about its business with methodical expertise. It was a surprisingly cerebral group of taxpayers, somewhat light on street wisdom but heavy in intellect and accomplishment. Many had graduate degrees and some had previous jury experience. The members included a U.S. District Court judge's wife, an engineer, a nursing supervisor, a business administrator, and an educator. There was no shouting, no pressuring, no abrasion. From the first secret ballots, they'd split along predictable lines: one third guilty, one third innocent, and one third with their fingers to the wind.

After a few hours, a juror who'd been arguing against Titus listed the strongest items of evidence—the montage, Celia's ID of the car, the temporary license plate with its three matching numbers, the gewgaw hanging from the rearview mirror, the brown vinyl folder, the Marlboro butts, the pen that could have been used as a weapon, and several other items—and said, "Now assume that there's only a fifty-fifty chance that each point shows he's guilty. Do you realize the odds against him by the time you get to the eighth or tenth item in the string? *Astronomical!*"

Someone urged the speaker to reread the instruction book issued to all jurors. It was right there in black and white: jurors were not to consider odds or probabilities; a criminal trial was not a poker game or a lottery wheel. There was reasonable doubt or there wasn't.

"Well, what's reasonable doubt?" the mathematical juror asked. "One in a million? One in *ten*?" But he graciously admitted that he shouldn't have mentioned odds.

Later in the first day of deliberations, the discussion turned to the fuzziness of the police evidence, the contradictions, the amateurishness of the Port cops. The majority agreed that the investigation and some of the testimony had been less than inspiring, but no one sniffed perjury or dishonesty. "We perceived police as helping little old ladies across the street," a juror explained later. "Our worst naïveté was that we believed that police would *never* fabricate evidence."

By the morning of the second day of deliberations, the secret ballots showed nine to three for guilty, then tightened to ten to two. As the hours wore on, subtleties and technicalities became lost in the stress. The guilty-voters kept insisting that it didn't matter if time frames varied a little, if colors were slightly off, if testimony wasn't consistent in every last detail. People under stress never got things exactly right. Did anyone expect a rape victim to take notes? Cops were overworked and made honest mistakes.

The hard-liners insisted that the case came

down to a simple question: whom did they believe? The angry, nervous, *intense* Steve Titus, up there trying to talk his way to freedom, or the poor abused child who had nothing whatever to gain? Sure, Celia was shopworn, a Sea-Tac Strip type, a little . . . common. But those tears, those buckling knees, that terrified look—who could doubt her honesty, her sincerity? *She'd been afraid to approach Steve Titus. Why would she react that way if she weren't positive he was her rapist?*

The last holdout against a guilty verdict was a silver-haired high school teacher who listened with a fatigued expression on his face as the others explained the defects in his thinking. For the first time, voices were raised and gentle aspersions cast. "I'm sorry," the teacher said, "but—I've still got a reasonable doubt."

They ran him through their points one more time and countered each of his doubts with rhetoric. He crossed his forearms on the table and lowered his head. It was almost 6:00 P.M. on the second day of deliberations, and the judge had indicated he would hold them through the evening.

The teacher's head stayed down for a long time. Then he raised it and said, "Okay."

61

Mona Jean Imholt had spent the day comforting Steve, starting on the morning drive to the gloomy old King County Courthouse and continuing at every break in the action. But she hadn't been able to calm his fears. "What's taking the jury so long?" he kept saying. "Does the truth have to hit them in the face? Can't they see through the goddamn lies?"

She'd fallen back on the prevailing defense wisdom: the longer the jury was out, the better it looked for Steve. At worst, it might mean a hung jury and a new trial. But the next time around, the defense team would know what to expect; the time jiggling and last-minute switches and revisions would be locked into the record.

But Steve didn't seem to hear her. "Don't you get it, Mona?" he said in an anguished voice. *"I can't go through another trial!"*

Mona and the frail Jacqueline Titus held hands in the front row as the jurors filed in and took their places just after dark. Steve seemed to crumple as the verdict was read. His head fell forward and he moaned.

Hillier asked that the jury be polled, and twelve times the word "guilty" pierced the air. When the last juror had confirmed the verdict, Jackie Titus slipped to the floor.

Mona took two steps to the defense table and grabbed Steve from behind. "Please sit down!" the judge ordered. He was a substitute who'd been brought in to accept the verdict. Judge Johnson had left for the day.

Mona shook her blond hair from side to side and hugged Steve harder. She thought they were going to put him in jail and keep him there. She knew nothing about appeals or bail. She was afraid she wouldn't see him again.

"Please," the judge repeated, "you must take your seat."

"No!" she yelled.

Steve's body quivered beneath her touch. A few steps behind, Mrs. Titus clasped her hands and sobbed. Steve's dad was gesturing and talking in a loud voice.

The judge ordered the bailiff to take the jurors out for their own protection. Then he banished Mona from the courtroom. As she strode down the hall, she slammed her purse against the ashtrays, producing a trail of broken glass. She was an angry kid again. One of her childhood nicknames had been "Mean Mona Jean."

Someone yelled that Steve was being taken downstairs on his way to jail, and Mona ducked into an elevator. On the street floor she spotted a deputy leading the jurors across the high-ceilinged entrance hall. "You're wrong!" she shouted. "You don't know Steve! Every damn one of you, you—are —WRONG! How can you be so *stupid*?"

A policewoman told her to back off.

"I won't!" Mona screamed. "I'm gonna say what I'm gonna say. We still got freedom of speech."

She jabbed her fingers at the well-dressed jurors as they edged along the wall toward the exit. "You goddamn bastards!" she yelled. "You're gonna pay!" She knew she was making a spectacle of herself, wailing and screaming, blond hair whipping back and forth, bangs bouncing, mascara dripping from her chin. "Steve didn't do anything," she called down the hall. "You guys are gonna be sorry!"

. When she dug into her purse for a hankie, a bystander yelled, "Look out! She's got a gun!"

The policewoman took a step toward her, then dropped back as the handkerchief appeared.

In a few minutes another elevator door opened and Steve was led out by two cops. He was handcuffed behind his back. He couldn't even wipe his nose.

Mona rushed up and squeezed him again. The cops were nice about it. "It'll be okay," she kept repeating. "It'll be okay." Steve didn't answer. His reddish skin had turned pale. He looked as though he were having trouble breathing.

She drove through the early evening rush hour to her favorite cousin's house. She knew she sounded uptight, but she couldn't help herself. "Do me a big favor," she told her cousin. "If Steve and I have to leave the state, will you tell the kids we love 'em?"

One way or another, she was going to get him out of jail.

62

Juror Edward Carl was having trouble getting to sleep. He was a chemical engineer at Boeing, a big thoughtful man with a brassy laugh, an ear for classical music, and a strong sense of fairness. Married with children, he lacked a few weeks of celebrating his thirty-ninth birthday. "I'm a statistical person," he liked to say. "Shit happens." But he didn't like it to happen on his shift. And now he was entertaining his first small doubts.

When he'd caught the Titus case, he told himself that he would approach it as though his own son were on trial. But he also remembered a college field trip and a get-acquainted lunch with the self-improvement group at McNeil Island Federal Penitentiary. Every convict had sworn he was innocent! Every convict had sworn he'd been railroaded! All through the Titus trial, Ed kept that in mind.

Like most of his fellow jurors, he'd been moved by Celia Dalton's courtroom breakdown. From that point on, he'd felt that Titus was probably guilty and it was up to him to prove otherwise. But the guy had turned out to be an unconvincing witness on his own behalf. He'd been caught in a couple of lies, like the one about his age, as reported by the airport cop who'd stopped him the night of the rape. Nothing important, but . . . wouldn't a defendant who lied about his age also lie to stay out of prison? And maybe convince his parents and friends to lie on his behalf? Or bend the truth a little?

Ed Carl had voted "guilty" from the first vote to the last and hadn't been shy about saying so. He'd been the promulgator of the probability explanation and had been happy to withdraw it even though it still made sense to him. He'd been comfortable with his decision until . . .

"When the verdict was announced, he let out a moan," Carl confided to his wife. "It seemed to come without conscious thought." He struggled to find the right words. "It was like it came straight from the gut—valid, unfakable. It was—it was the most pathetic moan I ever heard. And I thought, *Son of a bitch, this doesn't fit in! This sounds like an innocent man.*"

The engineer couldn't comprehend his own feelings. He was still a statistical person, reasoned, orderly, and now he was finding himself deeply influenced by a convicted felon's cry of pain. And yet he remained convinced of the accuracy of the verdict.

When he couldn't get to sleep, he phoned Chris Washington for reassurance. The prosecutor still seemed sure of his position. His attitude was that Titus had moaned for the same reason that many convicted criminals moaned: because they'd just come up against the hard fact that they were going to jail; they weren't going to get away with their crimes. Carl had to agree that the idea made sense.

But he elicited an earthier reaction when he phoned Tom Hillier at home. By now it was past midnight, and the defense lawyer had drunk his way across Puget Sound on a jumbo ferry and then finished drowning his anger at a Bainbridge Island bar with a teammate from his softball team. Hillier sounded ashamed that he'd let Titus down. "This is it," he said. "Piss on it. I'm leaving the law."

Carl tried to console the man he'd lobbied against in the jury room, but the lawyer didn't seem consolable. "We blew them out of court," Hillier said. "I can't understand where you guys got your verdict."

"Hey, Tom," Carl said as though they were old friends, "don't feel so bad. There's nothing more you could've done."

"I quit," Hillier repeated. "I'm hanging it up."

Carl insisted, "You did the best you could."

He went back to bed and tried to sleep, but he kept hearing Titus moan.

Early the next morning a fellow juror phoned. "I just found out that our boy failed a lie detector test," she reported. "They kept it from us."

Thank God, Carl said to himself. If there was ever any doubt, it's gone now. The guy's guilty as hell.

When he reported for work at the Boeing plant in Everett, he noticed an artist's sketch of a suspected "open house" rapist on the paint hangar's bulletin board. He was surprised to see how much it resembled Steve Titus.

63

With the approval of Christopher Washington, Mona Imholt was permitted to attend Steve's bail hearing on her promise to behave. Judge Johnson was back on the bench, and he released the prisoner on $2,500 cash bond. Not a minute too soon, Mona said to herself. Look at Steve, a wreck, all pale and shaky. His clothes hung like a Halloween outfit.

In the hall he hugged her and his parents and kept repeating, "We're gonna fight this. We're gonna *fight* this." But he didn't look them in the eye, and his hoarse voice lacked punch. He sounded like someone trying to convince himself.

Tom Hillier had gone from 178 to 160 pounds since taking the case. Out in the hall, Mona told him he looked as though he was the one who'd spent the night in jail. "Maybe I should have," Hillier said. He wasn't smiling.

A Titus family member suggested that they tell their story to the *Post-Intelligencer* or the *Times* or one of the TV stations. "No," Hillier recommended. "We'll win without them." So far, the case had barely been mentioned in public.

.

As Steve steered south toward home in the midday traffic lull, he told Mona that he'd intended to hang himself in his cell. "I was looking for a place to tie the sheet. I didn't know I'd get out today. I thought it was forever."

Mona stroked his arm.

"I wouldn't make it in prison," he said. "Do you know what happens to rapists? I'm not a big guy, you know."

She knew what he meant. Despite his masculinity, there was a certain beauty to him, with his blond curly hair, his deep blue eyes, and his smile. Everyone knew what happened to pretty boys in the penitentiary.

He seemed so hurt, so . . . shredded. She thought his spirits might revive when they reached home, but he just fell into her arms and started sobbing again. "You'll never know what it feels like," he said, "to be so disbelieved."

Sentencing was set for April 21, six weeks away, little enough time in which to prove his innocence. Somewhere in this urban area of a million souls, a bearded man drove a blue Chevette, wore a cream-colored vested suit, smoked Marlboros, and raped women in the airport woods. All they had to do was find him, drag him in, and prove his guilt. The nightmare situation reminded Mona of movies where the beleaguered hero had to clear his name while chased by cops and killers and vicious dogs. Like most horror film clichés, it was easier to watch than endure.

∎

They started by trying to understand the *why* of the arrest and prosecution. Who stood to gain by putting him away? Who had the motivation? Ronald Parker was clearly the prime mover, but to what end? "I never did a thing to that man in my life," Steve told Mona. "Why is he so dead set against me?"

He was convinced that there was a connection between his ex-wife Phyllis and the Port detective, and all they had to do was ferret it out. What else could explain the cruelty, the venality, the energetic distortion of evidence, except the blood feud he'd had with Phyllis over child support and visitation rights and every grievance under the sun? Maybe there hadn't even been a rape. Maybe it was pure hoax, pure vendetta.

A friend at the phone company produced a listing of Phyllis's outgoing calls, and days and nights were spent dialing the numbers to try to get the names and addresses of her contacts. She'd once dated a man named Tom Parker; to Steve, that was too big a coincidence. There were Parkers galore in the phone book, but no verifiable connection between Ronald and Tom. Steve and Mona staked out Tom Parker's home with a long-lens camera, waiting for Phyllis or Ron Parker to appear. Some nights Steve would drive Mona back home to get some sleep, then resume the stakeout till 4:00 or 5:00 A.M. But no Parker showed up, not even Tom. Evidently he was out of town—"on the lam," as Steve explained, more convinced of the "conspiracy" than ever.

■

Steve phoned Port police headquarters so often that the operators began refusing his calls. He tried using a fake name and was informed, "Personnel information is *strictly* confidential, Mr. Titus." The dispatcher wouldn't even acknowledge Ron Parker's existence, let alone confirm that he worked for the Port. One of Steve's friends heard that the crooked cop had gone to school in the naval shipyard town of Bremerton, across Puget Sound to the west. Steve asked a schoolteacher friend to check the files, but she turned up nothing.

To Steve, Detective Corporal Ronald Parker was evil personified, and yet decent people seemed to be covering up on his behalf. He saw Parker's hand behind every dead end, behind every denial or refusal to cooperate. He imagined Parker capable of great feats of influence and pressure. A law officer who would lie and fabricate evidence and persuade others to lie, for the sole purpose of railroading an innocent man—what *wouldn't* a guy like that do? Murder and mayhem were more justifiable offenses. This Parker was about forty; he must have left a life-long trail of deceit and dishonesty. But how to turn up the proof when no one would even discuss the guy?

Steve went off in every direction. On weekends he dragged his son Kenny on his investigative rounds rather than miss out on his visitation rights. He would have preferred their usual round of video games and sports events and junk food binges, but time was short. Steve had already explained to his son that the case was "no big deal," and the nine-year-old seemed satisfied. Above all else, Steve didn't want him upset. Kenny was a nice kid, and he'd suffered enough in the divorce.

Close friends Peter Rago and Kurt Schaefer took time off from their own jobs to help in the gum-shoeing. The intense black-haired Kurt seemed as aggrieved as Steve. "I don't care if it takes the rest of my life," he promised. "I'm not gonna rest till you're cleared."

Schaefer was still chagrined that twelve of his fellow citizens had taken him for a liar. "If they'd believed my testimony," he lamented, "no way they could've believed that Dalton girl." He wanted to take a lie detector test and shove the results under the prosecutor's nose. But the cheapest examiner charged $175, and Steve doubted that Chris Washington or Mary Kay Barbieri would look at the results. They'd won their case. Wasn't that the name of the game? Besides . . . what if Kurt flunked?

The amateur sleuths focused their attention on the coincidence of the temporary license plate, spending almost three weeks visiting car dealerships, examining Department of Licensing files, running down rows of numbers till everyone was red-eyed and exhausted. Steve paid a helpful DOL employee to work through a weekend, but she found nothing useful. A block of licenses starting with similar numbers had been shipped to dealers in the Tri-cities area, just east of the Cascades, but none had been issued to a Chevette. Temporary licenses had been assigned to numerous blue compacts in the Seattle area, but Steve's was the only one that came close to the numerical sequence recalled by the victim.

■

The neophyte detectives soon learned how hard it was to buy professional assistance. A private eye charged hundreds of dollars to inveigle her way into Celia Dalton's room in Tacoma and report that it was "a slop pit, a biker's paradise"—interesting information but useless.

Steve took to sitting in his car on the shoulder of the Sea-Tac Strip, keeping watch for the bearded rapist and the blue car. He trailed a likely subject all the way to Tacoma and jotted down the address and license number. When he returned home, he realized that he didn't know what to do next and turned again to the private agency. The "suspect" proved to be a camera salesman who'd purchased his car long after the rape. This time the bill was $1,500.

After a few weeks he ran out of money. His legal billings had reached $5,000 and he wasn't making payments. Tom Hillier told him not to worry. Of course, an appeal would cost two or three times as much.

Mona continued waitressing at Denny's, but Steve hadn't drawn a salary in weeks and was about to be removed from Yegen's books. Everyone at the company remained loyal—top officers even wrote letters of protest to the judge—but parents of Yegen's female employees had protested the employment of a convicted rapist. And Steve was in no shape to continue as an administrator anyway.

With his lawyer, he pored over the presentencing report. Hillier warned that a rookie judge like Charles Johnson was unlikely to deviate from its recommendations. The probation officer's phraseology was chilling: "◡ . . Celia Dalton became concerned and told *Mr. Titus* she wanted to get out of the car. . . . *Mr. Titus* replied, 'I won't hurt you I am going to rape you. . . .' *Mr. Titus* stated, 'Remember that I have a knife.' "

Now that the jury had ruled, Steve realized that he was no longer considered the "alleged" or the "accused" rapist; he was no longer the "suspect"; he was no longer innocent until proven guilty. By due process of law, Steve Gary Titus was now *the rapist of Celia Dalton,* and all subsequent proceedings would proceed from that assumption.

He reached the portion of the probation report that quoted others about his behavior and reputation. His parents reported: "Loves the Lord our God, loves people, generous and compassionate . . . Loves to be with people and has an abiding need for them. He has always honored his mother, father and brother. He loves and honors his son Kenny." Under "bad points," his mother and father had listed "a slight temper" and "does not dress good enough for his work."

He hadn't expected his ex-wife to sing his praises to the presentence investigator, but he was upset to read her comments. Phyllis claimed that he'd cheated on her during their marriage, slapped her, kicked her and threatened her with a .22 rifle. He'd shown "little affection or consideration" for their son. It was her opinion that marijuana abuse had turned him into a rapist, and that he needed to change his personality if he wanted to avoid further entanglements with the law.

Steve's mouth fell open as he came to the presentence investigator's final recommendations. He remembered their interview almost word for word. He'd taken pains to explain to the busy woman that he was innocent and needed time to prove it. Clearly, she'd thought he was lying.

"In my opinion," her report declared, "Mr. Titus has demonstrated he is capable of violent behavior and cannot be considered safe to remain in the community. A recommendation for treatment at Western State Hospital does not appear to be a viable alternative at this time based on Mr. Titus' continued denial of the offense and his need for treatment. Mr. Titus' failure to participate in an evaluation with our staff psychologist and his failure to notify us in any way also demonstrates, in my opinion, a lack of cooperation and motivation on his part to resolve his behavior problems. *I therefore recommend Steven Gary Titus be sentenced to prison."*

That could mean twenty years to life.

Mona read the report and reverted to the "Mean Mona Jean" of her childhood. She fired off a letter to the judge:

I know Steve better than just about anyone. I am soon to be his wife. He has never laid one hand on me intending to hurt. I also cannot believe you would take the word of his ex-wife. They have never for as long as I have known them *ever* had a decent word to say to one another. . . .

In her delicately wrought French hand, Jacqueline Titus wrote, "Steve and his family are crying for justice."

But the condemned man, his relatives and his friends had reached the realization that their cries would go unheard. They decided on one more roll of the dice.

64

Mac Smith couldn't remember such a cold, wet winter since his earliest years in Columbus. Despite his driveaway gasoline thefts and other petty scams, he couldn't pay the rent on the scruffy house he'd rented after his trailer had burned down, and the landlord sent an eviction notice. Mac's hard-working wife Nan had become so disenchanted that she told him not to bother finding another place; she would take the kids and move in with a friend. Mac could take a hike. Who needed a guy who couldn't do a damned thing right?

Nan's rejection came as no surprise. In six years of marriage, she'd never adjusted to his carousing and his lies. There'd been too many secrets, too many half-truths and evasions; any woman's faith would have eroded. He was sure that she still loved him, but her body no longer transmitted the message. He'd watched her change from sexually active to mechanical to inert. For a long time he'd manipulated her by playing on her marital obligations and guilt, but lately she'd cut him off completely. He'd told a few lies too many.

He unpacked his suitcase in a five-by-ten-foot shed on his heavily mortgaged Lake Sawyer acreage, brushed aside the rodent droppings, spread a sleeping bag on the damp floor, and set about surviving the cold with neither heat nor water. His job selling home security alarms was petering out and he barely had enough money for food, let alone pills and beer.

Only one satisfaction remained, and it produced the most intensely stimulating rush of all. The serious young man who'd once collected comic books, pennies and back issues of *Playboy* now collected victims.

PART FOUR

THE WRONG MAN

■

1981

65

It was a dismal Thursday afternoon, the last day of his screwy workweek, and Paul Henderson III was about an inch away from telling his bosses to shove it. He'd just learned from the *Seattle Times* bulletin board that after twelve years of working the night shift, after twelve years of living like a goddamn bat, he was being reassigned—to nights. How long would it be this time? Another twelve years? *Christ,* he thought, *I'll be fifty-five!*

At a confrontation with an unsympathetic editor, he was told in blunt language that the assignment couldn't be changed. The old promises reeled through his head: "Paul, you're the best police reporter in town, *blah blah blah*. . . . Just give us one more year on nights, *blah blah blah*. . . . This'll be good for your career, *blah blah blah*. . . ." He'd given them "one more year" plus an extra four months, and now they were handing him another bag of shit. The best police reporter in town realized that he'd been living in dreamland.

The turd plane circled overhead as he sulked at a corner desk as far from the city desk as possible. "The turd plane" was newsroom shorthand for catching an unbearably boring assignment—a schoolboard meeting, an interview with the oldest

Norwegian in Ballard, or, worst of all, updating the weather table with temperatures from Capetown to the North Pole. So far on this slow news day, the weather was about the only thing that was happening in Seattle. The biggest story in the daytime editions had been about a sack of money that bounced out of a Loomis armored car, scattering bills. Tonight the Mariners were opening their home season against the California Angels at the Kingdome, but Sports had the privilege of covering those losers.

Ducking behind his VDT, Henderson felt at the mercy of an assistant city editor famous for his outbursts. You never knew the guy's moods, and they changed hourly. First he'd be St. Francis of Assisi and then Attila the Hun. They'd had plenty of run-ins before.

Henderson's personal schedule called for getting off at midnight and drinking with his newsroom cronies at the 2–3–4 bar across the street till the first papers came off at 2:00 A.M. He looked at the clock on the newsroom wall: 4:45. Oh, shit, he thought, the turd plane's coming. He could see the headlines:

NEIGHBORS PROTEST ZONING CHANGE
BUDGET HEARING DRAWS CROWD

He was figuring out how many minutes were in seven more hours when the assistant c.e. yelled across the room, "Henderson, take this call!"

He picked up the phone as though it had quills. "This is Steve Titus," a man said. "Do you remember the name?"

The voice lacked spirit and Henderson didn't

think he'd heard it before. But something clicked. A few months earlier a waitress at the 2–3–4 had mentioned a friend of a friend who'd been convicted of rape. Not only was the guy innocent, the woman claimed, but he hadn't even been in town on the night it happened.

"Yeah, sure," Henderson said into the phone. "I remember you. I thought you were gonna call me. Where ya been?"

"My lawyer wouldn't let me."

"Wouldn't let you what?"

"Call the newspapers. He said we were gonna win the case. But . . . we didn't."

The phone went silent. Then Titus said, "I'm being sentenced next week. I, uh—I need your help."

"Aren't you the guy that was out of town at the time of the rape?"

"I wasn't out of town."

Too bad, Henderson said to himself. That was the angle that interested me—some poor bastard nailed for a rape when he was a thousand miles away. Blatant injustice had always pissed him off. It also made great copy. Weeks back, he'd even mentioned the Titus case to the city desk.

"Are you innocent?" he asked, pressing the phone against his ear.

"Yes, I am," Titus responded. It sounded weak. They were *all* innocent. He wondered if he'd live long enough to hear somebody admit he was guilty as shit. He looked toward the city desk and saw his nemesis wearing a phone on each ear. More stories must be developing:

PROTESTERS RAP SEWAGE PLAN
SEATTLE TEEN WINS SPELL BEE

Titus was mumbling something about tire tracks. Henderson observed the assistant c.e. scanning his troops. The turd plane was on final approach.

"Okay, Titus," Henderson said. "Where do you live?"

His rackety old car provided more justification for the evening's passion play of misery and self-pity. It was a ten-year-old beater, olive drab with a ratty vinyl top, nicknamed "the army staff car" by his friends. He'd taken the word of a preacher that the Dodge Dart ran like a watch and laid down $1,150 after a test drive in the church parking lot. Now he had to downshift into first to climb Queen Anne Hill to his apartment.

Lurching and spewing blue-gray exhaust, the army staff car took him south out of Seattle to Kent, where he refueled at a service station and knocked back three Rainier beers at a C&W bar. He picked up a six-pack for the road. You never knew when you might be calling on Methodists.

66

Titus's new "apartment community" turned out to be a monstrosity, maybe five hundred units, nestled in firs and rhododendrons. Henderson recognized it as one of dozens of similar developments where corn and squash had grown a few years before. Floodlights, buried in the shrubbery, were intended to give the place a look of nocturnal elegance, but there were bowling trophies in the windows and old pickup trucks in the lot. He drove over a dragon's teeth tire shredder next to a big sign: DO NOT BACK UP! He hated the goddamned things. A succession of speed bumps bottomed out his shocks and his mood.

Steve Gary Titus was shorter than he'd expected, maybe five eight, a lightly built kid with a thin beard and moustache, wavy ginger hair parted in the middle, blue eyes rimmed with red, and a baby face. He looked a little like the dancer Baryshnikov. The poor guy appeared unable to smile or make small talk. Every inch of his small second-floor apartment was covered with papers and documents and open phone books, and he couldn't get down to business fast enough. It developed that Titus and his fiancée Mona had spent the evening checking out his latest theory, which was that a hermit named Paul Liston and his hospital nurse had conspired to bear false witness—or something to that effect.

As the evening wore on, Henderson found the guy to be full of far-fetched conspiratorial theories—the prosecutor's office had been bought off, his former wife's boyfriend had helped to frame him, the polygraph examiner was helping the cops, the rape had never happened, etc., etc. On the more realistic side, Titus had worked up a list of seventy discrepancies in the case against him. The list was handwritten on notebook paper like a school kid's report, and some of his points made the state's case look dubious as hell—the absence of the victim's fingerprints in Titus's car, for example. The tire tracks that appeared and disappeared at the prosecution's convenience. The timetables that were curiously out of joint. The fact that this didn't match and that didn't match and that some of the police testimony had *p-e-r-j-u-r-y* written all over it.

Titus showed him a grainy photo montage that would have made a criminology professor cry—everything tilted northeast toward his picture. Goddamn, Henderson said to himself, somebody wants to send this poor guy away. I wonder why. Aren't there enough real rapists to prosecute?

He reminded himself not to give in too fast. Despite his surface cynicism and blunt manner, he was notoriously impressionable. As an army correspondent in Korea, he'd preferred stories about orphans and hungry peasants to puff pieces about the brass. In his cub year on the Council Bluffs *Nonpareil* in Iowa, an editor accused him of suffering from "terminal empathy.'' After nineteen years of reporting, he was still an easy touch, even though he spent most of his time with hard-liners like vice detectives, street people, and fellow reporters. His fiancée, the *Times* courthouse reporter Janet Horne, theorized that his softheartedness welled up from his childhood—he'd been raised by alcoholic parents who thought nothing of leaving him and his baby sister in the backseat of their Buick Roadmaster while they spent hours in a bar. Growing up on the East Coast, he'd been neglected until his compassionate ''Gramps'' dragooned him and sister Gale to the bucolic town of Beatrice, Nebraska, and provided them with warmth and security and a robust parental image.

Whenever Henderson worked a sob story, he had to avoid projecting his own sensitivities and scars. He'd been fooled, but he doubted that this Titus was capable of it. Anyone could see that the guy was bleeding in his shoes. His anguish, his outrage, his hurt—everything showed. He was so consumed with pain and anger that he couldn't even fake a smile.

But—that didn't clear him of rape. In fourteen years on the *Times*, most of them as a police reporter, Henderson had met his share of criminals with stories, and all too many turned out dirty. So he insisted on hearing the whole story, minute by minute, inch by inch, document by document, far into the night. Titus and his girlfriend weren't drinking, but a stash of Lucky Lager turned up in the fridge when Henderson's supply ran out. It seemed like a good omen.

67

Hours later, the baby-faced Titus had passed just about every test—at least for the moment. With his light blue eyes and his soft voice, he rang the right bells. If he was manipulative, it didn't show. But Henderson refused to relax the pressure. "You claimed you don't own a suit," he challenged. "Show me."

Titus opened a closet door. No suits.

"What's in the other closet?" Henderson insisted. Titus showed him Mona's clothes.

"Can I check around?" Henderson asked. Titus nodded. No suits were under the bed or in the kitchen cupboard.

"Ask my friends," Titus said. "Ask my brother, my parents. Ask the guys at work. Nobody's ever seen me in a suit."

"Thanks," Henderson said. "I'll do that." And he knew he would. That was the only way to avoid mistakes—hard checking, no easy assumptions, and above all no bleeding-heart sympathy.

"I want you to check every word I say," Titus said. "Then if you don't believe me, drop the case."

"You got a deal," Henderson said, "but let me rephrase it. If I catch you lying even once, it's all over."

Titus nodded. It was the closest he'd come to a smile all evening.

Driving north toward the 2–3–4 after midnight, Henderson stopped at a pay phone and told his boss, "I think this might be a good story. The guy seems to be telling the truth."

As he resumed his return trip, he thought again about the conflicting times and numbers in the material Titus had shown him. Two documents kept clashing in his mind: the victim's signed statement that she'd been raped at 7:00 P.M. and the phone bill showing the call from Steve's apartment at precisely the same time.

Even if you went by the prosecution's version of the facts, Henderson said to himself, the guy had had about a fifteen-minute window of opportunity in which to pick up Celia Dalton, drive her to the woods, rape her and return to his apartment. By anybody's time line, he was either the fastest dick in the West or the longest. But if he was crazy enough to commit an impulse crime like this, how had he managed to go thirty-two years without getting into trouble? And why was he spending his last few days of freedom opening his whole goddamn life to someone he'd met on the telephone, a guy who could only wind up finding more evidence against him?

The newspaper hangout, across Fairview Avenue from the old concrete *Times* building, swarmed with pressmen in newsprint hats, hard-drinking mailers, powerlifters from the loading dock, and nightside reporters babbling about the Mariners' opener. He tried to tell the Titus story, but no one seemed interested.

68

Mona tried to sleep while Steve rattled papers in the front room. It was after 4:00. Some nights he didn't come to bed at all.

Her first thought when Henderson had arrived was, *Oh, God, look what the paper sent! This bearded half-bald dude with the six-pack is gonna get Steve off? He looks like he couldn't find the men's room with a telescope.*

But after he left she had to admit he'd been a kick. For the first time since the arrest, Steve showed some spirit. "The guy *believes* me," he said after the reporter left. "He's gonna help us. Listen, Mona, we'll give him anything he needs."

She was happy to hear him speak above a dispirited whisper. A few days earlier he'd almost given up after Yegen's hit him with his notice. His job had meant everything to him: supervising seven restaurants, driving a company car, earning good money. He'd been in line for the next vice-presidency at thirty-eight grand a year. Then . . . wipe-out.

The sad situation hadn't been helped by a string of nighttime phone calls. "You're guilty, mother-fucker," a male voice would say. "You're gonna die, man. We got a knife for ya!" Steve insisted it was Ron Parker.

Mona was afraid to open the door. The two of them sat around for hours, feeding each other's anxieties. Every time he took out the garbage, she stood at the door and listened for the sounds of a scuffle—or gunshots.

Steve believed that the whole world knew his face and considered him evil. "I'm afraid for my life," he told her. He shaved his beard and changed his hair style. Whenever they went out, he asked a neighbor to watch the apartment. The shades were permanently drawn. When a saleswoman arrived, Steve slammed the door in her face and yelled, "Nope! Not interested!"

He'd lost the sparkle and spontaneity that always made him so different. If Mona asked him a question, he acted irritated or didn't answer. Sometimes he tried to lighten up, but it was never more than a minute or two before the pained expression returned. He demanded reassurance and griped at her if she didn't maintain the proper level of enthusiasm about his cause. Every day he accused her of lacking faith.

But through their worst hours, she never doubted his love, or her own. At fifteen, she'd made the mistake of marrying a father figure to get out of the house, but she'd never known romantic love till Steve. She couldn't imagine waking up in the morning and not seeing his face. She only wished she knew how to prove her love to his satisfaction. He'd become a bottomless pit of need.

At 5:00 A.M. she heard him heating water in the kitchen. Who else would work all night and then make coffee to keep himself awake all day? She wished she could bear some of his load, but she didn't know how. She'd already lost her own kids over the rape case. The final papers had come through in her divorce; her ex-husband's lawyer had demanded full custody, and the live-in girlfriend of a convicted rapist had no choice but to accept his terms. She'd signed her name and scrawled "Eat shit!" It made her feel better.

At last Steve's slender body slid under the covers. She looked at the clock: 7:35. She stroked his wavy hair and saw that the muscles on his face were relaxed for the first time in ages. "We're gonna win, baby," he said. "Henderson's gonna make the difference."

Mona thought, He won't survive another letdown. This reporter character better be the real thing. She just wished he hadn't sucked up so many beers.

69

The throbbing in Henderson's head had lessened by the next afternoon when he drove the army staff car to the scene of the rape. It was a cold, wet March day and of course he'd worn loafers. The condemned neighborhood was grown over with prickly devil's club, poison oak, vine maple, blackberry runners that nipped at his socks. Faintly marked driveways led off crumbled asphalt streets. Thistles and weeds choked yards; orchards were unpruned.

He came to an empty shell of a house with stair patterns and floor separations etched on the bare walls. The place gave him the creeps; it looked like a set for a snuff film, with jet engines drowning out the victim's screams.

He noodled around for an hour or two trying to find the right driveway, then left without being sure.

Back at work after his weekend, he asked Titus to drive the fish company's Chevette to the *Times* parking lot for a closer look in daylight. There was an ugly scar on the front seat where the Port police had cut a swatch as evidence. "But they didn't produce it in court," Titus explained. "It would've wrecked their case."

"How so?" Henderson asked.

"Celia Dalton said the car had soft seatcovers, velveteen or velour. Look at these."

The Chevette seats were covered in cheap vinyl, hard and cool to the touch. "She said she was sure it was velveteen because she pressed her cheek against it," Titus said.

Titus's blond girlfriend piped up, "Can you imagine a woman who can't tell vinyl from velour— with her face?"

Mona slid into the front passenger seat. She looked tired. "Watch this," Steve said, flipping a lever on the door side of the passenger's seat. Mona's weight made the seat flop back.

Henderson asked, "What's that prove?"

"Dalton testified that the guy reached across her body to recline the seat and it took him a real long time." He flipped the lever again, and the seatback popped straight up. "It doesn't take a long time in my car," he said. "It's instant."

Henderson thought, Yeah, but your lever could've jammed. Or Celia could've been mistaken about how long it took. What the hell, she's just a kid and the guy was holding a knife on her. But he kept quiet. He was Titus's last resort, and he felt the responsibility.

As the Chevette pulled out of the *Times* parking lot, Steve turned and waved. Henderson thought, I really feel for this guy. There's sure as hell a reasonable doubt. . . .

Back in the newsroom, he corraled one of the top editors and outlined the story. He said he believed there was a good chance that Titus had been set up for conviction by a police department that was

Mickey Mouse at best and downright felonious at worst.

"That's a big assumption," the editor said.

Henderson nodded. He knew the professional risk he was taking.

"Go for it," the editor said. "We'll give you a couple of weeks."

He drove straight to the prosecutor's office for a talk with Christopher Washington. He wasn't expecting much cooperation—the state had its conviction and no reporter was likely to overturn it—but the moustached young deputy seemed affable and sincere. At the outset, he volunteered, "Did you know that Titus blew the needles off the polygraph?"

"No," Henderson said. It was disturbing news, but innocent people had flunked lie detector tests before. Despite what the public had been led to believe, polygraphy wasn't infallible. "Okay, Chris," he said, "but how sure are you *personally* that Titus is guilty?"

Washington smiled. "One hundred percent," he said, and began reciting his list of proofs.

Henderson thought, It must be nice to be so sure.

He arranged a meeting with a Port police friend, a smart cop who'd been helpful in the past. The sergeant confirmed that Ron Parker had plenty of problems, but added that he couldn't imagine a brother officer conspiring to send an innocent man to prison. A luncheon with Parker's supervising lieutenant produced more of the same, plus a few indulgent shrugs. Apparently the Port police department wasn't giving anything up. Henderson knew he would have to dig hard. But would he have time? The sentencing date wasn't far off.

Mary Kay Barbieri, chief of the newly created Special Assault Unit, sounded shocked when he told her his plans. "Paul," she said, "does the *Times* really intend to question *a jury verdict*?" She made it sound as though they were doubting Deuteronomy.

"You bet," he said. He laid everything on the Port police, how they appeared to have altered evidence and maybe even lied in court, and how Ronald Parker had a dubious record.

"Don't be so rough on the Port," she put in. "I remember that case very well. Parker came to us just before trial and said he had some concerns about whether he had the right man. He said he couldn't understand why Titus had been so cooperative if he was guilty. But I reviewed the evidence with Chris Washington, and it all pointed one way."

Henderson was aware of Barbieri's sterling reputation, but a clearer picture of Detective Corporal Ronald Parker was coming into sight like a photoprint developing in its bath. Wasn't it possible that the cop had suffered an old-fashioned case of jitters and gone to Barbieri to cover his ass? He'd twisted the facts and his neck was out a mile. *If I don't pull this off, I could go to jail. So I better put in a little disclaimer to convince the prosecutor I'm bringing an honest case. If she agrees that we look weak, we'll just back off and nobody gets hurt. . . .*

Obviously the Special Assault Unit had elected to go forward on Parker's word as an honorable officer. And what had the rogue cop done as soon as he got the green light? If Titus was right, he'd rushed out and created more evidence! Just before the trial, he'd managed to get Celia and her waitress friend Shirlee Watson to change their time frames, then altered the information about the tire tracks. Cops had gone to prison for less.

Henderson decided to drive to Sea-Tac Airport and confront the spit-and-polish chief, Neil Moloney. He knew there was a chance he'd be shut out. Five years earlier, he'd written a prize-winning exposé on waterfront theft, and the main culprits turned out to be Port of Seattle officials. The Port had been ignoring wholesale theft to avoid a confrontation with longshoremen and Teamster truck drivers. The larceny was so widespread that dock workers openly displayed stolen goods at Saturday morning flea markets in the union hall. Henderson hadn't spoken to Moloney since the story had run. He regarded the chief as a corporate yes-man, but not everyone shared his view. There was a rumor that Moloney was ticketed to take over the State Patrol. If so, he wouldn't be eager to discuss another hot potato.

Seated in the chief's pleasant office, Henderson repeated Titus's claims about inconsistencies, contradictory testimony, and lack of evidence. Moloney seemed to listen thoughtfully as the rumbling sound of taxiing aircraft filtered into the air-conditioned room.

"Between us, Paul," the chief said, leaning forward confidentially, "I've had concerns about Ron Parker for some time."

Henderson thought, What happened to the stonewall I expected?

"He got into a big hassle with one of his superiors on Port property," Moloney continued. "Called him every name in the book. And there's been— other stuff." He promised that if Titus's allegations were true, he would personally see to it that Parker went to jail. "My people know where I stand on things like that," he said. He talked a hard line, but he also put in a polite refusal to let Henderson conduct his own interviews with Port personnel.

"Thanks for coming in, Paul," he said, shaking hands. "I'm gonna assign Dave Hart to look into this. They don't come any better." Henderson nodded but withheld judgment.

Driving back to the *Times,* he warned himself not to be too cynical. Give Moloney a chance. This isn't a stolen TV or a hijacked load of cigarettes. This is a man's life.

70

When he reached his office, he found a note on his desk. The prosecutor's office had called. Out of respect for the *Times,* Barbieri and her superiors had agreed to review the case.

He couldn't wait to tell Titus. That poor bastard hadn't heard an encouraging word since the day he'd been handcuffed in court.

"Steve," he barked into the phone. "I've got good news and *good* news. The Port's gonna reinvestigate. And so is the prosecutor. The sentencing's been put off for two weeks."

A long silence followed, then a choking sob. Mona came on the phone and whispered, "Steve can't talk."

The charged response gave Henderson a warm feeling. If Steve overreacted a little, so what? The poor guy had spent the last six months of his life worrying about being butt-fucked at Walla Walla. He was entitled to show some emotion.

Then Steve's voice said, "That's just swell, Paul." What a strange word, Henderson thought. *Swell.* So old-fashioned. What a simple, decent guy . . .

"Steve?" he said. "*Steve?*"

The line was dead.

·

Henderson wandered over to the copy desk and flopped in an unoccupied chair. Years ago, before VDTs and extended keyboards had turned newspaper offices into Mission Control, he'd worked the rim on the *Omaha World-Herald;* with its smell of fresh-sharpened pencils and its canny old news heads in glasses and eyeshades, the copy desk was a convivial place where the turd plane seldom flew, or so it seemed back then.

But before he got too comfortable, he felt a sudden impulse, the kind he was famous and infamous for. He realized that sooner or later Ronald Parker would have to be given a chance to respond to whatever the *Times* published about him; it was a standard journalistic practice known as "simultaneous rebuttal," and it was also vital insurance against lawsuits. So why not call the guy right now and lay it on the line? Why give the son of a bitch time to make more mischief? If he's dirty, let him stew the way Titus is stewing.

A reporter named Jan Smith was sitting across the rim reading galleys. He asked her to pick up the extension and monitor his call. If Parker copped to something, it would be nice to have corroboration.

He was surprised to find the policeman's home phone number in the book and more surprised to find that Ron Parker sounded calm, friendly, and reasonable. But then he thought, This asshole is trying to handle me the same way he handled Titus on the night of the stop. Disarming, easygoing. Scheming. Controlling. Was he another goddamn sociopath?

Henderson cited the obvious discrepancies in

the state's case. "Titus came to me in desperation," he said. "The guy swears he's innocent, and I gotta tell you up front, his story makes a hell of a lot of sense. Is there, uh, any chance that you went after the wrong person?"

Parker paused, suggesting thoughtful reflection. When he spoke, he sounded like a typical good-guy cop trying to help an old pal from the press. "Have you seen the trial transcript, Paul?" he asked.

"It hasn't been typed up yet."

"Well, I'll tell ya, Paul"—Henderson grabbed for a piece of paper, couldn't find one, and took his notes on the back of a phone book—"I think that if a person were to sit down and read the entire transcript, you would know that Steve Titus is guilty. Maybe he just blocks it out."

The detective said he wished he could reveal a few tidbits of inside information. "Then you'd be convinced for sure, Paul." But Port police procedure prevented him from commenting on a live case. The hang-up was friendly.

Henderson thought, This monkey tells the prosecutor that he's not sure Titus is the right guy. Now he tells me he's totally convinced. Bullshit! Ron Parker *is* dirty. Henderson didn't know exactly what made him so positive. Sometimes inflections meant more than words. So did instinct.

He looked down at his scribblings. "Well?" Jan said from across the rim.

"That bastard. He didn't tell me shit."

"What'd you expect?" the woman replied. "You think he's gonna admit he framed somebody?"

Jan's right, he said to himself. Parker's holding all the cards, probably using this case for promotion to sergeant. Henderson anticipated the slugging match of a lifetime, a fine-print investigation that could take a month or more. He'd barely started to dig. The *Times* had its faults, but it was a money-maker and gave its reporters plenty of rope. He knew his professional reputation and it didn't bother him. He was slow but meticulous, a persistent pain in the ass, a bulldog. Except, he said to himself, I'm prettier.

The bulldog's next problem turned out to be the judge. Rookie or not, Charles V. Johnson wasn't afraid to take command, and he made it plain that he didn't intend to defer sentencing much longer.

Henderson decided that the fastest way to spring Titus was to find the actual rape car. Somewhere in the dusty files of the Department of Licensing, there was a 667 or a 776 or something close that had been issued to a blue compact with velveteen slipcovers and a passenger seat that was slow to recline. There might even be semen stains. He fantasized making one phone call to Olympia and scoring a hit. If reporting were only that simple!

He knew that his future was at stake. But what if his investigation proved Titus guilty? Would he write about *that*? Lately he'd noticed several sets of executive eyes peering his way, and he'd never felt more vulnerable. The turd plane was being refueled.

71

Mac Smith found himself another girlfriend, a pretty kid barely out of high school. He was confused by his feelings—he still loved Nan, still dropped in on her and the kids, but it felt good to be with Crystal, too. She loved him and showed it. And when they went out, men gawked. If he had a few bucks, he took her to places like the Raintree Tavern on the Sea-Tac Strip, his favorite stretch of road. Sometimes she let him sleep with her, but the sex didn't reach the intensity he'd once known with Nan. Maybe that would come with training. Or maybe Nan would let him back into her bed. He still had hopes. A mutual friend from his real estate days had recently quoted her as saying, "I really love Mac." But Nan had also said that she'd learned one thing from their years together: love wasn't enough.

Working on his new job selling home alarms, Mac often pondered his open house rapes. How exciting it had been to go after classy, clean, well-dressed chicks instead of a bunch of scuzzy delinquents and whores. At night he masturbated to the memory of the tall blond sales agent, the one that pissed him off by offering him forgiveness. Who was *she* to forgive *him*? He'd enjoyed his taste of upscale rape, but he realized that it was dangerous duty. The newspaper description had come a little too close. Luckily, in this era of full-bearded moustached young men, it also came close to a ton of other guys. Otherwise, he reminded himself, he might be back in jail.

Late on the morning of Thursday, April 16, 1981, two weeks before Steve Titus's rescheduled sentencing date, Mac drove his beautiful black Mustang through the tree-lined suburb of Lynnwood, north of Seattle. It was the first community he'd lived in after fleeing California five years before, and the memories flooded back. What a future he'd had! He pictured himself in his cream-colored suit, shooting his cuffs and ordering drinks for his staff. He should have known that his high-rolling real estate career wouldn't last. Nothing good ever lasted. As Ruby the witch had always said, You can't change the cards, only rearrange them a little. He thought, What have I ever done but fuck up? Twenty-eight years old and I haven't done squat.

He remembered the time Ruby warned him he was headed for prison, and the way his dad always treated him as though he weren't worth the effort. Well, he thought, I proved Dad right. I've lost my wife, my kids, my job, my house, my pride. The brief interlude of self-respect was over, and he was back in the role of Mac the nerd, the drunk: Mac the badass. Any day now the dealer would repossess the Mustang; he'd told about fourteen lies on the loan application. And every cop in the northwest was on the lookout for a man of his description.

His spirits picked up when he cruised past a big "for sale" sign on a split-level rambler and spotted a

cool-looking woman with short black curly hair staring outside. He circled the block and returned. She
was still framed in the picture window, looking kind
of expectant. Well, he thought, why disappoint the
lady?

He tucked into a bar for a glass of draft, his
usual mitigating precaution ("I was drunk, judge. I
didn't know what I was doing"), then returned to
the sale house and backed into the driveway. He
signed her guestbook "Mike Drake" and added a
fake phone number. The woman seemed pleased to
encounter a potential buyer; how well he knew the
feeling. She said she intended to move out of state
as soon as she sold her house. He followed her
through the rooms and told her he had twenty
grand available for the down payment. "Oh, that's
plenty," she said enthusiastically.

As she measured a closet on her hands and
knees, he thought, How can you beat this setup? She
won't be around to make a fuss; she probably won't
even file a report. If she does, the police won't work
hard for an out-of-state victim. Most of these local
cops didn't know dick anyway. He'd made a career
out of suburban rape and considered himself an expert. It was no longer true that Mac Smith didn't do
anything right.

He slid the buck knife from its sheath.

72

Lynnwood plainclothesman Brian Burkhalter, twenty-seven, a former linebacker with an altar boy's cherubic face, was finding himself increasingly grossed out by sex criminals. For six years, ever since finishing his law enforcement course, he'd dealt with flashers, porn peddlers, sadists, child molesters, rapists, and other freaks. In college he'd studied psychology; he knew the poor dears couldn't help themselves, they'd been mistreated by their mommies and dadas, *there but for the grace of God* and all the other bleeding-heart bullshit. But that didn't keep these dirtballs from polluting his dreams and interfering with his private life. When he interviewed a typical child molester it was a struggle to keep from breaking the guy's jaw.

For some reason there'd been an explosion of sex crimes in the Northwest since he'd joined the Lynnwood force in 1975. It made him cringe to sit across from some potato-faced asshole and hear comments like "I know I shouldn't of touched the kid down there, but God, you should have seen her with her pants down! And she enjoyed it, she begged for it!" He tried not to carry such conversations home, but it was hard, especially since he worked sex crimes exclusively.

His latest case was a perfect example. He looked at the preliminary report on his desk:

When she had her back turned she was grabbed from behind with the suspect holding a knife across her throat. The suspect then told her to get on the floor while he kept the knife to her throat. She kept pleading with him then and throughout the incident to put the knife away. He kept telling her how sharp it was and how if she struggled or didn't do what he told her, she would be hurt.

The victim then went down on her knees with the suspect still keeping the knife at the victim's neck. He made her unbutton her blouse and then he pulled it partially down, pinioning her arms. He then unzipped his pants and pulled out his penis. He then held the knife to the side of her neck and told her to . . .

He skipped ahead to the part where it said the rapist "was partially flaccid" and "told her to give him a 'hand job' to get him hard again." How many times had he read something similar in a rape report? People thought rapists were hot young studs, but most of them were underendowed little simps who couldn't get it up. That was one of the reasons they raped.

The investigator shrugged his wide shoulders and walked outside to his car. He visited the victim's house with the intention of conducting a reinterview, but she wasn't ready for him. Two days had passed since the attack, and she was still in a mild state of shock. He showed her a composite of a suspect drawn up by earlier victims and she shrank back as though she expected the guy to jump from the page. He decided to return when she'd calmed down.

The phone number left by the rapist turned out to be bad. Two Michael Drakes were listed, but their ages and descriptions were off. Burkhalter had expected the information to be false, but everything had to be checked. Rapists had been known to sign their real names and addresses on motel registers. In this era of scrambled brains and attitudes, you never knew. He sent out a Teletype to Washington police agencies describing the perpetrator and the offense.

Within a week he learned that the guy was no cherry. He'd raped at two open houses in Everett, once using the Drake name, and he was suspected in a string of others. But who the hell and *where* the hell was he?

Burkhalter made photocopies of a composite sketch drawn up by King County police and spent his day off distributing them. He was feeling good about the possibilities—this asshole had left tracks—when his phone rang.

"We're in Michigan," the victim's husband announced. "We won't be coming back."

"Not even for a trial?"

"She's in therapy. She couldn't handle it."

Burkhalter pleaded, but he could tell he was on another bummer. He went to the evidence room

73

Paul Henderson's plan to track the rapist's car soon
bogged down in the same numerical swamp that
had stopped Steve Titus. In two weeks of hard work
the reporter established only two facts that weren't
totally useless: every temporary tag issued to car
dealers by the Department of Licensing for the
thirty days starting September 15 had begun with
"66," and one whole batch had been sent to dealers
on the eastern side of the Cascades. Personal calls to
fifteen dealers failed to turn up a match for the rape
car, nor did a canvass of the registration cards of
Sea-Tac Strip motels.

Henderson talked the *Times* into putting up two
hundred dollars to test Kurt Schaefer on the lie box.
The young alibi witness passed without a twitch, con-
firming vital entries in the defense's time line. But
the prosecutor's office shrugged the test off. Hadn't
the rapist taken one and failed? Whose test was
more significant?

Henderson was baffled and frustrated. As sentencing time approached, Titus was pushing his theory that the rape was a teenage girl's fiction or a
careful hoax. In his myopic eyes, everyone from his
ex-wife to the judge was after his ass. He argued so
compellingly that there were times when the re-

porter almost fell into his mythology. Working with
Titus was like baby-sitting a terminal cancer victim.
Henderson tried to jack him up, crack a joke, but
nothing worked. The poor guy's human warmth
had been squeezed out.

"Before this happened to me," Titus confided
one day, "I was a free spirit, a cheerful guy, kinda
reckless in my ways." It was another of his old-fashioned expressions: *kinda reckless in my ways*. Mona
confirmed that he'd never wanted to do anything
but have a good time and stay a buck or two ahead
of his bills. Henderson found it hard to envision a
happy-go-lucky Steve Titus. The guy was a walking
temblor, in constant motion, every cell quivering,
leaping from theory to theory, excitedly phoning to
recite his latest brainstorm. He never seemed to
sleep.

Henderson pored over the trial transcript and ex-
hibits, trying to find something that would save
Steve and produce a good story for the *Times*. All
day he studied the data at the office, stopping now
and then to buttonhole a fellow reporter: "Look at
this montage! Is this suggestive or what? Which
would *you* pick?" When his colleagues grew irritated, he fled to his favorite bar on Lake Union and
read and compared and checked and cross-checked
and rechecked till his eyes burned. It was a pleasant
place, quiet, uncrowded in the early afternoons, and
the cold beers kept coming. He would arrive home
all fired up and bend Janet's ear till 2:00 A.M. "Just
read this report! Look! *Did you ever see such
crap* . . . ?"

It didn't take long to discern the outlines of a

conspiracy, though nothing as broad or as calculated as Titus imagined. From the first night, Ronald Parker had run the show like an animal-act impresario. When he reworked a report or altered a log to improve the case, certain of his colleagues seemed to fall into line. If he "forgot" a piece of exculpatory information, some of his sidekicks seemed to suffer the same pinpoint amnesia.

Crucial data appeared and disappeared according to one criterion: did it make Titus look guilty or not? For example: Celia had told police she'd spotted a brown legal-size folder on the backseat of the rapist's car. So, it now turned out, had Ron Parker, in the back of the Titus car. Funny thing, though; the patrol cops who'd originally photographed and inventoried the contents of the Chevette, logging items as inconsequential as the number of cigarette butts in the ashtray, had made no mention of the folder. Unfortunately, the original inventory had been mislaid or never made, depending on which Port cops were telling the story, nor could they put their hands on the photographs. But there was no equivocation about the tire track pictures. Every print and negative had been logged by number, sent to the prosecutor's office—and lost.

When Henderson pressed for explanations from Parker and his assistants, he was informed that Chief Moloney had ordered every scrap of evidence reassessed and every available witness brought back for questioning. Until the results of the in-house investigation were in, the Port cops would be unavailable.

74

On hands and knees, Henderson studied the rape scene for missed clues: a cigarette butt, a used Kleenex, a tire track the cops had missed. My God, he thought as he slapped at a spider hanging from the lip of his white golfing cap, this place is a rapist's Shangri-la! He found nothing new except a previously unnoticed basketball backboard shrouded by blackberry tangles on the side of a driveway. Was this where the rape had occurred? From the original police reports, he couldn't be sure. He drove back to the office as confused as ever.

Then the turd plane made a bomb run at his balding head. In quick succession, the King County Prosecuting Attorney's office and the Port of Seattle P.D. announced that their exhaustive investigations had cleared everyone involved—except, of course, the rapist Titus. Henderson was surprised, then angry. You stupid son of a bitch, he said to himself. You thought those guys would do a competent job. Shake hands with the tooth fairy.

He demanded a session with the Port police brass. Lumbering down the I–5 freeway in the army staff car, he squeezed the steering wheel till his knuckles blanched. In one month he'd gone from bemused to frustrated to thoroughly pissed off. He hated to be diddled; it made him turn red and hyperventilate. He figured his sensitivity was a throwback to his early childhood, when he'd been ignored and left to fend for himself. Whatever the reason, he preferred lies and evasions to being ignored. Lies and evasions could be checked out.

He was sorry to see that the airport conference room was devoid of key players. Evidently the *Times*'s chickenshit investigation wasn't important enough to merit Chief Moloney's personal attention. Detective Corporal Ronald Parker wasn't there, nor were any of his hands-on assistants. That left a lieutenant, Tim Kimsey, who'd already made it plain that he considered Titus guilty as hell, and the former Seattle P.D. hotshot, Sergeant Dave Hart, who'd led the reinvestigation, plus several uniforms who had no apparent connection with the case. Henderson thought, Every one of these guys looks like somebody just farted. I'd rather face the KGB.

He made his points methodically, starting with the convenient last-minute shifts in the prosecution testimony. The room was silent except for his sharp voice. No one smiled or nodded or offered concessions. God damn, he said to himself, these fuckers are ruthless. Just that morning Mona had told him that she wouldn't be surprised if Steve killed himself. He wondered if any of these cops would give a shit.

"Look at this," he said, waving one of Parker's original reports. "Titus makes a routine lane change and it's held against him. He tells Parker where he's spent the afternoon and night, minute by goddamn minute, and nobody checks it out. Your men haven't interviewed one alibi witness! Christ, that's elementary procedure. Explorer Scouts would do a better job. Why—''

"Henderson, you're outa line," one of the uniforms snapped. "Are you accusing us of a dishonest investigation?"

Before he could answer, someone else said, "An officer has a right to report his observations, doesn't he?"

Henderson saw that the wagons were circled, but he couldn't shut up. "Why did Parker drive Shirlee Watson and Celia Dalton to the trial?" he asked, stabbing a finger at the lieutenant.

Kimsey said he'd interviewed all three parties, and they'd agreed that the subject of the case had been meticulously avoided.

"Oh, I believe them," Henderson said sarcastically. "What'd they talk about, Lieutenant? Their fucking stock holdings?"

"Detectives always review testimony with witnesses," Hart interjected. "There's nothing wrong with that."

"Is that how their stories got straightened out at the last minute?" Henderson shot back. "Is that how they knew to roll back their times?"

"They *corrected* their times," Hart insisted. "I interviewed the Red Lion waitress myself."

Henderson decided that he was being bamboozled. He grabbed his papers and walked out.

Back at the office he warned himself to deal with the facts as they existed and quit worrying about irrelevancies like fairness and honesty and simple human decency. No amount of logic or common sense was going to change the minds of beleaguered police officials or a crooked detective like Parker or a victorious prosecutor. It was against human nature to expect bureaucrats to admit they'd fucked up, especially when they had twelve honest citizens to hide behind. "Don't blame us. He was convicted by a jury. . . ." It would take *hard* evidence to turn things around. And he didn't have a shred.

Five weeks had passed since the first call from Titus, and sentencing was a few days away. Henderson wasn't sure he could prove Titus innocent or even produce a readable story. Overconfidence had never been one of his problems. But the time had come to write.

75

He'd hardly taken his place in front of the VDT before he learned that the editorial luminaries of the newspaper had ticketed his piece for the section known as *Scene*. The news sections were tight, an editor explained, but *Scene* had room for a maximum effort, including graphics. The idea seemed absurd. *Scene?* That was for stories on fashion and visiting movie stars and ruminations on cellulite.

As usual, he typed with sweaty fingers, leaning forward and rocking in his chair. He had to sum up five weeks of research in three days, and he couldn't think of a lead. When at last he'd squeezed out two columns of copy, he hit the wrong combination of keys and erased every line from his screen. It took four hours in the computer room to reassemble the lost paragraphs.

On his second day of writing, he became aware of a baneful presence monitoring his efforts on the screen of an adjoining VDT. He knew who the guy was but preferred to ignore him. Dick Cheverton was newly hired from the *Philadelphia Daily News* to edit *Scene;* he was five or six years younger, stiff and straight, with the apparent charm of a tax auditor. His fellow editors referred to him as "Chev," but newsroom grunts took note of his expression and his beard and dubbed him "the Ayatollah." Henderson had him pegged as an asshole.

On the third day of writing, Henderson was still hunched over the keyboard when *Scene*'s copy deadline arrived at 4:00 P.M. The Ayatollah didn't comment.

At 5:00 P.M. Henderson still hadn't finished. Out of the corner of his eye he saw Cheverton sitting patiently. When was the guy gonna say something? His whole damned section was being held open for the Titus piece. Henderson couldn't help muttering, "Hey, man, I'm sorry."

"No sweat," the new editor said. "I've been reading your takes."

By 7:00 P.M. Henderson was still polishing. "I'm sorry," he repeated.

"Good things are worth waiting for," the Ayatollah said.

The finished copy went to the printer four hours late. Henderson cautiously suggested a nightcap at the 2–3–4. By the time their second round of beers arrived, he was calling the Ayatollah "Chev."

76

Even the insecure Henderson was satisfied with the product that hit the newsstands on the morning of Friday, May 15, 1981, three days before Steve Titus was due to be sentenced. The *Times* had allotted more space than Henderson could remember for a single story. Under a top headline, "ONE MAN'S BAT- TLE TO CLEAR HIS NAME," the piece covered the front page of *Scene* and jumped inside to another column and a half. Cheverton's layout was professional as hell. Right under the masthead, a sad-looking Steve Titus walked out of the airport woods into the reader's face. The caption noted "70 discrepancies in the state's case." The photo montage was tucked into the lower right corner, where readers could see how prejudicial it was. In the lower left, a fierce vis- age stared out over the message: "Kurt Schaefer swears he was with Titus at the time of the rape, but the jury didn't believe him. Later Schaefer passed a lie detector test."

No detail had been omitted or cut. The story opened with the contradictory descriptions of Titus, the assailant, and the rape car, and closed with a poignant quote from defense attorney Tom Hillier: "I lie awake at night dwelling on this case. The rest of us can walk away from it. But Steve Titus can't."

▪

Late that afternoon Henderson walked down the aisle of a rush hour bus and saw two newspapers opened to his story. In a restaurant, he leaned over a man who was reading the article and asked, "Whattaya think of that?" Friends, acquaintances, and strangers phoned all weekend and encouraged him to keep slugging. It seemed that half of Seattle had read the story.

On Monday, May 18, three days after the article appeared, Judge Charles V. Johnson granted a final continuance until June 1, two weeks away. He made it plain that he was not entirely pleased. "You have had more than the normal time to prepare for sentencing," he lectured Tom Hillier. "I think we should conclude this matter as soon as we can."

The defense prepared motions aimed at setting aside the verdict or reducing the charge, but such last-ditch efforts seldom prevailed. The Special Assault Unit and Chris Washington resisted every move; it was obvious that they believed in their case and weren't going to be affected by a newspaper story, no matter how lengthy or eloquent or well researched.

Henderson and his new friend Chev realized that their job wasn't finished.

77

This time they intended to attack the prosecution's time line, making the point that it had been deliberately altered. The two journalists mushed back to Paul Liston's sagging house and collected a crucial page from the old man's diary. "I appreciate your help, Mr. Liston," Henderson said as he was leaving. "If we don't get Titus off, he's going to prison."

The retired carpenter blinked back the pain from his cancerous stomach. "I'm going in the hospital Tuesday," he said, offering a weak handshake. "I like his chances better'n mine."

Henderson had always been touched by the ordeals of old men, maybe because of his love for his Gramps back in Nebraska. He hoped there would be a light in the house when he returned.

He retraced the escape route taken by Celia Dalton the night of the rape. The young victim had insisted that it took her thirty minutes to walk from the crime scene to Liston's house. In the black of night, with Cheverton timing him, Henderson made the walk in three minutes. He repeated the trip, this time making every possible wrong turn. Elapsed time: eight minutes. "Just to make it fair," he told Janet later, "I stopped to take a leak." The state's major witness against Steve Titus had been confused, mistaken—or lying.

Once again *Scene* blared a Steve Titus story, this time under the headline, "GUILT IN RAPE CASE MAY HANG ON THE TICK, TICK, TICK OF CLOCK." Once again the town talked about the case and sent letters of praise to the editor. A defense fund was set up with a box number. But a friendly lawyer commented, "Paul, it's a good reporting job, but I doubt if the judge'll consider it new evidence." As the prosecutors kept insisting, the law didn't permit the judge to order a new trial unless evidence was presented that "could not have been discovered through reasonable efforts prior to trial." If Henderson and Cheverton could make time-checks with a stopwatch, the reasoning went, so could Hillier and Titus. And they should have done so before *State* v. *Titus* was heard.

Judge Johnson stretched the sentencing date one more week. If nothing new or significant turned up, Steve Titus would be on his way to prison on Monday morning, June 8. The minimum term was ten years and four months.

78

Henderson's legs dangled from the stone fence overlooking a scene of hot competition among his friends and colleagues. It was 3:00 A.M. in north Seattle, raining hard, and his heart wasn't in the killer croquet game or his can of beer. He asked himself, What kind of self-indulgent dick am I, boozing it up while Steve has a week of freedom left?

But he just didn't know what to write; he'd run out of information and ideas. Or was it just that he hadn't been trying hard enough? It was his turn to play and he was in perfect position to drive his colleague John Saul's red ball into Snohomish County. He handed the mallet to Cheverton. "Gotta go home," he mumbled. He poured his beer in a potted plant and left for Queen Anne Hill.

Weak sunlight poked under the living room blinds when he finally trudged upstairs to the bedroom. He'd gone through every official document in his files; he'd reread key testimony; he'd reviewed notes scribbled on legal-size yellow pads, spiral notebooks, damp napkins, ripped-out phonebook pages, matchbook covers . . . and come up empty. The last item he'd reviewed was the presentence report, with its harsh conclusion that Steve had exhibited "violent

behavior" and "cannot be considered safe to remain in the community." In an obvious effort to
influence the publicity, the prosecutor's office had
leaked the confidential document to the *Times*. It
seemed a conniving thing to do—but only one of
many.

As he quietly prepared for bed, his anger turned
toward the faceless scumbag who'd started the
whole mess by raping Celia Dalton. The Titus story
had been picked up by every local radio and TV
news show, and unless the rapist was deaf, dumb,
and blind, he knew that an innocent man was taking
his fall. Henderson wasn't surprised. The guy had to
be a sociopath, and they were the coldest sons of
bitches on earth. *Who, me? I'm not guilty. He did it!
THAT GUY OVER THERE!* They were always happy
to shift the blame. Wolf eels lived by a higher code
of morality.

He lay back and listened to Janet's soft breathing. She'd been covering a half-dozen felony trials
and still found time to commiserate with him, run
the house, balance his checkbook, and pay the parking tickets that accumulated on the floor of the
army staff car. He was tempted to wake her up and
ask her advice. She was a journalistic natural,
headed straight for an editor's job. He wondered
how he would react the first time she vectored the
turd plane in his direction.

Somewhere in the brief span between wakefulness
and sleep, he flashed on an idea so simple that he
wondered why he hadn't thought of it earlier. He
sat straight up in bed.

Shangri-la! He remembered saying to himself

that the airport woods looked like a rapist's Shangri-la. If so, wouldn't there be other victims? What would *they* recall about their rapes and their rapist? For one thing, they'd sure as hell recall that he wasn't Steve Titus!

He nudged Janet awake and outlined his idea. He would contact local police jurisdictions and ask them to review anything resembling a sexual abduction and compare it to the October 12 Dalton rape —the suspect's description, his car, M.O., weapon, his patter, the dates, places, times, and anything else that came to mind. Like so many criminals, rapists seldom quit till they were caught. If the asshole wasn't in jail, it was a good bet he was still doing his thing.

He wrestled with the bed sheets for an hour and then grabbed for the phone. For years he'd made daily checkup calls to police agencies from the Canadian border to Oregon; they were called "cops checks" and served as his standard start-up procedure when he worked the police beat. He dialed old contacts in Kent, Des Moines, Renton, Normandy Park, asking them to peruse their files. It was his day off, but he'd stopped logging his overtime weeks ago.

He slurped a cup of cold coffee, pulled on his clothes, and aimed the army staff car at King County police headquarters. If any agency would have a handle on look-alike rapes, it would be the new Sex Crimes Unit that had jurisdiction over every unincorporated area in the county. He hardly knew the unit's commanding officer, so he went directly to his office.

Sergeant Harlan Bollinger, a taciturn detective with a thick shock of brown hair, didn't send out convivial vibes. Henderson knew how a reporter was viewed in this stuffy little office: as an intruder, an outsider, one of *them*—maybe even a threat. The Port police would be given the benefit of every doubt by this elongated brother in arms. Cops didn't like to pick up their colleagues by the nuts.

It was plain enough that Bollinger had other things on his mind. Golf, maybe. He didn't seem to pay much attention, then stood up and said abruptly, "Okay, I'll look into it." Henderson was almost sorry he'd come.

79

When attorney Jeffrey Jones met Henderson for the
first time at the 2–3–4, the reporter looked him up
and down and said, "You're twenty-nine, a U.W.
graduate. You got a law degree from Seattle U.
You're a hell of a soccer player. And you used to
hang out at Vito's."

Steve Titus's newly hired lawyer was momen-
tarily piqued that this superannuated police reporter had gone to the trouble of checking him out.
Later that day Tom Hillier told him not to take offense; Henderson was a Roman candle of a guy who
wore everybody's heart on his sleeve, but he was also
a case-hardened investigator who wouldn't have
dealings with Mother Teresa without a preliminary
check.

To the incoming Jones, the outgoing Hillier appeared devastated by the case. And after Jones had
reviewed the paper work, he could see why. Hillier,
an honorable man who expected honesty in others,
had been bushwhacked by dubious new evidence,
late shifts in testimony, and a prejudicial in-court
identification. It seemed to Jones that Titus
wouldn't have been charged if the Port police or the
prosecutor's office had employed the most elemen-

tal screening procedures. But the verdict stood, and that was the reality the young lawyer had to face as Titus's new counsel.

He ran into his friend Christopher Washington at a meeting and asked him what the hell was going on. Why were the prosecutor's assault troops so intent on sending an innocent man to prison?

"He's not an innocent man, Jeff," the deputy prosecutor insisted. "There's just too many coincidences, plus the eyewitness ID, plus the lie detector, plus . . ."

By the time Washington was halfway through his bill of particulars, it was clear he sincerely believed in the verdict. "Jeff," he went on, "I'll be the first to admit it's a strange case. Titus comes the closest to being a normal, everyday person of any criminal I've prosecuted. That makes it tough. But he *is* guilty."

Jones was unmoved. There were plenty of indications that Washington was just plain wrong. If Titus were guilty, for example, why hadn't he jumped at the chance to enter the state's Sexual Psychopathy Program—two or three years in a hospital instead of ten or twenty in a prison? By insisting on his innocence he'd rendered himself ineligible for the program. Sex therapists couldn't treat a man who wouldn't admit he needed help.

Jones was convinced that his client had been railroaded, but he couldn't decide who was the engineer. Certainly not Chris Washington. No one in the prosecutor's office was capable of an act so inimical to the canons of the legal profession, let alone ordinary human decency. But they sure as hell were capable of being overzealous and muleheaded. Chatting with Washington, he realized that Mary Kay Barbieri's Special Assault Unit was dug in.

For a while the new defense lawyer fought a delaying action, filing motions, seeking postponements, hoping against hope that Henderson or someone else would turn up more exculpatory information. Everything had to be done fast. Briefs that should have taken weeks were churned out in hours.

Titus and his relatives were still too bitter to be much help; they continued to waste time railing against the legal system. "Look," Jones told the family after a frustrating strategy session, "I don't blame you for being upset, but you're paying me a hundred and ten dollars an hour to talk about the law, not the system. We won't get a new trial without new evidence. And we just—don't—*have it*!"

Another continuance was out of the question. "If I put this over for one more week," a frowning Judge Johnson had asked at their last discussion in his chambers, "are we gonna get another article in the paper?"

"No, sir, Your Honor," Jones said. "I guarantee there won't be any article. I *promise*!"

The tall judge waved his hands in front of his face and said, "Nope, *nope*! Don't say that! I don't want to be reading that I tried to muzzle the press."

"Oh, no," Jones replied agreeably. "That won't happen, Judge."

"I hate to see my cases tried in the newspapers. Is that gonna happen, counselor?"

"You have my word, Judge," Jones repeated.

A glum-sounding Henderson phoned the lawyer and confirmed that the *Times* planned no further coverage. Steve Titus was soon to become a number.

80

Early on a Wednesday afternoon, five days before the final sentencing date, Henderson's office phone rang and a gruff voice said, "I found something you might be interested in."

"Who's this?" the reporter asked.

"Bollinger."

"Hold everything, Sarge. I'll be right down."

The desk was littered with files. "Rape cases," Bollinger explained, beckoning Henderson to a wooden chair. It looked as though he'd done a case-by-case review of every sex offense since Loeb and Leopold. "Take a look at this," he said, handing over a sheet of paper.

Henderson tilted back and started to read. It was an offense report dated October 6, 1980, six days before the Dalton rape. The victim, Julie Whitehurst, described the crime scene as an abandoned driveway in the airport woods, off Twenty-second Avenue South. The fifteen-year-old hitchhiker said she'd been raped by a man of twenty-five to thirty, well dressed, with a reddish brown moustache and beard. He drove a light blue compact car. On his way to the scene, he told the girl, "I have to stop and see my sister Liz." He warned that he had a knife. He said, "I won't hurt you as long as you do what I say."

Henderson looked up from the report and said, "Jesus Christ, sergeant, you've just saved an innocent man from prison."

"Hold on," Bollinger warned. "Your boy's not off the hook yet." He explained that one of his detectives was speeding south to the Whitehurst home in Tacoma with a freshly prepared montage that included a photo of Steve Titus. If Julie failed to make him, he was home free. But if she picked him out, he could be facing another charge of rape.

On a hallway pay phone, Henderson called Titus. "We got a break," he said. "Get up to my office fast!"

When Titus arrived at the *Times*, Henderson was already roughing out a lead on his VDT. The two men talked in a side room. "What were you doing on Monday, October sixth?" Henderson asked.

"October . . . sixth?" Titus touched his brow and frowned. "Gee, I don't know. Working, I guess."

"Can you prove it?"

"Maybe by my time sheets."

After the long enervating battle, the poor guy seemed resigned to defeat. He wanted to talk about a New Jersey priest who'd been falsely convicted and served twelve years. Then he discussed his troubles with his fiancée. Henderson had already heard from Mona on the subject. It seemed that Steve had turned quirky and was asking her questions like "Why are you hanging around me? Why don't you just leave?" He was trying to avoid rejection, trying to push her away before she left on her own. Mona understood and refused to go. Henderson had advised her to hang in. She was good at that.

He drove south to Tukwila to check out Titus's expense reports himself. He was happy to see that the folks at Yegen's remained cooperative. Their position seemed to be that they believed in Steve's innocence, but they were afraid that his personality had deteriorated to the point where he couldn't perform in a management role. He'd already received his pink slip and six months' severance pay.

It took a supervisor five minutes to produce the Titus expense report for the new rape date, October 6. It showed that he'd logged ninety-one miles in a company-owned 1979 Pontiac LeMans station wagon, driving from his Kent apartment to a pair of restaurant supply houses in Seattle, from downtown Seattle to an Ivar's Seafood Bar east of Kent, southward to the company's store in the town of Federal Way, and finally back home. Every minute of the rape time was accounted for by signed logs and receipts.

The Yegen executive also volunteered a document showing that Titus's new Chevette had been delivered four days after the earlier incident. If he couldn't have committed the first rape, could any rational person believe he'd committed the second? Of course not, Henderson told himself. But would the hard-ass prosecutor's office see it the same way?

Back at his desk, he took another call from Bollinger. "The October sixth victim?" the sergeant said.

"Julie Whitehurst? She didn't give the Titus picture a second glance."

Henderson typed out a lead, zapped it, and tried again. And again. And again. It was like the old days on the *Omaha World-Herald* when he'd filled wastebaskets with take after take before getting it right. He needed to create just the right tone: not superior, not final or triumphant, but surefooted, clear, and persuasive. He finished the main piece and two long sidebars at midnight. As usual, Dick Cheverton sat quietly by, offering help when it was requested.

Galley proofs were pulled, and the night staffers walked around patting themselves on the back. The head blared "TITUS CASE" in 48-point type, and the subhead read: "Another Sea-Tac assault: Did Titus take the rap for a well-dressed rapist who struck twice?"

The stories left no doubt of the answer.

Henderson was sipping a beer at the 2–3–4 when he remembered to call Steve's new lawyer. "Jeff," he said, "you can relax. We found a look-alike rape."

Jones sounded drugged. "What the hell time is it?" he asked.

"Quarter to one," Henderson replied.

"Regular office hours, huh? Can't this wait till morning? I haven't slept in three days."

"You'll sleep better when you hear this, pal."

"Paul," Jones asked, "did you write another story?"

"That's my job, man."

81

Chris Washington, still supported by his boss Mary Kay Barbieri, insisted that the *Times* articles weren't evidence. In court papers, he tagged Jeff Jones's latest motions "a red herring defense." The new information should have been introduced at trial, he claimed, and was now inadmissible. He suggested that Judge Johnson pay no heed to "a discrepancy in times discovered by a newspaper reporter . . ."

Then Washington took a roundhouse swing at the media, the *Times,* and Paul Henderson. "In addressing this issue," the deputy prosecutor wrote, "it must be noted that the pressures created by the media, primarily the press, has been extraordinary. The public sentiment expressed in letters of personal opinions has undoubtedly been affected by the publicity the facts of the case have received. That sentiment, however, must be seen as the engineered result of newspaper articles written with the expressed purpose of gaining a new trial for the defendant. This advocacy by the press should not be confused with the facts . . ."

Henderson read the angry words and threw up his hands. Apparently the prosecution wasn't going to quit till it was hit by a truck. He wondered where to find one.

82

Late on the Friday afternoon before the Monday sentencing, the reporter was rereading his third and final piece in *Scene* when his office phone rang. It was a suburban policeman who wanted to pass along a story he'd heard: Titus was dirty, the cop said, maybe not in the Dalton case but in others. A Kent officer had checked out a Chevrolet involved in a gas driveaway, and in the course of his investigation, a teenage girl identified Titus from his driver's license picture. But the case never went to the prosecutor because the victim refused to testify.

"What color Chevrolet?" Henderson asked. "What model?" Under his breath, he said, *Please, God, don't let it be a blue Chevette.*

"I'm not sure," the cop said. "Green, blue, whatever. It mighta been a Nova."

Henderson's heart raced. He was so flustered that he forgot to jot down his informant's name.

He dialed the Kent dispatcher, asked for the detective division, and was told by an answering machine that the office hours were 9:00 to 5:00 Monday through Friday. He looked at his watch. It was 5:05. He had two-and-a-half days to wait before he could check the information out.

He dragged into Cheverton's office and broke

the news. "Oh, shit," the editor said, taking a deep breath. "I think I need a drink."

"This thing sounds fishy to me," Henderson said at the 2–3–4. "But if it's true, I'm gonna be writing obits for the next twenty years. My ass is gonna be grass."

"*Our* ass is gonna be grass," said Cheverton, a weary look on his face. "Look," he added, "you proved Titus is innocent. Goddamn it, the man did *not* rape Celia Dalton."

"What's the difference, Chev? A rapist is a rapist. Do you think the public gives a shit who he raped?"

The weekend passed a tick at a time. Henderson's moods were up and down. It seemed as though he'd spent most of the last two months playing the optimist for Steve and Mona and the lawyers and everybody else. Now he wondered, Has this guy been playacting all along? Am I the patsy here?

He couldn't stop imagining the worst. *If Titus is a rapist, I libeled a whole bunch of people. The Port and the prosecutor will crucify the* Times. *And I'll be the patsy. I'll be working nights till I'm ninety-two.* . . .

Janet tried to cheer him up, and Cheverton arrived on Sunday morning to join in the wake. After two days of worry, the bearded editor looked uncharacteristically downcast. "What irony," he said. "We should be celebrating this weekend, Paul."

In a few short weeks the two journalists had become as tight as old friends. Henderson thought, I'll never forgive myself if I drag Chev down.

∎

Late Sunday night he located an old contact on the Kent P.D. "Yeah," the veteran cop said, "I remember that case. Bill Ross worked it. Relax! Titus wasn't the rapist. It was an asshole named Smith."

When Henderson called Cheverton at home, a loud sigh of relief came over the phone. Then the editor said, "Who was nervous?"

83

Jeff Jones stepped uneasily into the courtroom and sat next to his client. The judge had set the hearing for 8:00 A.M. to allow plenty of time for presentencing argument. Unlike some jurists, Charles V. Johnson didn't telegraph his rulings in advance, and no one knew which way he leaned. Attorney Jones had already briefed Titus on how to act if he were led away in handcuffs again.

The courtroom was packed, a queue of would-be spectators stretching far down the hall. Jones nodded to Henderson, tightly squeezed into the second row. The reporter looked as though he'd spent the weekend being tumbled at a Laundromat. Next to him sat his girlfriend Janet, covering for the *Times* and looking nervous herself. Jones also recognized a star reporter from the rival *Post-Intelligencer*. Up to now, the venerable *P–I* had barely mentioned the case, but Henderson and the broadcast media had made it too big to ignore. Mary Kay Barbieri slipped in, her short arms balancing a stack of files.

Jones had needed every bit of his soccer player's stamina to prepare his arguments through the night, and when he stood up to speak, his throat felt as though he'd swallowed cotton. He was grateful that the verbal arguments were mostly a formality, a touch of courtroom theater. There was nothing new to say—both sides had made their points in carefully worded briefs filed over the weekend, and everyone knew that the judge had studied them and probably reached a conclusion. Still, Jones was surprised at the intensity of Chris Washington's presentation. The deputy prosecutor came on like a crusader whose mission was to protect American womanhood from a dangerous criminal. Washington was respected for his verbal arguments, and this morning he was at his best.

For once, Henderson took no notes. He held hands with Janet on one side and his grown daughter Leslee on the other. He was sure he'd proved Titus's innocence to the satisfaction of everyone who read his stories, but his readers weren't sitting up there in black robes. All that mattered now was how Judge Johnson interpreted the law with its whereases and wherefores, its stupidities and contradictions. The truest words ever spoken were "Justice is blind." Stupid, too, Henderson muttered to himself. Titus looked like a man attending his own hanging. In an hour or so, Henderson thought, he'll be heading home at the wheel of his car, or on his way to jail.

As the arguments continued and the judge interjected a question or two, Cheverton flashed thumbs up or thumbs down from further down the row. Henderson thought, Chev can't read this judge and neither can I. He just doesn't inkle.

By the time the last argument had been made, his friend's thumb had been well exercised.

■

After a short recess, the former Arkansan returned to the bench, straightened his robes, peered through his glasses, and began refuting the defense contentions as though he were swatting weevils. It was simply not true, he observed, that the state had failed to prove the aggravatingelements of first-degree rape. As Henderson flinched and Titus shrank in his seat, the judge also disagreed that the jurors had committed egregious error. To the contrary, they'd been "serious, alert, and attentive," and there was "absolutely nothing wrong in the decision of the jury." Henderson heard the turd plane approaching from twelve o'clock high.

Then the judge turned to the final defense motion, "a more complicated matter," as he described it. Speaking in slow, measured cadence, he framed the issue: "whether there is newly discovered evidence and surprise testimony that would cause the court to grant a new trial."

He took note of the fact that "the defendant is extremely serious about the motion for a new trial," in marked contrast to petitioners who went through the motions merely to protect their record on appeal. The crowded courtroom fell silent as Johnson remarked that judges are reluctant to overturn verdicts "because juries perform a very vital role in the American system of justice. Since it is the jury's duty to decide the facts, the court is very slow to exercise its discretion to disturb a jury's verdict. . . ." Cheverton's thumb went up.

The judge observed that the information about the October 6 look-alike rape had been placed in the files of the King County P.D. long before Titus's trial and conviction, and therefore it had been available to the defense. Cheverton's thumb went down.

Then the judge began discussing the tire-track evidence, the surprise testimony, the last-minute time shifts by key witnesses and other issues. God damn, Henderson thought, he's Patrick Fucking Henry, blabbing past our first deadline. Why doesn't he just send Steve to jail and be done with it?

It seemed like hours before His Honor paused for a sip of water. Then he wiped his lips and stared at Titus through his glasses. The guilty verdict, he announced, was null and void. He was granting a new trial.

At first Titus didn't seem to comprehend. "We got it," Jeff Jones said in his ear. "We won!"

Titus slumped forward. Jones grabbed him across his narrow shoulders and squeezed. Jacqueline Titus's scream of relief pierced the air. Spectators gasped. Tears filled the eyes of Steve's dour father, David. Mona Imholt jumped up and down like a cheerleader, her light hair in disarray. "Aw right!" she yelled. *"Aw right! . . ."*

Jones helped his client to his feet to face the well-wishers who swept past the rail. It took Henderson several minutes to reach the man he'd saved. The two friends hugged hard, crying and pounding each other's back. Even the reporter from the *Post-Intelligencer* seemed pleased.

When order was restored, Chris Washington demanded that the judge reconsider his decision on the spot. Johnson declined, and before his firm refusal had echoed away, Mary Kay Barbieri gathered her folders and strode down the aisle, her heels thumping loudly as she made her exit.

Reporters who expected to interview an exuberant Titus in the hall were surprised. He spoke just above a whisper, his eyes still moist. "They've taken my dreams away from me, my life," he murmured. "I spent eight hellish months trying to solve this thing, and it took the *Seattle Times* newspaper to help me." He stepped back and rubbed his eyes like someone who'd walked from darkness into light.

Jeff Jones stood to one side, wondering if his client had heard about the fat lady and her song. There was going to be a retrial, and anything Steve said now could bite him in the ass later. The exhausted lawyer winced as he heard Titus suggest that there'd been a fix and add, "We should all be shocked that something like this could happen in America."

Jones thought, Didn't you just hear a judge grant you a retrial? That happened in America, too. The surest way to antagonize Chris Washington and Mary Kay Barbieri was to attack them in the media, exactly what Steve was doing at the moment.

A reporter asked Jones, "Do you have any comment about the job your predecessor did?"

"Mr. Hillier?" he responded. "He tried the case exactly the way I'd have tried it myself. He did a hell of a job."

"Then who screwed up?"

"Just say . . . the system." He grabbed Titus and hurried him away before he said too much himself.

∎

Henderson had little time for handshakes and congratulations. Janet had to write the breaking story, and the second morning deadline was approaching. They ran two blocks to the *Times*'s downtown bureau in the creaky old Dexter Horton Building and produced a joint effort that ran on page one under Janet's by-line and the head: "STEVE TITUS WINS NEW TRIAL ON RAPE CHARGE." The long piece included a prediction from Titus that he would be vindicated at a second trial and his promise that "I won't be the nice guy that I was last time in court."

That night, after the troops at the 2–3–4 had viewed the last local newscast with its extended coverage of the day's events, someone doused Henderson's receding hairline with champagne. He licked his lips and asked, "Did we run out of beer?"

He toasted Dick Cheverton with a pint of draft. The Ayatollah had turned out to be a newsman and a half, and a great guy to boot. They raised their glasses to Bollinger, Paul Liston, Mona, Kurt Schaefer, Hillier, Jones, the nightside printers, the newsboys, the judge, and the crew that cleaned the men's room.

84

On that same night, Crystal Parke and her parents poured her boneless boyfriend into a spare bed in their Kent Valley home. It was so unlike Mac to get drunk; he seemed devoted to Crystal, and he'd always made a good impression on the family. But after the family poker game was over and everyone watched the 11:00 P.M. news, he'd looked upset and knocked back one drink after another. They figured he was probably coming down with something.

PART FIVE

MANHUNT

■

1981

85

In the run-down offices and cubicles of the King County Police Department in downtown Seattle, where the name "McDonald J. Smith" had popped up fitfully from year to year like a ghost on a cheap TV, the head of the Sex Crimes Unit wasn't happy. If Steve Titus was clean—and Harlan Bollinger was an absolute believer—then some scuzzball was still out there raping. How many Tituses had gone to prison for this asshole's crimes? The guy *had* to be nailed. It didn't take the plainspoken sergeant long to communicate his feelings to the overworked men in his command.

Bollinger was surprised when Christopher Washington phoned and demanded new work-ups of the last two airport rapes—the one for which Titus had been convicted and the carbon copy six days earlier. The dogged young prosecutor made it plain that he didn't care whether the investigation circled back to Titus or turned up someone new, but he preferred to read the results in official police reports rather than *The Seattle Times*.

86

Two nights after every newspaper and broadcast station in the northwest had trumpeted Titus's victory, a seventeen-year-old girl stood outside Ernie's gas station near the Kent exit of State Highway 18. Liza Cimino was using her customary mode of transportation: her thumb. A black fastback pulled over and a nice-looking man with blondish hair and a light complexion beckoned her inside.

Liza was impressed. The car smelled new and had two side mirrors, a digital clock and a tape deck. She thought it might be a Mustang. The driver apologized for the sponginess of the ride and said he needed to put air in the tires.

"That's okay," she said pleasantly. "I don't mind waiting." It was already 2:00 A.M.; her parents wouldn't be any angrier if she arrived home an extra five minutes late.

The nice-looking man pulled into a gas station, fiddled with the tires, then took the well-traveled Kent-Kangley Road toward the center of town. At 116th he hung a sudden turn, drove under a big tree, and stopped. "Excuse me," he said. "I gotta take a leak."

How weird, she thought. But she figured a little craziness came with the free ride.

When he stepped back in, the man pressed a knife to her neck and forced her to commit oral sodomy. Then he made her undress and raped her. "Now get out and lay facedown on the ground," he ordered in an angry voice. "And don't look up or I'll come back and hurt you."

When he left, she staggered to the main road and called the police.

87

Patrolman Bill Ross was sipping coffee in Denny's when the county dispatcher advised all units to be on the lookout for a black Mustang fastback with two mirrors. He held the portable radio to his ear and jotted details on a napkin.

The filthy crime of rape had been on the young officer's mind ever since he'd almost nailed McDonald J. Smith a few months back. He could still feel the frustration of learning that one victim couldn't ID the guy and the other refused to bring charges. That left the guy free to do his thing right here in Kent, the same SOB who'd been raping for five or six years and previously served time in California.

When the dispatcher signed off, Ross studied the scribblings on his napkin: "Wht, 6 ft, full brd, well drsd, knife. Vict. 17, hitching . . ."

He remembered Mac Smith's preference for young hitchhikers and the fact that he'd flashed a knife on Joanie Kay Finley and an earlier victim. Smith dressed well. Smith had a beard and a moustache. Smith wasn't a six-footer, but rapists looked tall to their victims.

The young cop reminded himself not to rearrange the facts to suit his suspicions. That was the mistake the Port police had made. Besides, there were aspects of this latest rape that didn't fit the pattern. Smith had always operated in the isolated area south of the airport. Why would he drive all the way over to the east side of Kent to snatch a victim in an unincorporated residential area?

Ross decided this was probably a different rapist. Then he remembered reading in the *Times* that Steve Titus lived in the Comstock Apartments. My God, he thought, that's three blocks from the crime scene! Is this jerk dumping a rape in Titus's backyard? Is anybody that rotten?

The last time that Ross had dealt with Smith, the guy was driving a green Chevrolet Nova. But the green car had been abandoned on the street and returned to the rental agency.

The young cop wondered if he'd saved the montage from the driveaway gas theft. Months had gone by since the case had fizzled out. He drove to Kent Police headquarters and rooted around in a desk. The slightly faded faces in the photo laydown stared at him from the bottom of a drawer. He sped to Valley General Hospital on his siren.

The latest rape victim was dressed in jeans and sitting on the edge of a bed in the emergency treatment room. She was short and childlike and angry.

"Would you mind looking at some pictures?" Ross asked. "Take your time. Don't say anything till you've looked at 'em all."

He'd had experience showing montages. You watched the victim's eyes, and you hoped that just once in your life she would jump up and down and yell and scream and say, "That's him! Absolutely, positively, *that's him*!"

The girl stopped at one picture and frowned. Then her eyes lit up and her forefinger poked hard at the laydown. "That's the guy," she said. "That's him! *This is the guy!*"

The King County deputies huddled around as Ross peered over her shoulder at the picture. It was Mac Smith.

Ross thought, Oh, damn, if I'm in uniform for fifty years, I'll never forget this. I'll beat-feet to Smith's last known address and bust him. If he's good for this rape, he's probably good for more, including Titus.

Then one of the King County officers stepped up and Ross remembered who had jurisdiction. He handed over the photo array for evidence and returned to his overnight job of writing speeding tickets and making Kent safe for its citizens.

88

On the next morning, June 12, 1981, Mac Smith confided to his pal Mike Drake that he had to get out of town fast. "Things are getting too hot around here," he explained.

Drake figured that his friend must be caught between his wife and his girlfriend again. Or maybe he was worried about the cops. They'd come sniffing around the realty office looking for him—something about a rental car.

Mike's 1976 Dodge had been repossessed and he was having a hell of a time getting around. The Kent Valley was big and wide and it was usually six miles to the nearest men's room. It was no cinch to sell home security systems by bus. Sometimes he bummed rides with Mac in the new black Mustang, but that system was coming to an end. Mac liked to brag that he still hadn't made his first payment.

Mike thought how far down the two friends had slid since the days when they'd sold suburban houses and sipped single-malt Scotch and worn rep ties. Leaving town might not be such a bad idea. Montanans didn't take well to hobbles, and everything he'd accumulated in his years in Seattle would fit into a suitcase. "If you go," he asked Mac, "where ya going?"

"Probably L.A.," Smith answered. "I've got family there."

"Mine are in Helena."

Mac said, "Let's split, man. I'll drop you off."

Not much was said on the long drive. They didn't get away from Seattle till after dark and took turns at the wheel as they crossed the Columbia River and drove past the rolling wheat fields of western Washington. At a Spokane motel, Mike noticed that his companion had a knife with a six- or seven-inch blade. Mac said it was for protection.

Back on Interstate 90 the next morning, the two friends fell into a rare intimate conversation. Mac almost never discussed anything significant; hanging out with him meant listening to a stream of small talk about women and booze, business, sports. But now he was saying that he'd seen his girlfriend Crystal for the last time; he'd said good-bye the day before and promised to return soon, but it wasn't in the cards. The affair hadn't worked and he had himself to blame. "She's just one more failure in my life," he lamented. "What a nice chick. I just couldn't see past the sex."

After a while he confessed to lifelong feelings of inadequacy. With a little prompting, he acknowledged his sales talents and a few other useful characteristics, but he said they didn't overcome his faults. "I'm like a guy I read about in the papers," he explained. "No matter how much success he had, he saw himself as a dork. Then one day he got passed over for a promotion and jumped out the window."

"You're no dork," Drake insisted. But Mac

seemed to be enjoying his self-pity and there didn't seem to be any point in debating the subject.

An hour after leaving Spokane they wound around the deep blue curve of Lake Coeur d'Alene and headed into the gold mining districts of western Idaho. "I won a bike when I was a kid," Mac mused. "I set a record for stolen bases. But, shit . . ." His voice trailed off.

Drake wasn't accustomed to seeing his friend in the role of whiner; in the worst of the real estate doldrums, Mac had always talked a good game and seemed cool.

"You'll be okay, man," Drake comforted him. "It'll turn around. It always does."

They arrived at the Drake family home in Helena just after dark. Mac stayed the night and then took off. "Gotta shag ass for Vegas," he said. "See my dad again." He promised to keep in touch.

89

The trouble with being a detail man, Detective Milton Stewart complained to himself, was that the brass never gave you enough time to handle all the details. That made this new assignment a plum to be savored. It was even worth postponing his usual weekend round of golf.

Stewart was one of five investigators assigned to the Sex Crimes Unit of the King County Police Department, and on any given day he carried twenty to thirty active cases. Sergeant Harlan Bollinger's operatives were swamped. The detectives agreed that a sex perversion virus was epidemic in the Seattle area and someone had better develop a vaccine. Perversion was becoming a bigger growth industry than Boeing.

At forty-three, Mick Stewart was one of the unit's "old guys," everybody's uncle. Before landing the sex crimes job, he'd worked as a jailer, spent four years on patrol, seven more on a bike, then three years in the fugitive unit serving warrants. He was the sex unit's closest approach to a western bounty hunter. In the police cliché, Mick Stewart could "track a piss-ant across a bowling ball."

A few weeks back, he'd caught a routine case—the October 6 rape of Julie Whitehurst—and struck out. The victim's listed address proved to be her mother's place in Tacoma. The upset mom said she'd lost touch with the fifteen-year-old child. When three days of tracking failed to turn her up, Stewart had been forced to inactivate the case.

But now the airport rapes had been reassigned to him on a priority basis, and his current cases were distributed among the other detectives. Harlan Bollinger and Deputy Prosecutor Chris Washington minced no words: the rapist had to be brought in without delay. This Titus case had become an embarrassment.

Stewart was still wading through the reports on the Dalton and Whitehurst cases when he got his first break. A sharp-eyed Kent patrolman named Bill Ross fed the name "McDonald J. Smith" into the computer system as a possible rapist. According to the Department of Licensing, Smith had owned five vehicles and wrecked two or three. Stewart decided the guy must be cross-eyed or a drunk. He sent to Olympia for a driver's license photo. The guy wasn't cross-eyed.

It took a week to locate the particular Smith vehicle that came closest to the description of the car used in the airport rapes. Unfortunately, the blue Ford Fiesta was scattered all over the service floor of a west Seattle dealership, in the final stages of being parted out. Stewart impounded the Michelin tires, a few body panels, and the front seat with its crank wheel for adjusting the seat.

He looked up the temporary license plate originally assigned to the car. The number was 644-182, and Stewart noted how different it was from Steve

Titus's 661-677. He thumbed through the thick file on Celia Dalton and discovered that she'd reported seeing "667" and/or "776" on her assailant's license. Stewart was puzzled. If Smith was the rapist, how come she'd remembered one digit from his car but five from Titus's? It made him wonder if the fish salesman wasn't good for the rape after all.

But the crime lab reported that Smith's Michelin treads were a perfect match for the first tracks photographed at the scene. And the crank wheel in the Fiesta corroborated the victim's statement that her assailant had to reach over and work for a minute or two to lower the back of her seat. That could only mean she'd been in Smith's car, not Titus's. To a pro like Mick Stewart, the picture was coming clear.

It was time to go hunting.

He drove to the Smith family's last known address, a burned-out trailer at Lake Sawyer. No one answered his knock. A neighbor who said she'd been picking up mail for the Smiths volunteered that she hadn't seen "Mac" in a week and provided his estranged wife's address.

Stewart prowled Nan Smith's new neighborhood, ran some license checks, but found no signs of the husband. A neighbor directed him to a realty office in Kent, where he was told that Smith had quit to sell home alarm systems. The head of a security company in the nearby town of Federal Way reported that Mac hadn't come to work in days. Someone had seen him at a nearby landscaping business.

A sex unit detective named Leo Hirsch checked out the tip for Stewart and learned that a young man named Smith had been dating the landscaper's daughter, Crystal Parke. Hirsch said the parents described Smith as "a nice guy." The family thought he might be in Las Vegas, visiting his sick father.

On Thursday, June 18, Stewart got word that rape victim Julie Whitehurst had returned to her foster home. He sped thirty miles south to Tacoma and showed her a photo array. The haggard-looking girl passed over Smith's mug shot, but said she thought number six looked familiar. She popped her gum for a few more minutes before giving up on a car montage. Not much help, Stewart admitted to himself.

He decided to check Celia Dalton's reaction to the same photos. At 1:32 P.M. he met her in Vip's Restaurant, across from the Hyatt House on the Sea-Tac Strip. He was surprised at her appearance; she was eighteen now, nearly as tall as his own six feet, a good-looking kid who put him in mind of some of the golfers on the ladies' tour. She promised to cooperate and came across as genuinely upset by the articles in the *Times*.

Stewart asked her to describe how the Port police had presented the original montage. "They told me the guy was there," she said, "and it was up to me to pick him out."

The old pro clucked softly. That was *exactly* the wrong procedure. The Port police montage had stunk in the first place; it looked like something whipped up at a barber college. No wonder this girl had picked the wrong man. But . . . would she pick the right man now?

He spread six black and white pictures on the

table and watched as she squinted and stared. After a short pause, she looked up and said, "I'm not sure."

Jesus Christ, Stewart muttered to himself. Are we ever gonna solve this goddamned thing?

Then she took another look. "I think I was wrong before," she said. "It's this one." Stewart leaned over and saw that she was pointing to Mac Smith. "My God," she said, "what have I done to Steve Titus?" She started to cry.

Stewart handed her a pen. "Here," he said. "Sign across the back." Then he laid down pictures of seven different compact cars. She selected a Ford Fiesta exactly like Smith's.

At headquarters he showed her the impounded parts of Smith's car. She looked at the rear quarter panel and said the color was right. She brushed the velveteen seat covering against her cheek and said it felt the same as the covering in the rapist's car. And she described again how the man had reached across her body to twist the seat back knob.

Stewart stepped into a side office and dialed Deputy Prosecutor Washington, seven flights upstairs in the courthouse building. "I think you better come down," he said.

90

Late that night, Attorney Jeff Jones was still at his desk. In addition to preparing for the coming legal war, he was fighting a losing battle to quiet Steve Titus down. King County Prosecuting Attorney Norm Maleng still hadn't announced whether his office intended to retry the case, dismiss it, or appeal Judge Johnson's ruling. Over and over, Jones was compelled to advise his client not to tweak the dragon's tail.

But Steve had become God's angry man. For eight months he'd been branded as the lowest form of animal life and he intended to redeem his reputation at the top of his lungs. He pushed Jones to file an immediate suit against the Port police and the prosecutor's office for false arrest, false imprisonment, malicious prosecution, libel, slander, malfeasance, misfeasance, nonfeasance, and every other feasance in the statute books.

The lawyer agreed that a strong civil action was shaping up, but it was much too early to file. Depending on the damage-control plans of the prosecutor's office, Titus could find himself back in court on a charge of rape. Granted, he would have a better chance in a second trial, but it was still a roll of the dice. In Jones's eyes, keeping his client out of jail was the first priority.

So he listened closely when his adversary Chris Washington interrupted his nighttime labors with a phone call. "Jeff?" Chris said in that silken voice that was so impressive to jurors. "I want to tell you something, but first I need your assurance that you won't tell your client till I authorize it."

"Okay," Jones agreed. As officers of the court, opposing lawyers often had such private dealings. The cozy practice annoyed clients, but it was time-honored and served the purposes of both sides.

"Jeff, we have a suspect," Washington went on. "The car matches, the tires match, the M.O. matches, everything matches. This is the guy."

Jones thought, My God, we win! Steve can take a full-page ad. He can sue for the national debt. We—have—WON! But he tried to sound blasé. "Why can't I tell my client?" he asked.

"The guy's gone. And we can't find him."

91

Mick Stewart tracked Mac Smith's girlfriend to her parents' home. Crystal Parke struck him as a guileless young woman who'd fallen for a dirtball's line of bullshit. At first she refused to believe that her fiancé was suspected of rape. "He wouldn't," she cried. "He just *wouldn't*. He's such a . . . nice guy."

But after Stewart passed along a few telling details, she haltingly told what she knew. She'd last seen Mac on Friday evening, June 12. The detective remembered that Liza Cimino had been raped a night or two earlier, but he made no mention of it. At around 6:30, Crystal continued, Smith and his pal Mike Drake had left for Montana in Mac's black Mustang. He'd planned to see his sick dad in Las Vegas, then visit relatives in Southern California. He'd promised to be back in a week.

Crystal said he'd phoned her from Mike's home in Helena and again the next night from a pay phone in southern Idaho. She figured he was probably in Vegas by now.

"What'd he take with him?" the detective asked.

"His two jackets were on the backseat. One was green with a picture of a marijuana plant and the words GROWN IN KOREA. The other was beige with a hood. And he was wearing his Seattle Mariners baseball cap.''

Stewart realized that he'd just solved the June 11 rape three blocks from Titus's condo. Liza Cimino had reported the same items on the backseat, down to the "*S*" on the cap.

It was just before midnight when the detective said good night. A shaken Crystal promised to get in touch the next time Mac phoned. She said she was positive he would call. He'd always been a man of his word.

92

Maria thought her husband was kidding when he banged on their bathroom door in Harbor City and yelled, "Hey, your brother Mac's here!"

The Smith siblings hugged and squeezed and told each other how great they looked. Then Maria stepped back and asked, "Where's Nan and the kids?"

Mac paused. "Well, you'll find out anyway," he said. "We're separated. We're gonna get a divorce. I'm just taking a little time off."

Brother and sister gabbed nonstop, reliving the years when they'd had no one to depend on except each other. Maria felt bad about the breakup, but she'd always wondered if it was wise to marry a woman "just like Mom," especially when there was a fifteen-year age span.

Mac seemed fine otherwise. He was driving a new black Mustang. As usual, his pants were pressed and his clothes looked neat and clean; he hadn't forgotten their mother's example. They didn't talk much about their dad. Mac said he'd looked for him in Las Vegas but hadn't connected.

"When we were kids," Maria mused, "I didn't give a dime for our future. Now you're going great and so's Walter." It made her feel proud that they'd not only survived but flourished.

"How's Mom been lately?" Mac put in.

"Just fine," Maria told him. Her weight had ballooned, but their stepfather Ray didn't seem to mind.

"How's Lina handling her senior year?" Mac asked.

"Fine. But . . . she picked up some of Mom's ideas."

Mac didn't comment. Maria reminded herself not to mention religion again.

Every once in a while Mac slipped into the bedroom to use the phone, and once Maria overheard him call somebody "Honey."

"Come on, Mac," she teased. "Who is she?"

He confessed that he'd met a young woman from an old Washington family and intended to marry her after his divorce from Nan. But he didn't seem open to the subject, and Maria let it drop. She knew he wouldn't hold back when the time was right. His new fiancée was twenty and he was twenty-eight. Maria thought, That's more like it.

After a few days Mac left to visit his mother and stepfather in Westminster, twenty miles east. Then he phoned to report that he was headed for Washington and home.

93

Mick Stewart wondered if he would ever see another golf course. The one and only criminal investigation on his case load was giving him fits. Crystal Parke and her family had been as good as their word, phoning with the latest details of Mac Smith's wanderings, but the son of a bitch kept jumping around. The Las Vegas P.D. failed to turn up an address for a Calvin Smith. Crystal reported that Mac intended to visit his mother in Southern California, but she didn't know the address.

Every day, sometimes twice, Stewart drove the circuit from the Lake Sawyer trailer to Nan Smith's house to the Parkes' home to the security alarm company, checking for the black Mustang. He also collected and inventoried evidence, ran fingerprints, compared seat cover fabrics, vacuumed out cars for fibers and hairs and sent them to the crime lab, took pictures of seat back release mechanisms, and made up montages of cars and people. And he also wheedled more information from a long list of young women. As always, working with teenage victims was sticky business. Some selected Mac Smith in the montage and some didn't. Some picked Smith's car but not Smith, and vice versa.

Julie Whitehurst led Stewart to the scene of her

rape. Through a clearing in the woods, he could just make out the Dalton crime scene, sixty feet away. Damn, he murmured to himself, if only our office had handled both rapes. We'd have made the connection in minutes. A chip shot apart!

On his next contact with Crystal Parke, she reported that Mac was on his way back to Washington. The detective figured the guy must have switched cars. California officers had been sitting on the sister's home and hadn't seen a trace of the Mustang. Stewart shook his head in disgust. He was already investigating Smith for three rapes in three different cars: a Fiesta, a Nova, and a Mustang. The guy was a one-man auto show. But at least he was headed in the right direction.

94

Mac had been gone from his mother's house for two days when her phone rang. "Mom," he gasped, "I've been in an accident. You gotta come get me."

Dove scribbled the address, grabbed her seventeen-year-old daughter Lina, and sped up Highway 101 in the family car. It was a five-hour drive to the roadside town of King City. Mac was waiting for them at a street corner gas station. He could hardly walk and he was shaking from head to foot. He carried a gray toolbox and two jackets. His Seattle Mariners cap was pulled down hard on his head, concealing most of his brownish hair. He let out a moan as he slumped into the car. "Let's go," he said. "Come on, Mom! *Let's go!*"

As they drove south, he explained that he'd been in a head-on crash and totaled his new Mustang. Highway patrolmen had dumped him in a hospital but he'd escaped. Sister Lina thought, *Escaped?* Was Mac under arrest again? Her mother didn't pursue the subject. Lina remembered other times when Dove had failed to ask obvious questions. All she said now was, "Mac, you're hurt. You belong in the hospital."

He said he wouldn't go to a hospital even if his

ankle swelled to twice its size. All he wanted to do was crash at Maria's.

He nodded out on most of the drive, mumbling to himself. Once they heard him say, "I'm sorry, Mom. I'm just so sorry for everything." He spoke with such depth of feeling that the words seemed to well up from his soul. Sister Lina wished she knew what he was so sorry about.

95

The next day, Monday, June 29, 1981, Crystal Parke
called Mick Stewart with an urgent message. She'd
just got off the phone with Mac and he was in bed at
his sister Maria's house. He could hardly talk; he
said he'd totaled the Mustang in Utah. He promised
to call in the evening and left a phone number.

It was already 4:30 P.M. and the old bounty
hunter had to move fast. He dialed the prosecutor's
office and asked Mary Kay Barbieri to file charges
against Smith in the Dalton and Whitehurst rapes.
He called the L.A.P.D. and requested an address
check on Maria's phone number; it came back to
Harbor City, near Long Beach. He phoned the Utah
Highway Patrol and asked a trooper to run a computer check on Smith's accident.

Then he waded into the necessary paperwork,
breathing his customary silent thanks to the U.S.
Army for forcing him to learn touch-typing. In less
than an hour he'd tapped out an affidavit of proba-
ble cause, commitment papers, and an arrest warrant. At 9:00 P.M., he hand-delivered the warrant to
the home of a district judge for a signature.

Now he was ready to fly south. But the airlines
weren't. He'd missed the last Seattle–L.A. flight of
the evening.

He was about to sign out when the Utah High-way Patrol called back and said there was no record of an accident involving McDonald J. Smith or a black Mustang.

That's funny, Stewart said to himself. Why would he lie to his girlfriend? That car is vital god-damn evidence. Where the hell is it? Is Crystal lying to me . . . ? In his mind's eye he saw the fugitive speeding down a Mexican highway, whistling "La Cucaracha." He hoped the bastard hit a cow.

He dialed the L.A.P.D. fugitive unit again and spelled out the problem. A helpful detective named Ron Puckett promised to eyeball the Harbor City address. At midnight, he reported that the place was dark.

96

Maria was thankful that her dear brother hadn't been killed. Mac had such bad luck with cars, probably because he always drove as though he were the last man on earth, running lights and stop signs and blowing through crosswalks. He also did a fair amount of driving under the influence.

She still remembered how upset he'd been after hitting two men while test-driving brother Walter's new Pontiac. He'd feared that Walter would never forgive him, but the older brother had mellowed since leaving home. Maria was pleased that all the Smiths were on speaking terms. Who would ever have predicted *that*?

In the morning, Walter had dropped by to pick up Mac and drive him out to their mother's house in Westminster. Dove, little sister Lina and the stepfather had left on a vacation, and Mac would have the house and the pool all to himself for a nice long session of R&R.

97

On Tuesday morning, June 30, one day after the L.A. fugitive unit had looked for signs of Mac Smith at his sister Maria's, the phone was ringing when Mick Stewart reached his cubbyhole office. He'd just finished another predawn roundelay of checking Smith's haunts, unproductive as usual.

Crystal Parke was calling and said she'd heard from Mac. He was back at his mother's house in Westminster. This time he'd given her the phone number.

Stewart grabbed his handcuffs and briefcase, collected the arrest documents, and made Western Airlines' 2:17 P.M. flight out of Sea-Tac.

He'd been to L.A. often but was always surprised by the scented air and the fleets of rolling stock whirling around LAX like water bugs. Orange County deputies provided transportation and manpower for the sortie to Westminster. No one knew exactly what to expect. Smith's sheet showed priors for armed robberies and rape; otherwise he was an unknown quantity. But he was at bay and injured, and he had to be approached with caution.

98

Mac's ankle felt a little better and he borrowed a friend's car to check out the turf he hadn't seen in five or six years—Redondo Beach, where he'd played in the surf; Long Beach, where he'd shined shoes; San Pedro, where he'd ridden water taxis out to the ships; Harbor City, where he'd delivered the Long Beach *Independent;* Carson, where the family had suffered together after his father deserted. He drove past the fast-food restaurants where he and Rudi O'Shay had worked, and he felt again the surge of excitement and power that came from holding a gun on another human being. Too bad about Rudi, he said to himself. His mom had written that he was semipermanently confined to the state penitentiary at Chino. Mac wondered what the prisons were like back in Washington.

If he kept using his head, of course, he would never find out. The odds against getting caught for rape were still eight or nine to one. Make that forty or fifty to one, he said to himself. Maybe higher, if I keep playing it smart.

He drove to his old playground in Torrance and walked around the bases that he'd swiped with such skill. Through the open door of the gymnasium, he saw a couple of beaner kids shooting free throws.

He went inside and spotted a red graffito advising him to *Chinga tu madre.* He remembered a scene from his final baseball game, just before his mother had discovered the fundamentalist church. He'd smacked a single into right field and stolen second, third and home. Some old guy had hollered, "Look! The Georgia Peach!" Jeez, he thought, if you could only steal bases for a living.

He headed back to Westminster and reality. Something was in the air; he could feel it in his throbbing ankle and hear it in the dead leaves rattling in the palm trees. Once again he had no job, no car, no money, no wife, no kids. He didn't even have Crystal. He was running downhill and didn't know how to stop—and wasn't sure he wanted to. He felt no shame; shame was for losers. Most people acted as though rape was a terrible crime, but it was just his sex life. Who was he hurting? Whores and delinquents? What a joke. Why stop now?

99

The neat little rambler was set in a middle-class neighborhood with flowers and shrubs of the kind Detective Mick Stewart usually saw on the best landscaped golf courses. Small swimming pools dotted the neighborhood, most of them aboveground. At 6:15 P.M. the sky was so bright that he wished he'd brought his biker shades. The temperature was in the nineties and the wind blew grit against his face.

He strolled up to the house trying to look like a door-to-door salesman. A young man asked his business. Even under the thick moustache and full beard and shock of brown hair that fell across his forehead, he looked familiar.

"I'm Detective Stewart, King County police," Mick said, holding up his bona fides. "I have an arrest warrant for McDonald J. Smith."

The man took an uncertain step backward. "Uh, he's not here right now," he said.

"Who are you?" Mick asked.

"I'm Mac's brother," the guy said. "My name's Walter." He smiled, revealing neat white teeth. His voice was soft and he didn't sound intimidated. "Mac had to go someplace. If you just come back—"

"Then who's this?" Stewart asked as the Orange

County deputies joined him. He held up Mac's "wanted" picture.

The man beckoned the officers inside. Through a side door, a swimming pool caught the afternoon sun in bluish glints and glimmers. A newscast flickered on a portable TV next to an aluminum chaise longue draped in towels. The occupant of the house had been taking his ease.

"I'm Mac," he admitted. He smiled and reached out to shake hands. Stewart thought, This dude ought to be pitching costume jewelry. What was it everyone had said about him? "He's *such* a nice guy."

At the sheriff's office in Santa Ana, Stewart guided his prisoner into an interrogation room and spelled out his rights for the second time. He made a point of not taking notes; there would be plenty of time later, and notebooks turned most people off. As the detective recalled the conversation later, Smith acted friendly, pleasant, and contrite.

"You're under investigation for four rapes," Stewart started out. "A man named Steve Titus was convicted of one of them."

He studied the dark blue eyes for a reaction. If Smith was chagrined, he didn't show it. Nor did he enter the righteous denial that Stewart had expected.

The air thickened till Smith leaned across the desk and said, "I know you're telling the truth about the rape cases. I want to be just as honest with you. I've told a lot of lies and half-truths in my life. This time I want to tell the whole truth." He hung his head and brushed the hair from his eyes. He sounded ready to accept his fate. "I've done some terrible things," he said. "I need help, I admit it."

The detective waited for more specific admissions. Smith promised to sign a waiver and make a full confession as soon as he'd had a preliminary hearing. His eyes glistened with sincerity as he spoke.

It was old stuff to Stewart. Most perverts came across as nice guys; they looked and sounded like the men who shared pitchers of margaritas at the nineteenth hole. Glibness and bullshit were their stock in trade.

He let his prisoner stew while he stepped into another room to take a call from his office. Sergeant Harlan Bollinger had checked with the California Highway Patrol and learned that Smith's Mustang wasn't in Utah; it was a twisted mess in an impoundment lot in King City, California. CHiPs had intended to question the driver in the hospital, but he'd walked.

Stewart perked up at the news that a Finnish filleting knife had been found on the Mustang's front seat. Had Smith intended to break the monotony of the long drive home? Could he have wrecked his car while rabbiting from another rape? The scenario fit. It sure explained why he hadn't hung around.

As the two men walked along the corridor of the Orange County jail, Smith muttered that he was afraid. "My whole world's tumbling down," he whimpered in a little boy's voice. The bounty hunter felt him tremble across the handcuffs.

"Oh, say, Mac," he asked offhandedly. "What ever happened to your Mustang?"

"I abandoned it up near Sacramento. I didn't have money for gas."

You son of a bitch, Stewart thought. Didn't you just tell me you wanted to be completely honest? Didn't you tell your girlfriend you wrecked the car in Utah?

But Stewart didn't challenge the lie. Let the guy sleep.

They spoke a few hours later in a holding cell, and this time Smith reverted to the familiar role of the rededicated young criminal who intends to change his evil ways. But he remained annoyingly vague about his crimes. Over and over Stewart offered variations on the same theme: "If you mean what you say, if you're a decent person, a just person, if you feel *any* concern about Steve Titus and the women you raped, then do the right thing and tell me the details right now."

Smith smiled, promised to help, and didn't give an inch. He talked remorse but gave the impression that his main concern was number one. To Stewart he was just another scuzzball, protecting his ass.

100

Maria was at work when her brother Walter phoned and informed her that Mac had been arrested. "What for?" she yelped.

"I don't know. The cop was from Washington. He must've been writing bad checks or something."

Maria broke into tears. It was bad enough that she saw her favorite brother so seldom; now he'd been dragged away before she'd even had a chance to hug him good-bye. "What's he say?" she asked.

"He honestly has no idea what it's about," Walter said. He sounded perplexed himself. "He said he hasn't done anything wrong, but they're gonna take him back to Seattle."

Maria rushed home. Just as she'd expected, Mac soon called from Orange County jail. "They're accusing me of rape," he told her. "Don't worry. It's a mistake."

She went into the bathroom and buried her face in a towel. She couldn't believe his bad luck. It almost seemed that he'd been put on Earth to atone for others' crimes. He'd been accused of rape before, but that had been a misunderstanding involving a ditsy old woman. Did the cops intend to badger him for the rest of his life because he'd made mistakes as a kid?

She considered the possibility that they'd arrested the wrong brother. Walter had a violent streak; he'd done everything but pitch their mother out the window before he'd left home for good. But Mac had never hurt a soul, never raised a finger. He was gentle and loving. She consoled herself that he would be freed when the mistake was discovered.

101

After an uncontested extradition hearing, Mick Stewart rented a car and chauffeured his prisoner to the L.A. airport. He reported to the pilot that he was returning a fugitive and received clearance to fly armed. He put Smith in handcuffs, belly chain and leg brace, and prepped him for the flight with an illustrative story from his own experience as a jailer. He told how a sawed-off Missouri sheriff had arrived in Seattle in cowboy boots and a ten-gallon hat to return a hulk of a man to the Ozarks. "This sheriff tells this killer, 'Son, you can go back as a gentleman sitting in the airplane, or you can go back in the hold as freight. So if you wanna fuck with me, go right ahead. We'll chip the ice off ya at Kansas City.' Get my meaning, Mac?"

Smith nodded.

"Good," Stewart said. "Now here's a few personal rules of my own. Use the toilet now. Once the plane takes off, we stay in our seats. When the food's served, I'll uncuff one hand and give you a spoon. The other cuff stays on the belly chain."

"I can't have a drink?" Smith said. He was shaking slightly, as though he had a fever. Or was it the start of the dt's?

"Don't ask," the detective said.

"Not even water?"

"No drinks, no bathroom. We'll be happier that way."

On the two-and-a-half-hour flight to Sea-Tac Airport, the prisoner remained politely evasive. He'd already declined to sign a rights waiver, which meant that Stewart couldn't ask direct questions about the rapes. There was nothing to prevent Smith from volunteering information, but he didn't take the hint. Instead he talked about his faithful wife Nan and how sorry he was that he'd deceived Crystal and how he knew he had a problem and intended to work on it.

Ho-hum, Stewart thought, and stared at the Sierras.

The plane landed at 7:48 P.M. A Port policeman provided a courtesy drive to the King County jail in Seattle. Nothing much was said on the way up I-5. Once inside, Smith said he was too tired to answer questions but asked for permission to phone his wife. Then he was booked for rape in the first degree.

102

If Paul Henderson hadn't felt such a rush of euphoria and vindication, he would have been highly annoyed. With the real rapist finally in custody, just about everyone involved in the persecution of Steve Titus had run for cover. The prevailing comment was, "Who, me?"

In dropping all charges, King County Prosecuting Attorney Norm Maleng tipped his hat to Henderson and the *Times,* but he couldn't resist insisting that "we, of course, analyzed the prior decisions made in this case [and] we believe that each decision made was correct at the time it was made."

Christopher Washington echoed, "I can't apologize to Steve Titus. I can't find in my analysis anything that was done incorrectly by any part of the criminal justice system." But he added that he felt bad about Titus's suffering.

Mary Kay Barbieri appeared more concerned than her colleagues, both by the faulty prosecution and her deputy's reaction. She summoned Washington and said, "Come on, Chris! We did a horrible thing to this man. But we didn't act in bad faith. It doesn't mean we're a couple of badasses. But of *course* we apologize that it happened."

Washington explained that he'd only meant to

say that he'd done nothing wrong personally and therefore didn't feel that he should shoulder the blame.

Neil Moloney, who had left his job as Port police chief to take command of the Washington State Patrol, said he could find no fault with the way the investigation had been handled. His hand-picked sergeant, Dave Hart, said, "We do feel bad about what happened, but I believe that everybody was just trying to do their job."

Detective Corporal Ronald Parker held his ground. "They're making a hell of a mistake kicking Titus loose," he said. "Tonight he'll be back in the airport woods." Parker warned that if Henderson wrote one more line about him, he would file a million-dollar lawsuit. "It was the jury that convicted that little prick, not me," he reminded a friend.

He had a ready explanation for the latest development: "In our profession we see assholes like Mac Smith all the time. This guy is nothing but a professional confessor."

Dewey Gillespie, the respected polygraphist who'd presided over Titus's failed tests, admitted that he was disturbed. "All I can say is that the polygraph can't be 100 percent accurate," he explained. He reminded the public that the lie detector was intended to be used as a tool, not as the last word.

Juror Ed Carl looked around his house for a stamp so he could mail a long overdue letter to *The Seattle Times*, castigating Henderson for making the jurors look bad. "You weren't in the courtroom," he wrote, "and you couldn't see how some of Titus's witnesses could be mistaken." He listed the seven items that confirmed Titus's guilt.

Before he could post his letter, Carl picked up the latest copy of the *Times* with the news of the Smith arrest. The good-natured Boeing engineer told friends later that he felt like being measured for a dunce cap. He saved his letter as proof of the system's fallibility, and his own.

Celia Dalton seemed to blame both herself and the Port police. She confided to friends that she'd been disenchanted with Ronald Parker ever since he'd paid an uninvited social call at 2:30 A.M. She'd refused to let him in and still wondered about his motives.

She confirmed that Parker and other Port officers had strongly influenced her from the beginning. After all, she explained, they were the experts. She described their interrogation technique: she would volunteer a hazy recollection; the officer would say, "But couldn't it have been *this* way?"; Celia would concede that the revised version was possible, and the officer would write it down as fact. She said she'd always had doubts about Titus's guilt but kept them to herself, and that she'd never been sure of her timetable or other facets of her testimony. She'd read that certain parties were now refusing to apologize to Titus. She didn't understand that attitude. She said that she felt extremely sorry for the man.

■

Henderson soon learned that the Port was sending backhoes into the airport woods and pushing up hummocks of dirt to block the abandoned roadways. They planned to ring the condemned land with wire fences. "I guess they decided not to bust any more innocent men," he cracked to Janet.

At the office he had the satisfaction of banging out a final story about the case. The headline said, "FINALLY, TITUS IS CLEARED."

It gave him a perverse pleasure to remind his readers of the probation officer's appraisal of Steve, made after the conviction: "Mr. Titus has demonstrated he is capable of violent behavior and cannot be considered safe to remain in the community."

This time the story ran in news space. The Pulitzer Prize came later.

PART SIX
RECKONING

■

1981–1986

103

Mick Stewart continued to savor the heady delight of having a single case on his schedule. Mac Smith had finally consulted with a lawyer, and the result was a plea of "Not Guilty." Now it was up to Stewart, as the prosecution's chief investigator, to put the case together, and for the first time in his eighteen years on the force his coffee was being caddied to his desk. He felt like a movie detective, bird-dogging a hot suspect while his colleagues picked up the rest of his work load. He had time to run down tips, interview witnesses, inspect locations, oversee crime lab work, even stay current on his reports. He also had time to assimilate the stacks of interdepartmental data that floated across his desk. What a luxury, he said to himself, to start each shift knowing what the hell's going on in the world . . .

The day after Smith's plea of innocent, Stewart was perusing the latest stack of flyers from other agencies when he came across "Lynnwood P.D. Bulletin No. 81–005. Confidential. For police use only." The composite drawing of a suspected rapist drew his attention. He held the picture to the light and whooped, "Hello, Mac!"

He phoned Brian Burkhalter, the suburban

Lynnwood officer who'd signed the original Western Area TTY. He remembered the busy young
charger; he seemed to be on a mission from God to
nail a guy who'd raped three or four women during
real estate transactions, only one of them in his own
jurisdiction of Lynnwood.

On the phone, Burkhalter sounded as hyped by
the case as ever. In fact, he'd just picked up a hot
new lead. So far, he said, he'd handled some twenty
suspects, including just about every known sex offender between Lynnwood and the Canadian border—and come up empty.

After comparing notes, the two lawmen realized
that they had a serial rapist on their hands. Cars and
descriptions matched, M.O.s were close, and the
perpetrator had twice used the name of Smith's pal
Mike Drake as an alias. That left only one problem:
how many complainants would identify Smith in a
lineup?

Burkhalter mentioned an open house victim
named Ann Carmichael, the wife of a Seattle policeman, who'd been so determined to nail her assailant
that she'd held his semen in her mouth long
enough to deposit it in a strategic spot for the evidence technicians. If the lineup was held at the
North Pole, Burkhalter said, this angry woman
would rent a dog team to attend. And if necessary,
her husband would push the sled.

Stewart decided to assemble the victims while memories were fresh. He wasn't hopeful about King
County's four teenaged complainants, and neither
was the prosecutor's office. Celia Dalton had already
put on a convincing performance in court while

identifying the wrong man. Joanie Kay Finley was in jail for bad checks. Julie Whitehurst was last seen rattling around the Sea-Tac Strip. Stewart didn't know much about Smith's final victim, Liza Cimino, except that she was another wild kid. These were the prosecutor's only potential witnesses at the moment. Even if they made Mac Smith at a lineup, would they be able to convince a jury that he was guilty beyond a reasonable doubt?

Stewart was glad that Brian Burkhalter and Ann Carmichael were eager to participate in the lineup. They could make the difference.

104

She'd followed the Titus case in the *Times,* but with no idea that she was linked. Fourteen months had passed since she'd been sodomized by the sad-eyed young man in Everett. For a long time she'd refused to hold another open house, and she resumed the practice only after colleagues agreed to accompany her or check in on her frequently.

Since the rape, she'd had problems with her marriage. Ann couldn't shake the vileness on the man's face, the hatred and anger she'd seen in his cold, sloping eyes. Her marital relations, once normal and loving, had flattened out. She wished she could stop turning the rape against herself. What had she done to make that sick little man glare at her in white-hot rage and shoot his slimy insult into her mouth? She wondered, Was it something I said? Something I was wearing? The way I moved or talked?

She could only conclude that it was her same old problem: she was a magnet for creeps. One day her color printer was stolen at the office and a nasty-gram left behind: "Fuck you you cont." She decided that her karma was as bad as his spelling.

∎

The nice Lynnwood detective drove her and her husband Phil twenty miles to the King County police headquarters for the afternoon lineup. On the way, Brian Burkhalter explained that the victim in the Lynnwood case had left the state. A third open house victim was still being sought in the northern part of Snohomish County. And he suspected there were some who hadn't reported their rapes but might come forward now on the wave of publicity.

Ann felt excited, committed, and scared. Over and over she made Burkhalter promise that the men in the lineup would be unable to see her. She was convinced that the rapist would finish her off with his knife. It had happened to another Washington woman. Phil said, "Relax."

A plainclothesman led her into the softly lighted viewing room in front of a tinted glass panel. In one corner a tall, slender girl rubbed tears from smudged eyesockets. A woman in a business suit stood by quietly, seemingly uninvolved—perhaps a lawyer or a policewoman. A young lawyer from the Public Defender's office represented Mac Smith's interests. A street-worn female somewhere between fourteen and forty chewed gum and beat a silent rhythm on her kneecaps with fingers that were gnawed to the quick. There were one or two others, but Ann didn't want to stare.

A graying detective named Stewart reminded everyone not to talk or compare notes. The subjects were paraded in front of the screen, each displaying full face and profile and repeating after the detective: "Now just do what I tell you and you won't get hurt."

Ann wished her heart would stop thumping.

She didn't know which possibility frightened her more: spotting the guy or *not* spotting him. Dear God, she prayed under her breath, if he's there, let it be very clear to me. If he's not, don't let me pick someone out of panic. Don't let me incriminate someone who's not guilty. Let there be no question. . . .

Then number six stood a few feet in front of her eyes. The tall girl in the corner cried and shook. Some of the others mumbled. The public defender took notes.

Ann breathed a silent thanks. It was the eyes that left no doubt. She'd never stopped seeing those sad, slanted eyes. The rest of his body had changed a little. His hair was longer and stragglier. He looked as though he hadn't been taking care of himself. He didn't seem menacing, just beaten down. She couldn't help feeling sorry for him. How could she ever have trembled in front of such a weenie?

105

Mick Stewart contemplated the afternoon's results and felt as though he'd hit his tee shot into a bunker. The footloose Julie Whitehurst, closely escorted by her probation officer, made a positive ID, but she'd previously picked the wrong man out of a montage and her testimony would be unconvincing at best. The cop's wife made a solid identification, thank God, but she was the only one who didn't equivocate, and her case was fourteen months old. Another Snohomish County victim was still to be located. Mick's colleague, Detective Jim Alley, had snared Liza Cimino; she'd been raped down the road from Titus's apartments less than a month before and she'd already picked Smith in a photo laydown, but at this in-person lineup she couldn't make a pick. And the most notorious victim of all, Celia Dalton, had been so shattered by the Titus mix-up that she refused to identify anybody, including her actual rapist.

The case against Smith was turning soft.

107

Defense attorneys advised Mac Smith that he had to make the final decision on whether to fight or deal, and he spent long hours in his King County jail cell trying to figure the odds. He'd never known better lawyers than the underpaid public defenders assigned to his case. They seemed to go out of their way on his behalf, keeping him on top of developments as though he were a high-paying client instead of an indigent.

One of the young lawyers conceded that there was a fair chance he could be convicted on two of the King County charges, but "we'll blow them so far out of the water on Celia Dalton and Joanie Kay Finley that the jury'll refuse to convict on the other two. And since all the cases will be tried together, you'll walk."

But the same counselor also pointed out that the Snohomish County cases were more threatening —the cop's wife would impress a jury; the victim who'd left town had reluctantly agreed to testify, and another open house victim had come forward and identified him from photos. Maybe the best plan would be to deal with the King County prosecutor—already embarrassed over the Titus conviction and eager to wrap up the case—and hope that Snohomish County went along.

Smith made a long-distance call and discussed the prospects with his biggest supporter. "They say I might be able to get into a hospital program for sex offenders," he told Maria, "but first I have to plead guilty."

"But Mac," Maria said, "you're *not* guilty."

"I know," he said patiently. "If I'm found guilty, I go to the penitentiary. Remember the old woman in L.A.? I was innocent then, too, but I still had to serve the time. It's the system, Maria."

His sister warned that the sex program would be crawling with perverts. "I've heard it's not too bad," Mac replied. "They keep you locked up in a hospital near Tacoma. My lawyer told me you sit around and look at dirty pictures and then talk about it in group therapy. After a while, you get so bored that you swear off sex forever." He gave a dry cackle into the phone. "That's the theory anyway."

"That's your choice?"

"I don't know yet. I can risk a sixty-year sentence or I can spend three years watching pornies." He said he would let her know his final decision.

A few days later an almost forgotten rape tipped the scales against him. Five years ago Betsy Winkler had been a fourteen-year-old hitchhiker and he'd been a hot-eyed newcomer to Washington. She read about his latest arrest in the *Times,* identified him in a photo lineup, and agreed to testify. That made eight complainants in all.

The final blow was a latent fingerprint lift that the relentless Brian Burkhalter had forwarded to the FBI crime lab. It had come from the scene of the Lynnwood rape, and it matched the left middle finger of Mac Smith's hand. If the prosecutor could get the print admitted into evidence at the trial, Mac was a goner.

His lawyers strongly recommended the Sex Offender Program, and he authorized them to seek a deal. A few days later he was advised that King County had agreed to a plea bargain but Snohomish County was balking. There was word that the Carmichael woman and her cop husband had threatened to sue the Snohomish prosecuting attorney if her case wasn't prosecuted.

Smith was demoralized. "I'm sick of being in this cellblock with criminals," he told one of his Public Defenders. They decided to go ahead with the King County deal and see what happened.

On September 18, 1981, McDonald J. Smith entered guilty pleas to the first-degree rapes of Julie Whitehurst, Celia Dalton, Joanie Kay Finley, and Liza Cimino. Then he sat for a long presentence interview with a probation officer whose conclusions would strongly influence the court. With his usual artistic blend of truths, half-truths and untruths, he painted the least damaging picture of himself and his crimes. He reminded the overworked probation officer that his earliest arrest, for auto theft, had been a mistake. He admitted one fast-food restaurant stickup but failed to mention the other eleven or the year-long war of fraud and theft that he and Rudi O'Shay had waged against a trusting employer. He characterized one of the California rape incidents as a shoving match when he was drunk. His one serious morals conviction had happened eight years ago in Redondo Beach, he pointed out, and the attack had been so mild that the court had reduced the charge to third-degree assault. He didn't mention his two previous brushes with Washington authorities, nor did these cases turn up in the records presented to the judge by the prosecution.

As for his latest difficulties, he explained in his diffident style that they'd been "spur of the moment things" and were committed when he was so drunk that he couldn't recall a single incident by name, location, or date. He drew a picture of a well-meaning person who lost control when he drank; it was the same "diminished capacity" alibi he'd worked out ten years before as a safety device if he were ever prosecuted. He stressed how disgusted he'd felt with himself after each rape and claimed that he'd sometimes thrown up. He described how his morale had slumped after the unfortunate loss of his home to fire. His entire Washington rape career, he confided to the presentence interviewer, had amounted to eighteen months, mostly while he was under economic and alcoholic pressure.

The probation officer inquired about his past efforts at going straight. Smith said he'd tried to contact a counselor at a University of Washington behavioral clinic, but hadn't followed through. After another rape, he'd dialed a priest and then hung up.

He emphasized that he was a different man now. He no longer derived a thrill from terrorizing or hurting women. His marital sex life was satisfying. He wished he could visit each and every victim and apologize personally. His beloved mother and faithful sister were behind him and promised to help in his recovery. He would *never* abuse another woman —they had his solemn word on that.

When the discussion turned to the subject of Steve Titus, Smith claimed that he'd been horrified when one of his attorneys had told him that he'd inadvertently caused the poor man such misery. The probation officer suggested that one way to atone for his crimes would be to help the Snohomish County officers clear their cases. Smith agreed, but said he would rather not discuss the Snohomish matters in this particular interview.

Toward the end of the two-hour session, he recalled that there'd been friction between his parents before their final separation but said he saw no connection between his childhood experiences and his crimes. He gave the probation officer three character references, all female. A woman who had bought a house from him told the investigator that she felt the charges against Mac were totally out of character. "As a salesman," the probation report noted, "he showed real concern for her as a consumer, and as a friend was always helpful and considerate. She never saw him angry or upset with anyone and felt he was a good husband and father. She did point out that he was the object of many arguments with his wife, who she thought tended to dominate him. . . . She said he never drank alcoholic beverages with them when they had dinner and felt that he must have been under extreme pressures to do so."

A real estate coworker described him as a "kind, gentle and considerate person" who was "never intoxicated" and was endowed with qualities of leadership. On the downside, he'd suffered misfortunes in business and his wife was too critical, leading to "friction."

His third female supporter described him as "gentle, a good father, and a good person." She'd never seen him display violence. After his trailer home burned, she explained, he'd lost his self-esteem because he was overwhelmed with financial problems and could no longer provide for his wife and children.

In a voluminous report, the probation officer advised the sentencing judge that Smith was facing "his first adult felony offense of great magnitude. The terror under which he placed the young women while he was raping them cannot be condoned. It is my belief that he should be offered an opportunity to change through the sexual psychopath program at Western State Hospital."

The first big hurdle was passed.

Clad in pale blue jail-issue coveralls, the defendant sat impassively at his sentencing hearing while Deputy Prosecutor Linda Walton went through the formality of telling the judge, "I would implore the court to impose a maximum of twenty years on each count. These were violent crimes against particularly vulnerable victims. I don't think there is any question the defendant is a clear danger to society."

King County Superior Court Judge Gerard Shellan ordered him committed to the Sex Offenders Unit of the state hospital for ninety days of observation.

Before the hearing ended, Paul Henderson passed a note to Smith's lawyer: "Did your client know that an innocent man was convicted of one of his crimes?"

Through the attorney, Smith refused to answer. Later Henderson heard that the lawyer had referred to him as "a pushy asshole." He took it as a compliment.

Outside the courtroom, a former real estate colleague of the convicted rapist tried to shed light on the Titus matter. "I'm sure that Mac knew what was happening," he confided, "but there was nothing he could do about it. He was in too deep. He kept hoping that the Titus thing would die down, but it didn't. By that time he was too afraid." The salesman shrugged his shoulders and added, "You can understand."

108

On his arrival at Western State Hospital for evaluation, Mac Smith made an instant impression. He was left alone outside the locked ward while his forgetful escort returned to the police car for the commitment papers. When Smith was asked later why he hadn't run away, the former star sprinter explained that he wasn't at Western to escape; he was there to change his life.

In preliminary interviews, he provided a few glimpses into his early sexual activities. From ten to fourteen, he said, he'd masturbated to fantasies three to four times a week. He'd been sexually involved with an eight-year-old girl and a four-year-old boy, including ten or twelve incidents of mutual fondling and oral sex. He admitted five involvements with a cat when he was fifteen and three with his stepmother at eighteen.

A report from the hospital to the court cited the intense childhood sexuality that foreshadowed his adult career as a rapist. Judge Shellan was informed that Smith "has readily confessed to at least five forceful rapes during 1972 through 1974 in California, of which he was never apprehended, and he's admitted seven more forceful rapes in the Seattle area from 1976 to 1981." Throughout the ninety-day examination period, the report continued, Smith had caused "minimal behavioral problems" and "presents himself as a cooperative and motivated member of the program." Although the experts adjudged him "not safe to be at large," it was felt that he was amenable to treatment. The report, signed by three officials of the Sex Offender Program, assured the court that "we will give him an opportunity to behaviorally demonstrate his willingness to conform to treatment expectations and to alter his behavior."

Judge Shellan suspended a forty-year sentence on condition that the patient successfully complete the hospital program. If Snohomish County went along, Mac Smith could be back on the streets in three years.

Superior Court Judge Dennis J. Britt studied letters from his constituents while considering what to do about the three Snohomish rapes that Smith had now confessed. Brian Burkhalter had written: "I am convinced that this man has been committing rape, usually with a deadly weapon in his possession, for many many years." The Lynnwood officer theorized that the rapes to which Smith had confessed were "simply the tip of the iceberg" and "whenever the day comes that McDonald Smith is released from custody he will again commit rape and possibly more violently than he has in the past."

Ann Carmichael wrote of "the humiliation, the overwhelming fear and panic I felt as a knife was being held at my throat. . . ." She described her months of therapy with a psychologist from the Seattle Police Department and the help she'd received from "my wonderfully understanding husband and, most of all, our Lord, who gave me strength, faith, and a forgiving heart." In a neat hand, she'd written, "I think back now on how lucky I truly was on that April 15, 1980, while all through this horrible ordeal the Lord was protecting my unborn child; for unbeknownst to me, I was already one month pregnant. I thank God every day that my life was spared and that my husband and I were blessed with our very special baby girl—our little Rachel Marie." She told the judge that she didn't envy his position and prayed the Lord to give him wisdom.

Judge Britt was inclined to send the rapist away for life, but before making up his mind he turned to still another evaluation by the busy directors of the Sex Offender Program. Their second report noted that Smith had been assigned a diagnosis of pedophilia and paraphilia and appeared to qualify as a "sexual psychopath."

"As far as safety to be at large is concerned," the hospital officials noted, "Mr. Smith's pattern of sexual deviancy appears to be compulsive and somewhat long-standing. He has little insight into the reasons for his sexual offending and no knowledge of controls necessary to avoid reoffending. . . . In our opinion Mr. Smith is very similar to the average candidate returned to us for treatment. He seems to pose no greater threat to the community in this facility than most other rapists we retain for treatment."

Judge Britt was unmoved. He ordered Smith to serve sixty years in the state penitentiary with a mandatory fifteen-year minimum. After minor confusion between jurisdictions, the prisoner was driven to "The Walls," Walla Walla, the toughest prison in the state, three hundred miles southeast of Seattle.

Smith took in his new surroundings and told a prison counselor, "There are animals in here." He had no intention of staying.

109

Mona Jean Imholt kept waiting for the happy end-
ing. She'd seen her fiancé's mood shift from relief
and jubilation to a permanent state of rage. There
were times when she thought he'd gone mad. He
wanted to get the bastards good and thought of
nothing else. He tried to hire the famous Wyoming
lawyer Gerry Spence, but balked at Spence's price
tag and ended up asking a Seattle law firm to file a
$20 million suit against the Port. From then on, he
spent every minute looking at videotapes, studying
the trial transcript, preparing for depositions. He'd
become a dervish of revenge.

Mona advised him to lighten up and live a little.
"You oughta be just thankful," she lectured him. "A
lot of guys might be in prison right now if they
didn't get as lucky as you. Just thank God that people cared, and go on from there." Other friends
made the same pitch.

Steve seemed to take the advice as betrayal. The
world might know he was innocent, but he still required massive reassurance and attention. If Mona
seemed less than totally supportive about his vendetta, he accused her of losing faith. A psychiatrist
confirmed that he was seriously disturbed, suffering
from "severe depressive illness . . . chronic feel-

ings of sadness, depression, loss of interest in the usual activities, insomnia, decreased sexual desire, reduced appetite, periods of tearfulness.'' The doctor warned that an untreated Steve Titus was a candidate for suicide.

In his obsessed state, he began to turn on friends and supporters. He bad-mouthed his defense lawyers in a TV interview and falsely accused Paul Henderson of trying to make a movie deal behind his back. He was out of money and still owed $2,800 in lawyers' fees even after his parents had mortgaged their home and contributed their $9,000 life savings plus the contents of Jacqueline Titus's bottle of coins. Yegen couldn't take him back and he'd gone to work managing fast-food stores—"a glorified Slurpee clerk," as he complained. He had no interest in the new job and often malingered. Mona's income as a waitress at Denny's barely kept them afloat.

By late 1982 he'd fallen further behind in support payments for his son Kenny, and the bad blood with his ex-wife heated up. Mona sobbed as she told a friend, "Steve lies to Phyllis, puts her off. When she comes to get Kenny, the poor kid's crying and Steve's saying, 'Stay here, Kenny!' and Phyllis is saying, 'No, he's coming with me!' It's like a tug of war. Jesus, this is the worst time ever. I think he's lost his mind."

Mona warned Steve that the situation was becoming unbearable. "I don't want to be depressed every time I come home," she told him. "I can't live like this."

"We're gonna be millionaires," he raved. "We'll own the goddamn Port of Seattle."

"Look, Steve," she said, "I was ready for anything when it was a matter of justice. But now it's—it's all money and revenge."

"You don't love me, do you?"

She thought, *That old argument again!* "Oh, Steve," she said, "I *do* love you. But I'm tired of feeling sorry for you. I've got two kids of my own, I really don't need three. You're too heavy to carry on my shoulders anymore, bud."

By November 1982 they'd been together for two years. Driving toward his parents' home for Thanksgiving dinner, Mona squeezed his arm and said, "Let's leave the case alone for one day, okay? Just tell your folks that Mona doesn't want to hear about it today."

They'd hardly entered the house before he was asked how the suit was coming, and an intense conversation began between Steve and his parents. Mona thought, They don't have to hear about this every day. I do. And I've had it.

That night at the apartment she told him that she was leaving in the morning. He didn't seem to take the threat seriously.

At dawn she started packing with her eight-year-old son. Steve asked her to stay, and when she refused, he turned to the boy. "C'mon, son," he said in tears. "You love me, don't you? Stay with me, son. Tell your mom to stay."

"Don't bring my child into this!" Mona snapped. Her voice was raw from crying and lack of sleep. "It isn't fair." Soon all three were crying. "Please," Mona said. "I'm sorry. I just can't stay, ya know? I love you, but I just can't stay." Her stomach ached with loss.

He wouldn't stop bugging her at work, so she quit Denny's and started waiting tables at the Elks. Night after night he shoved his way into the private club and implored her to reconsider. When he wasn't following her around, he was on the phone. He begged family members to intervene. He left a note on her car: "These are the reasons I love you. . . ." followed by thirty pages of reasons. He made his anguish public in a letter. "I lost my job, my faith in the system, my self-respect, my good name, my self-confidence, my trust in the police, and finally the girl I loved most of all," he wrote to *The Seattle Times.* "Is that justice?" He was quoted in the *L.A. Times:* "I lost my fiancée because I spent so much time dwelling on this. And I've changed. I'm not the person she knew." Mona noticed that all his public utterances seemed to center on loss.

After a few more months, he stopped bothering her. She heard that his arms had gone numb, his blood pressure had soared, and he'd taken medical leave from his job. She worried about him as though they were still engaged. The psychiatrist's suicide warning troubled her sleep and her appetite. Every time the phone rang she jumped. She was afraid it would bring her a message she couldn't bear to hear.

110

After four months of rubbing shoulders with studs, queens, jailhouse lawyers, lunatics, psychopaths, and other jailmates, Mac Smith sent word to his Public Defender that he'd come into possession of crucial information about a big murder case. He said he'd heard incriminating statements by a suspected killer named Armstrong while the two men were playing chess.

Deputy Prosecuting Attorney Linda Walton had just come off a string of difficult rape cases, and she told Smith's lawyer that she remembered his quiet client from the sentencing hearing in which she'd labeled him "a clear danger to society." She listened closely as the defense attorney outlined how Smith might be able to assist her and the state.

It was true that she needed help on this particular murder case. Thomas Blake Armstrong III, an unemployed airline ticket agent, had stabbed a fifteen-year-old prostitute to death and pitched her body out his apartment window. His guilt was clear enough, but there was a shortage of admissible evidence that the victim had ever been in his apartment. The trial date was approaching, and the aggressive Walton was afraid that the woman-hater would walk—and probably kill again.

■

Flanked by his attorney and a deputy sheriff, a hand-cuffed Mac Smith was led into a pretrial conference. He was so frail of voice that Walton often had to ask him to repeat. He quoted Armstrong as interrupting their cellblock chess game to tell him, "I fucked up. I shouldn't've wrapped the bitch in my blanket" and "I shouldn't have killed the whore in my apartment." He said Armstrong referred to women as "bitches" or "whores." He said the guy had scared him half to death.

It was exactly the kind of testimony that the state needed. Walton told her boss, Mary Kay Barbieri, "I didn't expect to like Smith. I expected to see somebody that I could easily despise and say, 'God, what an asshole, he deserved what he got.' But there's another aspect to him: his meekness, his humility. I asked him why on earth he was sticking his neck out and he said he just wanted to make up for some of the bad things he'd done in his life. And he said he was so shocked by this murder—he figured if Armstrong went free and killed somebody else, it would be on his conscience for the rest of his life."

Barbieri asked if she'd made any promises. "Hell, no," Walton replied. "He wants to get back into the Sex Offender Program, but I told him there was no way we could help him. I said that we might consider trying to transfer him to an out-of-state prison to protect his life, but that was the most he could expect. He said that was fine with him. He said if he had to spend his whole sentence in protective custody as a snitch, it would be worth it. He just wants to do the right thing."

The two experienced prosecutors had little

choice but to take the sincere young prisoner at his word. "He's gonna be great on the stand," Walton predicted. "The jury'll like him. I feel pity for him myself, and you know, Mary Kay, that's not like me at all."

Back in his cell, Mac Smith liked the odds. The deputy prosecutor had said exactly what she'd had to say for the record, that there was no way she could promise him a return to the Sex Offender Program. But her words weren't set in stone. If he helped her to convict a vicious killer, she might change her mind about the quid pro quo. He knew it had happened before.

On the witness stand, he kept his cool while Armstrong's lawyer tried to smear him as a rapist and snitch. On redirect examination, Walton set about cleaning up his image:

Q. —Mr. Smith, have I promised you anything in terms of reducing your sentence, getting you back to Western State Hospital, getting you into the Oregon State system? Have I promised you anything for your testimony here today?

A. —Absolutely nothing.

Q. —How about my office? Has anybody in my office promised you anything?

A. —Absolutely nothing.

Q. —Has any police agency made any promises to you?

A. —No . . .

Q. —Was it just your decision for you to agree to testify here today, Mr. Smith?

A. —Yes, ma'am . . . I hurt many people and I don't want to see that happen again. I feel it was my responsibility.

The state rested immediately after Smith's testimony, and Walton hurried to Barbieri's office. "He was our star!" she exulted. "You could've heard a pin drop. He almost had tears running down his face. 'I've done so many wrong things in my life. Yes, I've raped women, and I feel terrible about it.' On and on."

It took the jury two and a half hours to find Thomas Blake Armstrong III guilty of second-degree murder.

Three days later, Walton informed Smith's lawyer that the prosecutor's office was grateful to the public-spirited young felon and wanted to do something on his behalf. An official letter went out to Judge Dennis Britt of Snohomish County, the stumbling block to Smith's return to Western State Hospital and the Sex Offender Program. The letter informed the sentencing judge that "the case against Armstrong was entirely circumstantial and Mr. Smith's testimony was vital." It described Smith as "an excellent witness" and added that both Barbieri and Walton "firmly believe Mr. Smith is amenable to treatment in the program and deserves the opportunity to get that treatment. We urge you to reconsider

Mr. Smith's prison sentence in light of all the factors."

On May 12, 1983, Judge Britt took the rare step of suspending Smith's sixty-year sentence and relinquishing jurisdiction to King County "in an effort to insure consistent rulings in any subsequent proceeding." Three weeks later Smith was back in the hospital program.

111

The prodigal patient's first inclination was to continue with the cooperative approach he'd employed in his earlier stay in the mental hospital, getting along by going along, his modus vivendi. He decided to do everything that the staff asked of him—and more. He would gain the therapists' respect and sympathy, enlist them in his cause, and graduate with honors in the minimum time of three years. A new McDonald J. Smith would burst upon the world. He knew he'd broken similar promises to himself in the past, but this time he was getting professional help.

At the outset, he was warned by other patients that the personnel of the Sex Offender Program were highly resistant to scams. A psychotherapist advised him to abandon deceptions and lies, including the ones he'd told himself. But when he was asked how many rapes he'd committed, he automatically lied again. "Twenty," he said.

The therapist frowned. "Things in your past are like parking tickets," he advised. "If you put them in a glove box, they'll end up costing you a lot. If you pay right away, they don't cost as much."

The remark was unnerving. In a locked side room, a polygraph machine functioned as the program's enforcer. Smith knew that if he was caught lying about the magnitude of his offenses, he could find himself headed back toward the hell on earth known as Walla Walla—"The Walls." He took a staffer aside and confided that he'd underestimated his rapes.

"By how much?" he asked.

He said he would need a few days to reconstruct an accurate figure. He took pencil and paper and dug into his memory, listing every place he'd lived, every car he'd owned, every job, every friend, every triumph, every setback, every significant happening since his twentieth birthday, and then tried to recall the rapes associated with each. The job took three days. His final estimate was fifty to fifty-five.

The lie detector confirmed that he was telling the truth, a positive reaction that was noted in his record. But when he glibly suggested that he'd learned his lesson and no longer felt the urge to rape, he was rigged up to a penile plethysmograph, a delicate instrument that measured penis circumference with a loop-sensor while the patient watched slides depicting various types of sexual activity. According to the assessor's report, the patient showed "considerable arousal to violent sexual scenarios."

Mac was still a rapist at heart.

the church, *saved,* and neither she nor the Lord intended to surrender him to Satan.

Mother and daughter arrived in Tacoma on a cloudy August day. They were nervous and apprehensive, and the sight of the drab old mental institution made them feel worse. Escape-proof windows made the place look like a collection of aboveground dungeons. The low-slung red-brick buildings were spotted with moss, linked by cracked and pitted roadways, and surrounded by broad, open lawns where human husks sat in deep communion with themselves, staring at their feet. Here and there a platoon of patients trudged along at the urging of an attendant. Maria found herself searching for Mac and hoping she didn't spot him with the crazies.

The visitors were directed to a locked ward in a building that looked like a setting from *Oliver Twist.* To their consternation, they were forbidden to see Mac until they'd submitted to broad-range interviews with a psychologist who asked such questions as "Did you ever have sexual relations with the patient?" and "What is your own sexual orientation? Heterosexual? Homosexual? Other? Please explain."

Dove emerged from her session complaining that no one should be subjected to such an inquisition, and especially not church people. Maria took the process in stride. She'd never done anything with Mac that she was ashamed of, and her sexual orientation was straight. She was sure that the same was true of her mother. But the interrogation process seem a little heavy, especially considering that they were here to visit a man who didn't belong in a

dump like this in the first place. Maria thought,
These nosy hospital people should have seen Mac in
the days when he was selling papers and shining
shoes to put food on the table, back when he always
had time for me or anyone else who needed him.
Don't these people know they're persecuting a
saint?

A staff member showed the visitors around the ward
and described some of the equipment. "Mac's
changing already," he confided. "He's one of our
most promising patients. You two can help him do
even better. Convince him that it's crucial that he
tell us everything he ever did wrong, whether he was
caught or not. That's an important step in his treatment."

As mother and daughter recalled the conversation later, the staffer added, "Any incriminating information will never be shared with the criminal justice system. If our records are subpoenaed, we'll just
say they're lost. In fact, we had a case like that a
couple years ago. We just told the judge we'd mis-
placed our files."

At last they were hugging Mac. To Maria, he seemed
changed, run-down, a little distant. His shoulder
blades showed through his T-shirt. She thought,
What are they doing to him here? "Mac," she whispered, "are you being—?"

"—Treated fine," he said, patting her hand.
They'd always understood each other's fragments.

As the three Smiths arranged themselves
around a wooden table, Maria flashed on her
brother's real problem. It was simply that he was

here, in this sicko-creepo place, surrounded by perverts and leering doctors and obscene machines that measured erections and other icky things. He was in a snake pit, being treated for an illness he didn't have, classified as something he wasn't now and never had been. Who *wouldn't* look upset?

"There's something I have to tell you," he said in a voice even softer than usual. "I'm, I'm—"

Maria squinted across the table at her brother. What were the words that he couldn't get out? He stared into his clenched hands and his face was twisted.

"I'm a sexual, uh—psychopath," he said.

Maria was confused and asked him to repeat. At first she was sure he'd been ordered to make this fake confession. It was part of the drill, part of the game he had to play to qualify for his stay in the Gulag. She waited for him to wink, or nod toward a microphone concealed behind the drapes.

But when tears came to his eyes, she realized that he'd spoken the truth. She felt dizzy, disoriented; her polar star had flickered out. She couldn't remember the last time she'd seen her brother cry. Then Dove joined in. Maria wished they would stop. She didn't want to be committed to this nut farm herself.

"Oh, Mac," Maria said, "why didn't you ever tell me?"

"You always saw me through rose-colored glasses, Maria." He wiped his nose with a handkerchief. "I couldn't bear to change that."

He seemed more comfortable talking about the program. Maria thought, He's really into this deal. "It's mostly group therapy," he explained. "Thirty, forty hours a week. There's hardly any individual treatment." He described some of the techniques used to decrease deviant arousal. "They'll show you a movie of a rape scene, and just at the hottest part they'll pop an ammonia vial under your nose. Or some other terrible smell. They use covert sensitization, aversion themes—"

Dove said she didn't understand, and Mac told her he wasn't surprised; he didn't understand all of the techniques himself. "Basically it's a self-help program," he tried to explain. "They provide the guidance and the tools, but you have to want it, you have to go after it, and you have to work for it." His eyes narrowed. "And I want it. *I'm not going back to prison.*" Maria had never heard him sound so determined.

On the return to Los Angeles, mother and daughter tried to put the best face on the situation. "People can be healed," Maria said. "Mac's bright."

"He's trying," Dove said. "I know my son. With God's help, he'll have his victory over this."

113

Mona Jean Imholt decided to stop trying to anticipate the future and take things as they came. A year
ago she'd been convinced that Steve Titus was gone
from her life forever. She'd also thought that he was
going to choke on his own bile and wind up on a
slab. Now, to her great joy, she was finding that
she'd been wrong on both counts.

It was January 1983, fourteen months since
she'd packed up and left their apartment. He was
living with another woman and Mona was seeing another man. She bumped into Steve at depositions
for his lawsuit and agreed to join him for a drink.
The former lovers talked away the afternoon. Mona
was alternately baffled and delighted by the new
Steve. Or was it the old Steve? It was as if they'd
never parted, as if Ronald Parker had never blighted
their lives, as if Steve had worked through his ha-
treds and angers and reverted to the wild and crazy
guy she'd known. He joked, laughed, flashed his
dazzling smile, and reached across the table to take
her hand as though there'd never been a break in
their relationship. She wondered, Is this real? Is he
just a little too happy? Is this a big act to get me
back?

He filled her in on the progress of his lawsuit,

said his lawyers were finding solid evidence of a frame-up, and he was sure to end up a wealthy man. Among other things, he claimed that the Port police had rewritten reports and forged log entries to create the impression that his license number or a number close to it had been spotted during the rape instead of six hours later. "They arrested me and then they made the evidence fit," Steve told her.

"We always knew that," Mona said.

"Yeah, but we couldn't always prove it."

She was happy that he didn't belabor the subject. The old note of desperation was gone from his voice. He spoke with the assurance of someone who was solidly in the right and would have no trouble making his case in court. She thought, *What an improvement. He sounds so relaxed, so sure.*

"Somebody's going to jail," he said just before they parted, "and this time it won't be me."

They met again the next week, went to dinner, danced "The Titus," drank margaritas, and made love at her place till 5:00 A.M. It was almost like the old days in the Comstock Apartments, except that tonight he seemed a bit tougher and coarse; she supposed it was inevitable after what he'd been through. He made a point of telling her that he'd decided to do whatever he damned well pleased from now on. He was living with a beautiful woman, but if he felt like leaving, he would leave. No one would ever shove him around again; he would run his own life and the rest of the world could go to hell. Except Mona, of course. He still loved her, he said, and always would. He rambled on and on, talking fast in his chirpy little-boy's voice, his face flushed. There was a time or two when she wondered if he was faking it, when his exuberance seemed overstated, but she wasn't a student of human behavior and she didn't believe in analyzing miracles. Steve was the man she loved, the only man she could ever think of marrying. Some things weren't a matter of choice.

A few nights later she waited for him at Chichi's restaurant in Tacoma. She'd worked there and knew the staff, and she couldn't contain her excitement as she sipped coffee at the bar. Every time one of her friends walked by, she said, "Hey, I'm meeting Steve tonight!" She saw her happiness reflected in their eyes.

At 7:20, when he was twenty minutes late, the phone rang. He told her he was sick and couldn't make it. His voice sounded scratchy and weak, his words slurred. Mona felt angry. Had it all been lies? Was he committed to someone else after all? She was annoyed that he hadn't called earlier. Now everybody in the place knew she'd been stood up.

"What's the matter?" she asked him sarcastically. "Are you gonna run home to your girlfriend?"

"We'll make up for it next week," he mumbled.

She'd barely put the phone down when she wanted to call him back. But . . . where was he?

She thought, Everybody has off nights. Why was I so hard on him? She wished she could stop reverting to "Mean Mona Jean." She didn't feel mean at all. Just lost.

114

Paul Henderson was in the middle of a dream about his grandfather's store in Nebraska when Kitty, the *Times*'s veteran telephone operator, called with an early-morning message. Steve Titus had been rushed to the hospital with a massive heart attack.

Henderson could almost feel the pain. It made no difference that they'd had a brief falling-out. He'd always felt that Steve was entitled to act paranoid and bitter and a little unreasonable. Anyway, their misunderstanding had been cleared up and they were friends again.

He drove the army staff car to Valley General Hospital in Renton, yawing and slipping in a fresh snowfall that had caught the city by surprise and snarled traffic. He found the Titus family huddled in the reception room.

"Pray for him, Paul," Jacqueline Titus begged. Mother and father looked as though they'd been up all night.

He tiptoed into the private room. Steve was hooked up to tubes and wires. His eyes were shut and his face was pallid and contorted. His bony chest rose and fell to the hiss of a device that resembled a concertina. Henderson reached across the bed and picked up his friend's hand. Thank God, he thought, it's warm.

"Come on, Steve," he said, squeezing hard. "You can do it. Wake up! Fight it, man. *Wake up!* I'm pulling for you, Steve. . . ."

He stopped to poke away the tears. How unfair, he thought. How goddamn fucking unfair! The poor guy was only a few weeks away from winning his lawsuit, from total exoneration, exactly what he needed.

He left the room and exchanged reassurances with the family. Jackie's fingertips ran down the page of a Bible. She looked up and said in her French accent, "He's not going to die."

David Titus's arm circled his wife's thin shoulders. "The Lord'll help him whip it," the father said. "He'll be just fine."

Henderson assured them that they were right; of *course* they were right. But Steve had looked braindead to him.

115

Mona Jean Imholt was leaving for her nighttime job when a friend phoned and told her to turn on the five o'clock news. She heard the telecaster mention Steve's name, then some words to the effect that his $20 million lawsuit against the Port of Seattle was scheduled to go to trial in three weeks. Mona said to herself, *So what? Is that* news? Then the announcer reported that Steve had had a heart attack and was in a deep coma. *Oh, my God,* she admonished herself. *It's my fault.*

She phoned the KING–TV newsroom and learned that he was in Valley General Hospital. A girlfriend drove her to Renton. She felt like an intruder, but she'd read that comatose patients could hear voices, and she was convinced that Steve would wake up at her command.

"Mona!" Jacqueline Titus said with a wan smile. "I'm so glad you came."

David Titus was there, too, and so was Steve's live-in girlfriend. Everyone was nice except the doctor. When Mona announced that she was going into Steve's room, he said, "I don't want *anybody* in there right now."

Mona and her girlfriend waited in the lobby. By

midnight Steve was still unconscious, and they drove home.

Eight days later, her favorite soap opera was interrupted for a news flash. Steve was dead.

Someone misinformed her about the time of the funeral, and she arrived at the cemetery on the Sea-Tac Strip thirty minutes late. She almost fell as she stumbled across the mushy lawn in her high heels. She was crying; she'd cried all the way up from Tacoma. Her friend Joyce Martin had done the driving. Mona would never have made it on her own.

She came in sight of a group of people in dark suits and black dresses, standing around a flower-covered casket on uprights. *Oh, my God,* she thought, *is that Steve? No no no no no no NO! It can't be. . . .*

Jet planes drowned out the noises from the Strip. She recognized a friend, hurrying toward the exit. She wondered why it made her feel worse that a tough guy like Henderson was crying. The first time she'd laid eyes on him he'd demanded a beer and warned Steve not to give him any bullshit, and she'd thought, My God, is this the guy the paper sent to save us?

"Is Steve there?" she asked. "Is that . . . his grave?"

"Yeah, Mona," he said. He hugged her hard. "Steve's right over there."

He scribbled something on a piece of paper and continued toward the parking lot. The other mourners began to leave. David Titus pulled a flower off the casket and handed it to her. She'd never seen the old sergeant act so gentle, so soft. She thought, Death sure mellows people out.

Steve's new girlfriend came up and shook hands. "I'm really glad you came," she said. "Steve would have wanted you here." She said that some of Mona's things were still at the apartment and she could come over and pick them up, but Mona knew that she wouldn't.

After a while, she was alone with Steve and the gravediggers. It took a long time to put him into the ground and cover him up.

"Hey!" she yelled when a shovel clanked against the casket. "Watch it!" She felt like Mean Mona Jean again. The men smoothed out the dirt and left.

She slid to her knees on the wet grass, squeezing her face with her hands. "I'm sorry," she said. "I love you, Steve. I love you. . . ." She repeated the words till it turned dark and she had to go to her job tending bar.

116

With Titus in his grave, his lawsuit ground ahead on behalf of his son and heir, Ken, now fifteen years old and in the custody of his mother. It wasn't long before word floated up from the street that Titus had sought the solace of cocaine in the last few months of his life, buying grams of the white powder and cutting it himself, a dangerous practice. The news was a problem for his lawyers. Coke was known to decrease blood flow to the heart, and the other side could argue in court that the drug had caused his mental and physical problems, reducing the Port's responsibility. It would be a messy situation at best.

So the $20 million lawsuit was quickly settled for less. The Port's insurance carrier agreed to buy $875,000 in annuities for young Kenny, the proceeds from which would pay the boy and his lawyers some $2.6 million over twenty years. As another part of the agreement, the Port's executive director James Dwyer issued a public statement to the Titus family:

"I realize that no apology can atone for the events surrounding the arrest and conviction of Steve Titus. Nevertheless on behalf of the Port of Seattle, I hope that my apology can lessen the bitterness. I am truly sorry for the hurt caused Steve, each of you and everyone else who loved and cared for Steve. It deeply concerns me that an agency I now direct may have contributed to the sadness you now experience. Please understand that I too have that sadness. We shall make every effort to insure that similar events never happen again. My prayers are with you.''

No gracious response emanated from the home of David and Jacqueline Titus. Their life savings had gone to lawyers and private detectives. They'd remortgaged their home and were reduced to living off Jackie's income as a waitress and David's disability pension. They faced a difficult old age.

Visitors to Steve's grave were obliged to lean over to read the words engraved on the remembrance provided by his parents. The small bronze plate was set flush to the ground:

Our beloved son Steve G. Titus
1949   1985

He fought for his day in court
He was used, deceived, betrayed,
And denied justice even in death

117

As for Mac Smith, he was well on his way to completing the Sex Offender Program and returning to his family—or so everyone thought. He'd never stopped trying to impress the staff. If Western State Hospital had been an institution of higher learning, he would have made Phi Beta Kappa. He obeyed every rule, caused no disciplinary problems, made personal friends and advocates of the staffers. When there was a job to be done, he jumped in without being asked. The surest way to make the floor gleam was to hand him a mop. The smoothest way to run a group therapy session was to invite him in.

By the fall of 1985, his folder bulged with commendations and recommendations, from top ratings in important tests and examinations to everyday comments about his attitude and work habits: "Good involvement . . . Did some cleaning work. Functioned appropriately, interacted and was responsible . . . Job well done . . . Put forth much effort . . . Was very helpful, enthused and produced well . . . steady and conscientious . . . cleaned stairwells very well . . . Such a wonderful job! . . ."

Not only had the patient completed his treatment in less than the three required years, but he'd proved to be a leader with bright, innovative ideas. Using his own variation of the desensitization techniques, he claimed to have reduced his arousal to rape scenarios from 100 percent to 12 percent and increased his arousal to normal sex to a flat 100 percent. His prognosis was so favorable that his estranged wife Nan scurried back from exile on the East Coast to rejoin her man in couples' counseling sessions and plan for his release. Just as he'd always promised, there was a new Mac Smith in the world.

Or was there? Some of the administrators weren't so sure. Experience had made them professionally cynical about their patients and taught them to err on the side of caution. Behavioral modification techniques sometimes worked—the world was full of recovered claustrophobes, agoraphobes, acrophobes, drug addicts, alcoholics. But sexual deviation was rooted in earliest childhood, and offenders were resistant to change.

The program's own success record, insofar as it could be determined from graduates who sometimes reported inaccurately or not at all, was considered sufficient to justify the cost to the taxpayer. In some twenty years of operation, one out of five graduates had reoffended, whereas the recidivism rate of nontreated sex offenders ran at 45 to 50 percent. And the balance sheet would have looked even more impressive if judges hadn't made a habit of dumping hard-core sociopaths into the program against the wishes of the staff. By definition, such men were untreatable, and they severely disrupted the agenda before they could be weeded out.

So the program had worked, but not perfectly.

Unfortunately, its failures were dramatic and sometimes bloody and often made major news. Three patients escaped in a single week and committed various outrages. A wispy James Earl Ruzicka walked
away, strangled a seventeen-year-old girl and hanged
a fourteen-year-old girl, then went on a rape orgy
before he was recaptured. A patient who doubled as
a group therapy leader managed to commit several
rapes in the ten minutes allotted each morning to
travel to his job on work release. Another former
leader was arrested for a series of vicious rapes just
about the time local viewers were watching a TV special describing him as one of the program's most
successful graduates. Another escaped and was arrested in New Orleans for multiple bank robberies.
The place had always been a sieve.

Smack in the middle of Mac Smith's course of
treatment, more attention was focused on Western
State Hospital by another bizarre case. For two years,
women in the East Hills section of Kent had awak-
ened to find an intruder leaning over them with a
knife. While his time-delay camera whirred away on
its tripod, he raped the women and stole their
money and jewels. A few of the victims reported that
he hurried off at the sound of a beeper.

The "East Hills Rapist" proved to be Douglas L.
Jeffery, a 1975 graduate of the program who'd
served as an example of how the most heinous offenders could be rehabilitated. Jeffery's beeper had
kept him in touch with the nearby hotel that he
managed. He was sentenced to three consecutive
life terms, but not before the press and public had
reacted with anger. "This case and others have
raised new questions about whether the state should

be in the sex treatment business at all," the *Seattle Post-Intelligencer* editorialized. King County Deputy Prosecuting Attorney Rebecca Roe, later to be depicted on the cover of a national magazine as one of America's toughest prosecutors, was quoted as saying, "I don't think violent sex offenders are treatable," and "Western never should have made the statement that Jeffery was safe to be at large."

Local editors followed with a spate of scare headlines: "Dangerous transient back at Western State." "Dangerous mental patient flees." "Dangerous patient is on the lam. . . ." Dangerous patients had always walked away from Western State; it had been funded and built as a hospital, not a prison, but the media acted as though the phenomenon was new and blamed poor management. No one bothered to point out that the administrators had complained for years that the place was overloaded—two hundred patients in space intended for half as many, and another hundred waiting their turn in jails and holding tanks. And not all of them amenable to therapy.

A few Washington state legislators commenced the death of a thousand cuts. By late 1985, when the model patient McDonald J. Smith became eligible for work release, the Sex Offender Program was barely functioning. From a public relations standpoint, it was the worst possible time to unleash another uncured psychopath on the community. No one on the staff intended to make that mistake.

118

"We'd wondered about Smith from the beginning," Program Director Maureen Saylor explained later. "He was just too damned good to be true."

Saylor, a handsome woman with short blond hair, was a registered nurse and holder of a master's degree in psychology. She was known as a plain-spoken, reasonable administrator and a favorite with the press because of her simple, direct, jargon-free speech. She'd helped to treat sex offenders for ten years and had no illusions. "Every one of us can be fooled," she said. "Anybody in this business who says he can't be fooled will be fooled most of all. There are sex offenders who routinely fool therapists *and* machines, including the lie detector."

The first alarms about Mac Smith had gone off when he'd admitted under pressure that he'd committed some fifty-five rapes, not the eight on his rap sheet or the twenty that he'd acknowledged on first entering the program. "If we'd known about those fifty-five rapes before we admitted him," Saylor explained, "we probably would have left him in Walla Walla. That's a hell of a lot of rapes, a lot of *habituation* to rape.

"His first therapist was high on Smith, so we decided to make the best of the situation and watch the guy closely. And I must admit he was impressive. He presented well and he acted conscience stricken, eager to make up for what he'd done. He sounded sincere when he said he wanted to change his behavior. He was Mr. Nice Guy.''

According to Saylor, that was exactly the trouble. After seven or eight months on the ward, he'd been flagged for "inappropriate flat affect" by one of the staffers. Saylor had agreed with the diagnosis. "He was *too* damned nice," she explained. "He said the right things, never acted out, never warranted major intervention. He had too good a facade, too much control. It didn't mesh with his background. You ask yourself, Where the hell is the hostility, the rage and frustration that he exhibited on the outside? What happened to it? He hasn't done jack squat in here!

"Some of us got nervous and took a closer look at his background. His rapes had been violent and dangerous. He'd come from an antisocial background—drug and alcohol abuse, family dysfunction, friction, frustration, rage. He seemed to lack inner controls. Of course, that's not easy to gauge. On a locked ward, he didn't need controls. But we wondered what he would be like on the outside.

"I began to take a personal interest in him, even though I wasn't his therapist. The first thing you noticed, if you looked at him in the right light, was that he tried to affect the Jesus look—brown hair halfway to his shoulders, beard, moustache. The soft voice, the humility. But it was important to him to be seen. An expert in sexual psychology once said he found it easy to spot the sociopaths on any ward; they ran up and greeted him at the door. Smith always made a point of being acknowledged. He wanted you to know what he was doing, what he'd accomplished, how remorseful he felt. If a sociopath is being a good boy, he has to be recognized for it, or he has no other reason to be a good boy. Whereas the nonsociopaths, the people we can help with this program, tend to be more laid-back. They can't be bothered impressing others. They just want to be left alone to work on their problems.

"So we felt dubious about Smith from day one. There was something icy about him. He tried to show real emotions, real shame and guilt and remorse, but he seemed to be going through the motions. He'd studied normal behavior and learned how to simulate it. But he definitely wasn't normal.

"We came close to bouncing him several times before he came up for work release. But somebody on the staff would always make the point that we'd invested two or three years in him, we've come this far, and he's no trouble at all—he's really jumped through the hoop. So what the hell—let him stay a while."

After Smith scored high in a course on anger management, one of the final requirements of the program, the administrators were obliged to put him on supervised work release or recommend that the court return him to prison. The staff leaned toward prison and called in psychologist Irwin S. Dreiblatt for a second opinion. Dreiblatt was known for his skill in interpreting abstract personality tests. As Maureen Saylor put it later, "Irv Dreiblatt's a hard guy to fool."

119

In sessions a week apart in early December 1985 the psychologist ran Smith through the Minnesota Multiphasic Personality Inventory, Rorschach Ink-blot Technique, Rotter Sentence Completion Blank, and Draw-a-Person. He studied the star pupil's thick file folder and consulted with some of his therapists at Western State.

"I found Mr. Smith to be an intelligent and articulate man," Dreiblatt reported back, "who spoke impassively through our two interviews. On occasion a hint of depressed affect was evident. He seemed to fully understand the purpose of the evaluation and the manner in which the findings would be utilized."

Dreiblatt noted that the model patient hadn't stopped fantasizing rape, even going so far as to select targets among hospital personnel and to plan the locale. "Although he claims that such ideation occurred five or six months ago," the psychologist noted, "he reports one such fantasy during the week of this evaluation. Mac also has thought about escape, and had such a passing temptation the same week."

The patient's test responses, Dreiblatt continued, "show superficiality, simplistic thinking, and an avoidance of many of the serious problems he experiences. There is remarkably little subjective discomfort and little evidence of insight. This man's overall test protocol reflects an individual with a serious personality disturbance . . . immature, irresponsible, and quite self-centered." Smith's coping skills were limited, his behavior under stress "poor." He tended to view the world around him as adversarial and dangerous. "He sees people in fairly primitive ways and has little empathy or understanding. . . . Aggression is imbedded in his view of human relationships."

Dreiblatt found disquieting discrepancies between Smith's spoken words and feelings. He quoted the patient as having thought about killing some of his victims in the months before his final arrest. "In my judgment," the psychologist reported, "it is quite likely that he could have begun to kill victims to reduce the risk of disclosure."

Dreiblatt found no signs of the behavioral changes that three successful years in the program were supposed to engender. "Since his arrest in 1981, Mac has continued in a very calculating, self-serving route. . . . There can be no question that intellectually he has mastered the concepts taught at the Sex Offender Program. Yet, when discussing his past offending, there is a profound lack of affect and very little felt empathy about the remarkable trail of victims he has left. . . . Psychological testing reflects a personality structure substantially unchanged and prone to aggressive acting out. . . .

"In summary, Mr. Smith constitutes a serious risk to reoffend if at large. In my judgment, the compulsiveness of his past offending, his almost total (adult) life commitment to rape, the strongly violent direction of his behavior, and his calculating, psychopathic personality style all underscore risk. . . ."

The consultant hinted that the best course would be to lock Smith up for life. At the least, he concluded, the patient should be observed under controlled conditions for another year before work release was even considered.

120

On February 14, 1986, officials of the Sex Offender Program acted on Dreiblatt's advice. They advised King County Superior Court Judge Gerard Shellan that "there is nothing more we can offer Mr. Smith" and it was "pointless to retain him any further." They recommended that Shellan, the original sentencing judge, order him incarcerated "for the maximum time allowed which would provide immediate protection for the community from further victimization." The final diagnosis was "paraphilia, atypical rape, alcohol and drug abuse disorder, and antisocial personality."

It fell to the blunt Maureen Saylor to call "the nice guy" into her office and break the bad news. A year or two earlier, his expressionless reaction might have surprised her, but now she found it predictable. "His initial response was nonresponse," she reported. "Of course he didn't break down and he didn't get furious; that would have been normal. He just sat there and showed his famous self-control."

But that night at a group therapy session, Smith inveighed against the administrators and suggested to his fellow patients that the program was "using me as a scapegoat." He said, "I did everything they asked. Everything! This isn't fair. I don't understand this.''

His aggressive change of mood inflamed the other patients, and for a few hours the late-night staffers had a minor revolt on their hands. Mac had always been a role model on the ward.

The next morning Maureen Saylor reacted angrily. "That's the whole goddamn trouble with these anti-social personalities," she fumed at a staff meeting. "They bend the others around their little fingers. Every single sociopath we've ever kicked out of here, we've had to pick up the pieces with his group. That's their main talent—making trouble."

Saylor and her colleagues assembled Smith's ac-olytes and tried to calm their fears. Ever since his blowup, they'd been demanding to know if it was true that they would be sent to prison no matter how much progress they'd made.

"The first thing you have to understand," Saylor announced, "is that Mac Smith is the excep-tion, not the rule." She outlined some of his prob-lems and explained that there'd been misgivings about him from the beginning. "As group mem-bers, you people don't have to take the responsibil-ity for Mr. Smith's actions," the psychotherapist concluded, "but—I do!"

Smith's final court appearance was pending, and Saylor ordered a close watch on him, not only against the possibility of escape but to minimize fur-ther damage to ward morale. "We needn't have bothered," she noted later. "He got himself to-gether and *kept* himself together. You could just see things click into place. He proceeded to do exactly what he needed to do to accomplish his goal of not going to prison.''

In March of 1986 Smith was formally discharged from the program and returned to King County Jail. His next destination would be up to the judge.

121

Maria and Mac agreed that he needed to counter the Dreiblatt report with a hired gun of his own. But who? He asked her to sound out a psychotherapist named Michael Comte. He said that Comte might be prejudiced in his favor since he'd once worked as assistant director of the Sex Offender Program and had observed Mac's struggle to change his ways.

From L.A., Maria phoned the therapist for a preliminary discussion. After they settled on a fee, she explained that she wanted the whole truth about her brother and nothing but. If he was cured, as Mac claimed and Maria firmly believed, she would expect the therapist to testify on his behalf. "And if he's still sick," she told the voice on the phone, "I want to know that, too. I love Mac more than anybody in the world, but if he's gonna reoffend, I'd rather he went to prison."

Comte said he wouldn't take the case under any other conditions.

122

The staff of Comte's and Associates, as the private clinic was called, administered the usual tests, including the MMPI, Hooper Visual Organization Test, Shipley Institute of Living Scale Vocabulary and Abstraction Test, and the Curtis Sentence Completion Test. Michael Comte interviewed the prisoner. His final report, filed in the court records alongside Dreiblatt's, placed slightly more emphasis on the stresses of Smith's childhood but otherwise paralleled the other psychologist's conclusions. Wrote Comte:

The origins of Mr. Smith's character pathology existed in his early developmental years and were reinforced by his early entry into sexual behavior. As he developed, he became increasingly sexually preoccupied, and themes of dominance and control became increasingly important and he began to center his life on the need to control others, probably because he experienced so little self-control. . . . He targeted women for discharging his anger from a young age and the pattern escalated unabated until his arrest. Psychologically, he evolved the sociopathic personality and he demonstrated his capacity to act without regard to the rights of other human beings. His pattern was sexually aggressive, violent, and predatory.

In a lengthy cellblock interview, Smith denied to his hired expert that he'd ever considered murder; Comte ordered a lie detector test on the subject and the operator reported that Smith showed no deception.

The psychotherapist quoted Smith about his rapes:

I told myself I really wasn't hurting anybody and if they fought back I would leave them alone. If they didn't want to be raped, they would fight back. With a prostitute, I told myself I was just taking their time. With hitchhikers, I told myself they wanted to be raped.

In his report Comte noted, "These cognitive distortions are typical of a rapist's thinking. However, many of Mr. Smith's victims were not prostitutes. It is apparent many of the victims never reported and Mr. Smith has made a case against himself in regard to his dangerousness, potential to reoffend, and his unamenability to treatment by his disclosures."

Comte described Smith as:

. . . a sociopathic personality with an excessive need for excitement and stimulation, and he obviously requires immediate gratification of his needs. He is concerned with short-term gratification and not the long-term consequences of his behavior. He was moderately defensive throughout the testing. . . . He attempted to present his new "image" and he indicated he was in no particular distress and had adequate ego defenses at the time of testing. His profile was surprisingly asymptomatic. There was no depression, anxiety, distress, or gross disorganization in his profile. . . . He indicated that he enjoyed being looked up to and respected. He appears to have some leadership potential. In the short run, he can conform to general accepted principles of moral conduct and can accept responsibility. Others are likely drawn to him because of his charm, his absence of anxiety, and the intensity with which he talks about his interests and commitments. Mr. Smith is definitely glib and projects himself as a warm and sincere person.

Comte attached a supplemental analysis of the patient by one of his staffers, Dr. Walter G. Peterson, who'd also been involved in the psychological testing:

He is basically a shallow, self-serving, narcissistic personality with preference for immediate need gratification and he has limited impulse control and is mostly concerned with external consequences of his behavior. He is excitement seeking and likely to choose friends and activities to meet this need. His judgment is poor. He makes a good first impression, but long-term contact reveals his immaturity, self-centeredness, demandingness, and irresponsibility. He is not above blatant power manipulations and his need for control in interpersonal relationships is excessive. He cannot empathize with others' needs and he easily excuses antisocial behavior and uses his good intellectual skills to rationalize his behavior. His behavior is controlled by external consequences and he is highly resistant to being told what to do and cannot be trusted to follow through with what is in his best interests.

. . . Mr. Smith's social relationships are probably poor and he tends to be exploitive, highly manipulative, and insensitive to slights to his personality. He has a limited ability to cope with rejection. He is a highly imaginative individual with an active fantasy life, which is likely centered on interpersonal success, power, and sexual competence. Insight and empathy is poor. There is a suggestion social censure can play a role in his self-control, and his ability to talk about sexual deviance is an important step to him. However, characterologically, he may not be able to put into practice his newfound insights and under stress he is likely to revert to his pattern of alcohol abuse and sexual misconduct. He is likely unable to evaluate his own stress level well.

To which Comte added:

Consistent with other convicted rapists, Mr. Smith is a sociopathic personality with the usual characteristics of impulsiveness, sexualized aggression, impaired conscience, and his history provides ample evidence of his self-centeredness, lack of insight, and disrespect for societal rules and personal boundaries. Dominance, control, and subjugation and humiliation of his victims along with sexual gratification motivated his predatory raping behavior, and two earlier confrontations with law enforcement failed to impact this pattern. There is no question he has left a trail of traumatized victims who for the rest of their lives will live with the consequences of his behavior.

As a practical matter, Comte urged the court to take note that eventually Smith would be freed one way or another. To minimize the "significant risk to the public," the sex therapist suggested that the court consider an alternative sentencing plan based on a closely supervised two-year work release program featuring frequent polygraph, plethysmograph and Breathalyzer tests, plus "intensive probation supervision for the foreseeable future." Like his fellow therapist Dreiblatt, Comte suggested that "Mr. Smith's history presents a good argument for a lifetime of supervision. . . . It would be ideal to have someone assigned to him for the remainder of his life. . . ."

But the psychotherapist also touched on "moral and ethical questions that are rather obvious." Smith, he said, had completed in-patient requirements of the program and had earned the right to be considered for work release. He'd been "operating in good faith" and "polygraph examinations suggest he was disclosing." His attitude and demeanor indicated "some sincerity in his desire to alter his deviant thinking and behavior."

To Mac and Maria, their hired gun seemed to be suggesting that his client had played by the rules and deserved a break. They only wished he would come right out and say so.

123

Reading and rereading the carefully worded reports and prognoses, Maureen Saylor and her colleagues were anything but sure they'd seen the last of Mac Smith's Jesus-like countenance. Intelligent sociopaths who "presented well" often wound up warehoused on the Sex Offenders ward despite staff protestations that they belonged in prison. The program was already in disrepute, and the courts seemed to take pride in routinely overruling the recommendations of its staff. Part of the judicial reasoning seemed to be that one institutional bed was as good as another, and prison populations were at their limits (there was so much overcrowding that a federal judge had ruled that incarceration in a Washington penitentiary constituted "cruel and unusual punishment").

Saylor could just imagine Mac Smith dropping in on a group therapy session, making his usual sly statements in hushed tones, calling the therapists "ma'am" and "sir," and undermining everyone's best efforts. As one who'd beaten the system, he would have more influence than ever.

Saylor reminded herself that there would be one small plus in Smith's return to the ward: He wouldn't be out raping real estate saleswomen and hitchhikers and innocent kids. It was small consolation. She hoped against hope for a sensible ruling.

124

The day before the probation hearing, Smith's latest Public Defender weighed in with an eloquent document entitled "Defendant's Probation Report." Attorney Scott A. Reiman blasted the Dreiblatt conclusions as exaggerated and inaccurate, "a totally unsatisfactory basis for a conclusion that Mac should be denied the opportunity for which he has worked since June 2, 1982." The young lawyer zeroed in on Dreiblatt's claim that Smith had started to escalate toward murder before his arrest.

"The impression left by this statement," he wrote, "is that McDonald Smith on multiple occasions or in a consistent and logical progression began to make plans towards the homicide of intended victims of sexual assault."

In fact, Reiman admitted, his client "did consider homicide," but "this was not with respect to any particular person or any specifically intended crime. His brief consideration of that possibility caused him to become physically ill. He never carried out such a thought, nor did he ever consider it again."

Then the defense lawyer turned to some of Michael Comte's "moral and ethical questions":

. . . This court offered Mac an opportunity
to rehabilitate himself through the Sexual Psychopathy Program at Western State Hospital.
It did this in full knowledge of the seriousness
of the incidents in which Mac was involved.
And, even though an exact number of incidents may not have been known, the court certainly was aware that Mac was a serious multiple offender whose behavior was out of control
at the time of his arrest. Mac has been subjected to consistent and extensive testing
through psychological, polygraph, and plethysmograph means. He has advanced step by step
through the phase of in-patient treatment at
Western State Hospital. Now, on the verge of
earning a limited and extremely restricted opportunity to begin his reentry into society, the
state seeks to commit Mac to prison as if he
had never been in the program at all.

"If anyone has ever earned the right to reenter
society based on institutional performance," Reiman observed, "Mac is that person."

The Defender asked Judge Shellan to view
Smith's successes in the program as "a predicter of
his future behavior" and summed up: "Mac has not
failed the correctional system. If his probation is revoked, the correctional system will have failed Mac."

Another powerful statement in the prisoner's behalf
arrived in the form of an affidavit from Linda Walton. She reminded the judge of Smith's cooperation

125

The cavernous courtroom was nearly empty at the unusually early starting time of 8:40 A.M. on April 17, 1986, when Judge Gerard M. Shellan opened the proceedings. Steve Titus had been dead for fourteen months and Mac Smith had never been more than a footnote to his tragedy. No reporters arrived to cover his hearing. *The Seattle Times*, its Pulitzer Prize tucked away, hadn't published a word about Smith since his arrest.

Maria sat with her husband and Mac's wife Nan. The Smith children, a nine-year-old son and twelve-year-old daughter, waited in the hall; they'd never been told why their father had been taken from them. If Mac was released, the plan was to drive him to Nan's small house for a reunion. In addition to the new suit he wore to the hearing, Maria had bought him casual clothes and stocked Nan's house with food and beer.

The state's big gun, Maureen Saylor, testified that there was nothing more the program could offer Mac Smith, and that three years in the program hadn't changed his basic nature, even though he'd come across as a model patient.

One of his earliest Public Defenders took the

witness stand and reminded the court of Smith's courageous appearance at the Armstrong trial—"he had done incredible numbers of terrible things in his life and he saw no other way to atone, in effect, other than to assist the prosecutor in prosecuting a murderer."

Michael Comte outlined Smith's history and admitted that he was uncomfortable with the state's attempt to return him to prison. "Here we are at the end of the process," the therapist told the judge, "where Mr. Smith has done everything he has been asked to do . . . and we are now saying to him, 'Hey, we don't think you've integrated what you've been presented with and we don't view you as a reasonable risk.' . . . My God, that's a real ethical and moral dilemma! . . . This hurts me. It hurts me to see that it came out this way, because the bottom line is that that man did everything that he was told to do."

Smith testified in his usual straightforward manner, leaning forward to make his points and brushing back his shock of brown hair. He sketched in his involvement in the program and his original motivation: "I decided sometime ago to turn my life around."

His attorney Scott Reiman asked, "What are your feelings about the crimes that you have committed . . . ?"

"I'm sorry about what I did," Smith said in his small voice. "I can't undo it. I wish to God I could. If I could, I would. And I certainly—I certainly—the thirty-five years that the prosecutor mentioned for imprisonment doesn't—certainly doesn't seem unjust to me."

There it was again, the impression that he'd always projected: Mac Smith, the most reasonable of men, being *fair*, even about himself.

After three hours of give-and-take, it was the judge's turn to speak. Gerard Shellan noted first that "this is the kind of case that can give a judge sleepless nights, because it is like a Greek tragedy that is unfolding before us."

He peered down at the defense table and commented that Smith had "a long and malignant history" and probably held the record for the most rapes in Washington state history. He read aloud from the reports submitted by both sides and reminded his listeners that in essence the behavioral experts didn't disagree.

Then the silver-haired judge invoked the ghost of Steve Titus in a courtroom where the name had gone unmentioned by either side. "Having reviewed all the files in this case," he said, "I do not believe that Mr. Smith will ever comprehend, even in his wildest dreams or during his most reflective moments, the damage, the harm, the hurt, the trauma, humiliation, and the scars that have been permanently inflicted on all of these victims over these years, including the person who was also unjustly accused and tried for a crime Mr. Smith had committed."

He paused and looked at Smith again. The big courtroom was silent as he finished his thought in slow, ponderous words that seemed to hit like blows on an anvil: *"To have committed that, in the Court's opinion, probably is the greatest mortal sin that any person can commit."*

•

Maria exchanged looks with her sister-in-law Nan and tried to comprehend why things seemed to be going wrong. At the very least, she'd expected to assist in Mac's transition to work release. But instead the judge was sitting up there on his throne reminding Mac that he was lucky he'd been tried for his crimes in an enlightened society instead of one "which undoubtedly would probably order execution or castration of a person who committed fifty or fifty-five rapes."

Maria winced, but Mac's blank expression didn't change.

At last it was time for the ruling. Judge Shellan said he saw no reasonable assurance that Smith wouldn't reoffend and no reason to continue his treatment. "Probation, therefore, is revoked," he declared, "and the defendant is committed to the penitentiary."

Under terms of the order, the prisoner was ordered to serve out his original forty-year sentence. He wouldn't be eligible for parole unless two psychiatrists or psychologists determined that he presented no danger to the public. Lacking such a finding, Mac Smith would remain behind bars till old age.

126

Maria and Nan escorted the two children to the King County Jail visiting room so that they could say a few words to their father through the double-thick glass. Everyone cried except Mac.

He asked Maria to look up their dad in Las Vegas and explain what had happened. "Oh, Mac," she said, "I haven't talked to Dad for three years and I—I really don't think I want to."

"Please," her brother said. "Ask him to get in touch."

"Mac, don't ask me to do this."

He insisted. "It's important to me," he said. Then he explained to his children that he wouldn't be coming home after all, but they would see one another on visiting days.

En route home, nine-year-old Michael said, "We don't even know what he did. Just tell me this, Mom. Did he kill somebody?"

"No," Nan answered.

The child seemed relieved. "Then it can't be that bad," he said.

A month after Maria had carried out her mission to contact Calvin Smith, Mac confided to her that he still hadn't heard a word from their father. But at the same time he was informing prison interviewers that he and his dad were "closer now" and that Calvin considered him "a good person." It was almost as though he couldn't bear to face the truth about their fading relationship.

Maria phoned Las Vegas again and asked why Calvin hadn't written. Her father hemmed and hawed, then said, "Well, it's very hard for me to get in touch with him."

"Yeah," Maria said, "but it's real hard for him, too. He needs us, Dad. He needs us."

The months passed and Mac heard nothing. "You shouldn't be surprised," Maria told him on one of their phone calls. "Dad was never there for us."

Mac confessed that he felt as though he'd been abandoned all over again, but added that his dad was probably busy with his music and would write eventually. Sister and brother agreed that they still had deep feelings for the strange little man who'd abandoned them for a witch. "It's odd we still love him, isn't it?" Maria said. "After what he did to us?"

Mac said it sure was odd.

EPILOGUE

i

Few who were involved with Steve Titus or McDonald Smith remained untouched by the experience.

Paul Henderson gathered up his Pulitzer Prize and his other journalistic awards and quit the *Times* to found Paul Henderson Investigative Services, a detective agency specializing in freeing the innocent. Within two years he'd cleared so many wrongfully convicted defendants that he was the primary subject of a one-hour HBO documentary called *Verdict: The Wrong Man*.

His wife, Janet Horne, was promoted to assistant city editor, but not in time to assign him to update the weather table. His former boss and sidekick, Dick Cheverton, no longer known as "the Ayatollah," traveled south to become an editor of the Orange County *Register*.

The lawyers landed on their feet. The tenacious Christopher Washington resigned from the prosecutor's office to enter private practice with a prominent firm. Jeffrey Jones continued to excel in his own practice and also on the soccer field. Thomas Hillier was named federal public defender for the western district of Washington, a likely stepping-stone to a judgeship or other political office. Mary Kay Barbieri and her friend Linda Walton gave up the practice of law for airier pursuits: studying for advanced degrees at Western Washington State University and running pack trips through the northern Cascades with a string of llamas.

The ultradignified Charles V. Johnson twice won reelection without opposition, but never again permitted a closeup identification of a rape victim in his court. Gerard M. Shellan retired as chief judge of the King County Superior Court and Johnson took over the prestigious post. Snohomish County Judge Dennis J. Britt also retired after a long and honorable career.

Celia Dalton married, moved to a village in the country, and gave birth to a baby girl. A boy was born to Joanie Kay Finley. Authorities lost touch with Mac Smith's other teenaged victims.

Ann Carmichael and her police sergeant husband entered counseling to break down the barriers partially formed by Mac Smith's attack, and after a year or two of readjustment, resumed a happy life with their daughter.

The lawmen who picked up Mac Smith's trail and followed it to the end, Brian Burkhalter, Bill Ross, Mick Stewart, and Harlan Bollinger, accepted the congratulations of their superiors and remained on the job.

Sergeant David Hart, Ronald Parker's superior officer, retired along with several other Port policemen involved in the case. Their former chief, Neil Moloney, went from head of the Washington State Patrol to head of the Colorado State Police and eventually returned home to Washington.

Mona Imholt moved from job to job, waitressing and tending bar, and helped her ex-husband raise their two sons. Every July 14, Steve Titus's birthday, she arranged fresh flowers on his grave and lingered for an hour or so, wishing he could hear the words she was saying.

Maureen Saylor retained her administrative title while the Sex Offender Program was being phased out at Western State Hospital. She was much in demand at seminars on the behavioral sciences, and her lengthy paper, "The Rise and Fall of a Sex Offender Program," was circulated widely among her beleaguered peers in other states.

The Smiths spread out and endured. Maria made a second marriage to a hardworking, prosperous businessman who supported her efforts to make life as pleasant as possible for her imprisoned brother, including providing him with a $2,000 Epson computer. On one of their visits to the penitentiary, Mac confided to his sister, "You know, I really didn't rape fifty-five women. They counted it as a rape if I had sex with a woman I didn't love."

Maria wanted to believe what he said, but she was afraid he was lying. It was just Mac's way. She loved him and would always remember the kindnesses and secrets they'd shared as kids. A therapist helped her to come to grips with their separation, but there were still nights when she cried herself to sleep thinking about her brother in his cage.

The youngest Smith sibling, Lina, married a man who shared her own religious convictions, but she was never quite able to forgive Mac his sins. When

Maria fretted that the prison didn't serve good cuts of meat, Lina said, "At least it's food, Maria! The homeless eat out of trash cans. Mac's got a roof over his head, he's not being abused, he's doing better than the women he raped."

Later Lina felt ashamed of her outburst and wrote her brother a letter. "I told him that even though we never really knew each other as children, I really loved him and I was sorry he was in prison and I was sorry that I hadn't written him for so long," she reported to Maria later. "I was bawling when I wrote that letter. I must've felt guilty. I waited weeks for his reply and it was as cold as ice. He didn't even acknowledge my letter, let alone comment on what I said or answer my questions. It hit me so hard. I thought, You know what he is? He's sick! He doesn't even care about me. I felt more and more bitter about him."

She never wrote again.

As he entered his thirties, the older brother, Walter, continued to rack up business successes, but he fell out of contact with Mac. "We each have our way of dealing with our childhood," Maria explained. "Walter's way is to act like it never happened. Who's to say he's wrong?"

Mac's mother forgave her errant son in the name of Christ Jesus and joined him in a seventy-two-hour trailer visit on the penitentiary grounds. "We had a nice time," she said afterward. "Just me, Mac, Nan, and the kids."

"Yes," commented Maria. "They had a nice

time, but only because they spent three days without talking about anything that mattered.''

Dove and her easygoing second husband moved away from Southern California and kept Mac's imprisonment a secret from their new friends and churchmates. She phoned her daughters frequently but refused to discuss certain subjects. Said Maria, "I understand what Mom did to me and Mac, but I can't get her to talk about it. She thinks I'm trying to punish her. She'll say, 'Oh, yeah, I was a *terrible* mother, wasn't I?' And I'll say, 'That's not the point, Mom. The point is, you did what you did. It *happened.*' But she won't talk about the way we were treated. I think this is called denial.''

Dove knew what had turned her healthy, happy, God-fearing son into a predator. At six, she recalled, Mac had almost died of flu. Every hour or so he would awaken from his coma, point to the wall, and yell, "Here comes another plane! There it goes! *It's . . . gone.*" After the fever broke, Dove told her husband that she hoped Mac hadn't burned up part of his brain. Calvin explained that the brain wasn't combustible, but she wasn't so sure about that.

A few years later, Mac cut himself on the leg and developed an infection. The doctor asked Dove to hold him down. "Please, Mom, *don't!*" the child begged. "He's got a knife!" Dove straddled his skinny frame while the doctor lanced the wound. Mother and son cried all the way home on the bus. Such medical traumas, Dove believed, could damage a person's mind. She couldn't think of anything else that might have twisted her son toward raping women at knife point.

Dove relaxed in the knowledge that her family

would receive its reward after death. "I'll be with my children," she predicted. "Mac backslid and didn't grow as a Christian, but he got saved in our church in 1962, and once you're saved, you can't be lost again. You don't have to be borned again and again and again." But she regretted that one of her offspring would never rejoin the others; Maria had forfeited her eternal reward by marrying a Catholic.

Calvin Smith continued to wander the country like Jerry Jeff Walker's "Mr. Bojangles," singing and strumming for drinks and tips. At a family gathering in Columbus he told his daughter Lina that he was augmenting his income by selling drugs to young folks, just as he'd once sold potatoes off the back of his truck. Lina told him not to come around her home till he changed his habits. "Until then," she snapped, "I don't want you near my kids."

Soon after, she heard that he'd separated from his second wife, Ruby the witch, bringing to eight the number of fatherless children he'd left behind. He'd always been contemptuous of women— "bitches," as he called them. Now he seemed to despise them more than ever. He spoke better of Dove than he had in the past, but he could hardly discuss Ruby without emitting a long string of cuss words. And he still showed touches of the same antisocial behavior that had landed him in a boys' industrial school in Ohio. When he was informed that a book was being prepared about Mac and the family, he said he would arrange to have his mobster brother Slim take care of the problem before the work could be published, " 'cause if it all comes out, my son'll spend the rest of his life in jail."

Mac Smith remained a model prisoner, a leader, an inspiration to those who were serious about their rehabilitation. Behind bars, he seemed well adjusted, tractable, a skilled practitioner of the fine old penological art of "walking the walk and talking the talk." He earned high grades in extension courses, taught illiterate prisoners to read, helped to prepare Braille books for the blind, and led group therapy sessions on subjects like marriage and sex. His behavior won him frequent connubial visits with his wife, who'd set up housekeeping in a nearby town. He also saw Nan and the kids on visiting days and swore he would rejoin them some day on the outside. His earliest release date was 2006.

ii

L'ENVOI

By the time the first rumblings of the funeral organ had sounded on the sunny spring day of June 12, 1987, dissension had followed Ronald Parker in death as it had in life. His eighteen-year-old daughter Donna wanted a plain gray casket, but his live-in girlfriend argued for electric blue. His daughter opposed an open casket, but the girlfriend and the Port police wanted his uniformed body to lie in state.

As a compromise, the casket was left unsealed until just before the services began. Parker's lover stepped up for a last look and the lid was lowered.

For outsiders who wanted to see what the loved one had looked like in life, a photograph of him and his K–9 partner "Acco," a handsome black German shepherd, was placed at the head of the casket.

The mourners overflowed Yarrington's funeral home and spilled into the street. Police cars, motorcycles and limousines were double-parked in both directions. The Port of Seattle chaplain presided, and several officers stepped to the dais to say a few words about their fallen comrade. One of them mentioned what a jovial man he'd been, how he'd kept his partners' spirits high while they made their rounds. Another mentioned his abundant love for his daughter.

Donna Parker shed tears with the others. It was true that she and her father had loved each other, but she didn't quite recognize him in some of the eulogies. Father and daughter hadn't exchanged a word in a year; the constant battles over support money had eroded their relationship. Before he'd deserted her cancer-stricken mother, he'd made sporadic efforts to do his duty as a father. But he'd also been a mean drunk, a two-fisted slugger who beat his wife bloody, a busy philanderer who once tried to move his pregnant girlfriend into their home. But he was the only dad Donna had known.

In the front row, a wizened little man of seventy wiped his eyes as the tributes rang out. Archie Parker had been fighting tears ever since he'd heard that his oldest son had died in the line of duty. The elder Parker was a retired shipfitter who lived in the family's old house on the far side of Puget Sound with his cat, his beer, and a few mementos. The old man only wished he could blot out his bad memories. His son Ronnie hadn't visited in seven years, despite numerous entreaties. Archie had a lyrical bent, and his latest invitation had taken the form of a poem from father to son. It began:

> I remember when you were born,
> Early on that Mayday morn.
> My happiness and joy knew no bounds
> As *you* made life's first beginning sounds. . . .

And ended:

> Son, this is just my way to say,
> I love, miss, and care for *you*.
> Can we get together sometime
> Soon for a day???

There'd been no answer, just as there'd been no reply to the Christmas and birthday cards he'd sent Ronald through the years. Archie explained to his ex-wife and his two younger sons that it wasn't that Ronnie didn't love him, but the boy was just too busy enforcing the law; police officers couldn't be too close to their families anyway, or they would expose them to dangerous criminals. Any day now, Archie had expected his first-born son to show up for a nice long talk.

But instead he'd received the formal announcement from the Port of Seattle:

At approximately 4:50 A.M. on Monday, June 8th, 1987, Corporal Ronald A. Parker, age forty-three, suffered a massive heart attack and

died almost instantly. Less than an hour before, Corporal Parker and two other Port of
Seattle officers had been involved in an alter-
cation with a theft suspect in the coffee shop
of the main terminal at Sea-Tac. After the completion of the arrest Corporal Parker left the
area and went to the officers' locker room.
Corporal Parker, a fifteen-year veteran of the
Port of Seattle Police Department, was just
completing a normal ten-hour work shift and
was preparing for his shift to end at 5:00 A.M.
when he was stricken. Attempts at reviving Corporal Parker by fellow officers, fire department
medics and Medic 1 personnel were fruitless.
Preliminary autopsy reports indicate that Corporal Parker died from natural causes and was
suffering from coronary artery disease at the
time of his death. During the course of his fifteen-year career with the Port of Seattle Police
Department Corporal Parker served as a patrol
officer, a detective, a narcotics detection K–9
handler, and a member of the Emergency Services Unit.

Archie Parker was pleased to see so many
lawmen paying homage to his son—he figured there
must have been close to two hundred, many in
fancy-dress uniform. Listening to the orations, he
tried to avoid thinking about Ronnie's childhood
and the battles the two of them had fought. He'd
been the baby of the family for ten years till his two
brothers arrived. Big and heavily muscled, he'd

turned into the angriest boy in the neighborhood, beating up other children, stoning them, looking for trouble. Once police had to take him to Juvenile Hall. When he reached his full growth at fifteen, he punched his scrawny father so hard that a splinter from Archie's shattered jawbone protruded into his mouth and scraped his tongue. Then Ronnie stomped his fallen father and broke several of his ribs. A few months later, after another set-to, Archie fired a shotgun at his son's car and tore the boy's knee open with shrapnel, revenge for the silver plate in his own rebuilt jaw.

When Archie had first heard that Ronnie was embarking on a law enforcement career, he'd remarked to a friend, "I would hate to be any person he arrested." As much as he loved his son, he was afraid that he'd helped to raise a troubled and troubling human being. He often wished that the two of them would apologize and shake hands, but by then they'd fallen out of touch.

And now the boy was lost to him for good. There would be no visit, no long talk. The old man's ears pricked up as the minister read a eulogy that Archie had composed at 3:00 A.M. the night before:

So now Dearly Beloved Departed Son, it is our most *fervent* of all prayers, that you have been, and are, a chosen one to fullfill "Almighty God's" *promise* that now, at the end of your earthly time, you may come for all eternity and dwell with him, in the house of the *Lord*. Forever—and Forever.

When the services ended, the preacher congratulated Archie on his eulogy and gave the old man a bear hug. Archie whispered in his ear, "Those were God's words, pastor. He just had me write 'em down."

The last note of the organ faded and the funeral procession snaked down the street toward Washington Memorial Cemetery. At intersections, moans on the sirens cleared the way. Forty police vehicles from as far north as Everett and as far south as Tacoma preceded the hearse, and as many followed. Motorcycles driven by cops in polished boots and helmets shepherded the procession in little arcs, spurting ahead and dipping their front wheels from side to side while their emergency lights twinkled and flashed.

At the cemetery on the Sea-Tac Strip, the lawmen stood at attention as an honor guard fired a salute over the flag-shrouded coffin. The two American flags were folded; one was handed to daughter Donna and the other to the woman who'd shared Parker's life at the end. The electric blue casket was lifted off the bier and slid into a crypt, joining sixty others in a high wall. The three-hour ceremony was over.

As the mourners trudged across the long expanse of lawn toward their cars, they passed Steve Titus's grave, two hundred yards down the slope. In death as in life, Ronald Parker was ascendant. A few months later, the Port of Seattle Police Department named him "Officer of the Year."